STILL HERE

AFTER OVER FIFTY WONDERFUL YEARS

To

Naumat-ullah Khan

Best wishes from

Mudassir

2008

Mudassir, Kath (Fernaz), Shahnaz and Suhail.

STILL HERE

AFTER OVER FIFTY WONDERFUL YEARS

By

Mudassir H. Khan

CREMER PRESS

First Published in Great Britain in 2008 by
Mudassir H. Khan
C/O Cremer Press, Blackburn.

First edition 2008

ISBN 978 1 898722 68 7

Printed and Bound By
Edmund Mercer, Cremer Press,
45 Harrison Street, Blackburn.
Lancashire. BB2 2JE.

ACKNOWLEDGEMENTS

My acknowledgements must firstly go to my wife Kath (Fernaz), our daughter Shahnaz, and our son Suhail, for their constant encouragement and support whilst I was writing my memoirs about the various landladies I have stayed with since I came to England.

Secondly I would like to thank
Salim Sameja our family friend
for all his advice, help and encouragement
during the time I was writing my life story.

I wish to thank all my past
colleagues and acquaintances.

Lastly I would like to thank Madeleine Fish, whom
I first met many years ago at William Birtwistle's,
for all her help in editing this book.

DEDICATION

I dedicate this book to my wife
Kath, (Fernaz),
and our children
Shahnaz and Suhuil.

I further dedicate this book to
my late Mother and Father
(Amma and Abba),
my late brother Muzammil,
my brother Mubashir,
and my two sisters Aapi and Beeda Baji
in Hyderabad (Sind) and Karachi.

INTRODUCTION

From the earliest immigrants from South Asia, to the present generation of 'born and bred' British residents of South Asian heritage, many communities still exist with strong cultural and religious values.

The rights of the individuals who are willing to express and celebrate their unique self-identity are often dominated by the most topical of social and political debates, before being lost within the stereotypical views of the masses.

For this reason there are very few from amongst these communities in present day Britain, who can truly claim any level of a successful lifestyle attained solely by grit and determination, but more importantly, with complete honesty.

The apt title ***'Still Here'*** was suggested by the author's son Suhail. The story itself is an autobiographical account of a very modest individual, of both the Indian and Pakistani heritage, who first sailed through the high seas as a youth, to reach his 'temporary' destination in Lancashire, England.

Mudassir Hussain Khan, affectionately known as Khan Sahib throughout most of his life, is the first amongst equals. In my opinion, Khan Sahib epitomises the true human values of care, compassion and modesty, without seeking any material gains or erroneous civic recognition.

Through toil has come his contentment with life's consistent rewards, surpassed only by the everlasting love of his family.

'Still Here' is an amusing, moving and sometimes critical account of one of the very first arrivals of the Asians in England, or to be more specific to Lancashire. Khan Sahib takes the reader through the trials and tribulations of being an 'alien' at a 'foreign' destination, all of this long before the days of unveiling multicultural Britain, followed by such media-speak as political correctness and community cohesion.

Despite being close to becoming a victim of ethnic cleansing from a post-colonial era, Khan Sahib unwittingly embarked on his life-changing journey from East to West.

As one of the earliest Asian arrivals in Lancashire, he has been in the thick of many changes across the regional landscape, sometimes as part of history - as was the case in Lancashire's textile revolution, and sometimes embryonic - as has been the case during the settlement of the South Asian communities throughout Lancashire and beyond.

'Still Here' reveals some fascinating real-life situations where tolerance on his part, brings Khan Sahib the ultimate rewards of work-life balance, without compromising family values, and more importantly, principles.

My genuine and warm friendship with him and his family over many years is a privilege. But for thousands of others he will always be their favourite Uncle Khan.

I have never known Khan Sahib to ever display any dislike, aggression or malice towards anyone, no matter what their race, religion or national heritage. This clearly becomes evident throughout this book, which incidentally has resulted purely due to his impressive ability to recollect fresh and fond memories from the distant past.

Personally speaking, I have considerable trouble remembering recent events from yesterday, let alone those that date back fifty years!

As well as Khan Sahib and Uncle Khan, he is also known as Mudassir or simply Khan by many others. It does not matter what name is used for him, for the respect due to him is still the same. He is indeed a very modest man, whose life has indeed served others as an example, whatever their skin colour, nationality or creed.

It is a great honour for me to have the opportunity to pen this introduction; but it is an even greater honour to have personally met and known Khan Sahib, who is now, and will surely become a role model for generations to come.

SALIM SAMEJA.

CHAPTER ONE

It was a dull, dark, cold and rainy morning in late August 1956 when two young men got off the train from Liverpool onto Blackburn Railway Station. Coming from a warm, sunny and bright climate, the first young man was terribly cold and miserable. He got more depressed as he looked around the station platform. The building seemed to be covered with black soot, and he could smell the odour of coal left behind by the engine's black smoke. Although the platform was well swept, and clean and tidy, he could still see traces of soot on the inside of the station shed and the surrounding walls.

The second young man was to catch a train to Burnley from Blackburn. As soon as that train left carrying his friend, the first young man remained on the platform wondering where to leave his two suitcases and holdall. As he pondered a porter in a black railway uniform approached him.

Without saying much they made each other understand that the young man wanted his luggage left at the station. The porter kindly obliged and wheeled the luggage to the Left Luggage Office.

Although the young man had a winter suit on, it had been made for winters in Pakistan or India. He was almost shivering with the cold. Walking out of the railway station he stood under the verandah, joining other people who were already sheltering from the heavy rain. Hovering nervously beneath the verandah the young man was still deciding what he should do next.

Looking towards the bus station at the buses and dark buildings he thought to himself, 'Ah, so this is Blackburn, the place that I have been dreaming about for so long.'

That particular young man was me taking my first steps on Lancashire soil. I'm Mudassir Khan, and the other young man who left for Burnley, was Mian Mazhar Hussain.

Luckily fate took a helping hand; I spotted a police officer actually sheltering underneath the same verandah. It was the very first time I had ever seen a British police officer. I had read and heard about British Bobbies, as to how big, broad and tall they would be, but I had never imagined them to actually be so huge. He was dressed in his full uniform, with helmet and cape, and looked so tremendously impressive.

Before leaving Pakistan I had been told that if I ever needed any help whatsoever, I should approach a police officer. I thought to myself, 'I have studied the English language for twelve years or so, and have passed all my school, college and university exams in English. I have also been practising spoken English with my friends in Pakistan prior to leaving for the U.K. so I shouldn't have any difficulty speaking to this policeman.' Having thus calmed myself, I walked over to the officer, and in my best English I began, "Excuse me officer."

"Yes," he replied in a deep and husky voice.

"Could you please tell me how to reach Alexandra Road?" I asked.

I watched him closely, as a blank expression crossed his whole face. I repeated my question.

He replied, but I couldn't understand a word that he said.

After a few minutes of this kind of conversation he took his notebook and pencil out of his tunic pocket, and held them in front of me, gesturing to me to write with them.

This time I realised, as it had become quite clear to me, that the English language I had learnt in India and Pakistan was of no use to me. 'My goodness gracious me,' I thought. 'In Pakistan, I used to be so proud of my fluency in English. Even on the ship sailing from Karachi to Liverpool, I didn't encounter that much of a problem.'

Taking the police officer's notebook and pencil, I wrote down, "I want to go to Alexandra Road."

The officer laughed cheerfully saying, "Oh, Alexandra Road, right!"

He looked around and beckoned a young man who was also sheltering just a few feet away, and they exchanged a few words.

By now the rain had somewhat slackened, and the young man looked at me, signalling for me to follow him.

Following this young man, I crossed the famous Blackburn Bus Station passing Queen Victoria's statue, turned left into the Cathedral's yard, passed by Lloyds Bank, and walked through King

William Street. We turned left again to reach a bus stop which was situated near a public house called the Ribblesdale Arms, right opposite King George's Hall.

Walking across the Boulevard I also noticed on my right the Star & Garter public house, the Adelphi Hotel, the *Lancashire Evening Telegraph,* and other buildings. Each one in turn was covered in dark soot.

A single-decker bus was already waiting at the bus stop, near the Ribblesdale Arms. Leaning over into the driver's cab, the bus conductor was talking to the driver.

My 'Guide', the young man, spoke to the conductor, who then turned to me, and putting his right hand on my shoulder, pointed to the bus door. I was sure that he meant for me to get on the bus. Both the conductor and driver gave me a big smile, so I climbed on.

At this point I felt as if I was both deaf and dumb, because so far all the people seemed to be communicating with me in sign language. To add to my misery I had got soaking wet walking to this bus stop, because I did not have a raincoat. To hide my embarrassment of shivering, I sat on the last seat at the very back of the bus.

I looked down the vehicle noticing that both the bus and its seats were very clean and comfortable, but the windows were all steamed up, so I couldn't see anything outside. More passengers boarded and when the bus was almost full it set off.

Sitting in the vehicle shivering and twiddling my thumbs, I was cursing the moment when I'd decided to come to England. I had never expected English weather to be so dull, cold or miserable. I tried to divert my thoughts by looking through the bus windows. I wiped the one on my right with my palm. Now I could see so much on the road, but the rain was pouring down again. The conductor started to collect the fares. It was so fascinating watching him collecting money and giving tickets to the passengers.

I noticed he was saying something like, "que, que," each time he handed a ticket to the passenger. At that time I couldn't understand this at all, but later on I came to know that in fact he was saying "Thank you."

He came over to me; I didn't know how much the fare was to Alexandra Road; as I had no loose change I gave him a pound note.

In return he gave me my ticket and what appeared to me to be hundreds of old pennies, with his usual "que."

Later on I realised that the fare was only tuppence-ha'penny, (about 1p now) but then there were 240 pence in the pound. I tucked these old, large pennies away safely in both side-pockets of my jacket.

By this time the bus was passing the front of Corporation Park; it turned onto West Park Road, then into Dukes Brow. I rubbed the steam off the side window and gazed outside. The trees and lawns of Corporation Park really pleased me. After another minute or so the bus stopped at a bus stop halfway up Dukes Brow, the conductor pointed out to me that this was **my** stop.

He very kindly got off the bus with me, pointed to Alexandra Road signposted on the wall, with the grand gesture, "Here you are."

It was raining heavily as I walked up the path looking at the numbers of the houses on my left. I looked at a house and saw that it was numbered 15 and the next was 17 then 19. At this point I got rather worried, as I wasn't at all aware of the odd and even numbering system on streets.

I thought, 'The bus conductor's dropped me off at the wrong place,' but I kept marching on. By the time I reached the correct number I was thoroughly soaked, water was dripping off my head and clothes.

I rang the doorbell and waited.

A few seconds later a middle-aged lady appeared at the door who turned out to be the landlady. As soon as she saw me in my drenched condition, she almost screamed, "Oh you poor boy, come in, do come in."

Her words were heavenly to me, because I could *almost* understand her.

She took me to her living room where a roaring coal fire was glowing. I was so glad to stand in front of the fireplace to get warm, and dry myself.

Briefly I wondered how my travelling companion was getting on. Hopefully he had reached his destination in Burnley by now, and was safely inside out of the rain.

The house on Alexandra Road, Blackburn, where Mudassir Khan lodged when he first arrived in Blackburn in 1956.

CHAPTER TWO

In 1956 I had finished my University education, gaining my degree of B.Sc. from the University of Sind in Pakistan. According to our family custom and traditions, I was at the age for getting married and, as I had finished my studies, there was really no excuse for me ***not*** to get married. Now and then, family members had been dropping hints about a potential wife for me.

In 1955 my father Mr Shabbir Hussain Khan had retired from his railway services as a Senior Station Master. He received his Provident fund with a pension from the railways. To this day I have no idea as to how much money he received, but I heard that a large portion of what he had got was going to be used for my wedding.

I had no intention of getting married, so to my father through my mother and sisters, I suggested that I would like to go abroad for some higher education. I also asked him if the money allocated for my wedding might perhaps be used for my education instead.

Following another family consultation, I was summoned by my father to explain my plans to him, as to which college or university, and which country I would like to go to? He also wanted details as to how much it would cost and how long I would be away?

At the start of the 1950s, following the end of the British Raj in India in 1947, Pakistan was barely established as a country, and was starting up various industries. Among the fast growing and popular ones was the textile industry. Foreign qualified personnel in this industry were getting the highest salaries compared to other industries. Besides very good remuneration, they also received other benefits such as a bungalow with large lawns, a chauffeur driven car, servants and suchlike. These benefits greatly attracted me so I decided to venture into this field.

I made contact with different textile mill owners and their senior staff, such as general managers, spinning, weaving, and dyeing masters in Hyderabad. They indicated to me that anyone who had qualified in England stood a much better chance in this industry.

A few days later I outlined my plans to my father. He listened to me attentively then told me to wait for his decision.

In our family, the boys, while they were still going through their education, were hardly consulted on important decisions. Our father's consulting panel consisted of my two sisters and my elder brother, as sometimes my mother would be ignored. My elder brother was only included in that panel *after* he had completed his education, started work and got married. My brother and sisters persuaded our father to let me fulfil my ambition to go abroad for my further education.

Once again I found myself in front of my father.

"To which country do you wish to go?" he asked.

I thought very carefully before answering him, "There are some colleges and universities in America, but Lancashire colleges in England are famous for their textiles."

Then he himself suggested, "Get in touch with the British High Commissioner and the American Embassy in Karachi, and also the British Council in Karachi."

I wrote to all three. The British Council promptly replied to my letter, forwarding the addresses of colleges and universities offering courses in textiles. I wasted no time at all in applying to almost all the colleges in Lancashire for admission. Although the response from other colleges was good, Blackburn College was the first to reserve a place for me, and advised me to send them £5.00 as my reservation fee. I promptly sent the requested money to Blackburn College through the State Bank of Pakistan.

I was very excited when I received the letter of confirmation from Mr D. L. King, Head of the textiles department at Blackburn Technical College.

Prior to, and during the 1950's, Asians who came to Lancashire were mainly students. They were mostly from well-to-do families, or they were offered scholarships sponsored by UNO or the Commonwealth.

Soon the news about me going to England for higher studies spread through my extended family and friends. At that time there were three local newspapers in Hyderabad and all three wanted to interview me about my plans.

My father intervened saying, "You must not talk to these people till you receive your passport."

To get a Pakistani International Passport in those days was very difficult. With an application for this document, one had to have a statement from the bank showing the bank balance of the applicant's sponsor, and a clearance certificate from both the Inland Revenue and the police; then there had to be a final interview with the chief passport officer.

As all these offices were in Hyderabad, I had no difficulty in obtaining the relevant documents, such as father's bank balance, clearance certificates from the Inland Revenue and the police; however the passport office was in Karachi. Armed with all these documents and an application form I therefore visited Karachi.

At that time, a cousin of a similar age to me was studying in Dow Medical College Karachi and, he lived in the college hostel. Whenever I went to Karachi, instead of staying with other relatives, I always stayed with him in the hostel.

The passport office was on Napier Road. The next morning I submitted my application for a passport, and a date was given for me to attend a formal interview with the chief passport officer.

The following week I travelled to Karachi for this interview. The passport officer examined my documents thoroughly, finding them both correct and in order. Then he spoke to me in English, asking different questions as to which college I was intending to study at, and what was the duration of the course? I was pleased that the interview was going so well.

All of a sudden the passport officer asked, "Are you familiar with English manners and using knives and forks?"

"Yes I'm familiar with manners, but I have never used a knife or a fork," I replied honestly.

The passport officer suggested that I should get in touch with the British Council in Karachi for some booklets and literature on the British way of life, and usual manners. He advised me to visit the Ritz Hotel's restaurant in Hyderabad at least twice a week for three weeks, and have English meals, in order for me to get used to using cutlery.

He made it clear to me that he would only issue me with a passport when I had completed this course. This made me wonder if he had some shares or something in that hotel!

Both my father and elder brother Muzammil thought it most appropriate for me to have some knowledge of English customs. They therefore allowed me to visit the Ritz Restaurant for my evening meals. The British Council in Karachi was very helpful and gave me a lot of booklets on British culture.

After three weeks of 'training' at the Ritz Restaurant, I went back to see the chief passport officer in Karachi. I assured and convinced him that I was now fully familiar with English table manners. Then he made sure that besides my other necessary clothing, I was taking with me a dinner-suit, and our Pakistani national dress, which consists of a black Sherwani, shalwar or Aligarh-trousers, and Jinnah or Liaquat cap.

I assured him that all these items were already prepared.

He then gave me a long lecture telling me to remember that I would be representing Pakistan in England, so I must not do anything that could tarnish the name of Pakistan. "You should be well-dressed, well-mannered, and well-behaved in England."

As he handed me my passport I felt I was already in England. I couldn't wait to reach my cousin in the hostel; I wanted to tell everybody about my passport.

Sitting in the crowded and noisy Karachi bus, everything around me looked so beautiful; the sounds were like sweet music to my ears. In my imagination I was already in England.

My cousin and his friends in the hostel were happy for me. The same evening I left for Hyderabad where almost everybody who heard about me going to England was pleased, but still there were just a few who were envious or even jealous of my new opportunity abroad.

The only person really close to me who **wasn't** so pleased with this news, was my mother. To her I was still a little boy, who was not able to look after himself. At this point my sisters and brother came to my rescue, and between us we managed to convince our mother that I **could** look after myself.

Top - My Late Father - Shabbir Hussain
Below - My late brother - Muzammil
and my brother Mubashir

***Mother (Amma) and Aapi,
with Beeda Baji standing behind
and Hajra and Beeda Baji below them.***

CHAPTER THREE

Mohammed Hassan was my college fellow; we had met a few times in Hyderabad before leaving for Blackburn. He too had managed to obtain admission into Blackburn College Textile Department.

Hassan and I had originally planned to travel to Blackburn together. However as he had already booked his seat on PIA, and my father wasn't in favour of me travelling by air, I had no choice but to try to get a seat on a passenger ship.

It was the last week of June 1956 and I had to reach Blackburn by September to join my course. Luckily I saw an advert for Anchor Line in *Daily Dawn* Karachi, stating that its vessel *RMS Circasia* was going to sail from Karachi to Liverpool in the first week of August 1956. I hurriedly wrote to them enquiring if there was a seat available on this ship?

RMS Circasia was a huge passenger ship which ferried passengers between Britain and Australia, calling at Port Saeed, Port Sudan, Aden, Karachi, Bombay, Singapore and several other ports.

I was terribly disappointed and worried when they wrote back saying that the whole vessel was fully booked, but in case of any cancellation, they would get in touch with me.

About a week later I received a telegram from Anchor Line in Karachi stating that due to a cancellation, a seat was available; if I wanted to accept their offer I should respond promptly.

By return I sent a telegram back to Anchor Line accepting it. I was so excited that the next day I went to Karachi to the office of Anchor Line at McLeod Road and paid my fare Rs 1200 by cheque. This was the very first cheque I had ever signed.

As soon as my college friends heard about my confirmed booking to England, they arranged parties for me. My long time friend Inayat held the first one; Nasir and Hadi arranged a second and third party to which my old college and university Professors and lecturers were invited.

Two Sind University Professors, who had studied in England for their PhD degrees, gave me some tips and contacts in England. The British Council and the Professor's tips helped me a great deal later on.

On July 30th 1956, I left Hyderabad for Karachi with my Mother, elder brother Muzammil, his wife, and my younger sister Beeda, as well as my very close friend Saeed Ahmed, who is now a successful doctor.

They all stayed with one of my cousins Mirza Islam Baig, whilst Saeed and I went to Dow Medical College Hostel to stay with my cousin Abdus Salam Khan.

The next day my father, my younger brother Mubashir, and my elder sister Aapi arrived from Hyderabad.

In Karachi too, we were invited by my maternal cousins in Khudadad Colony, Islam Baig, Faizul Ghani and others.

On August 4th we reached West Wharf Karachi seaport with about fifty relatives and friends, who had come from Hyderabad to see me off.

I couldn't believe my eyes when I saw the ship. It was huge, and appeared to be about a mile long to me. I had never seen a passenger ship before. It was painted white throughout and different types of flags were flying on top.

My holdall and big suitcase were loaded into the ship's hold; only the small suitcase stayed with me.

Everybody wanted to see my cabin on the ship, but nobody was allowed to go on board unless they were sailing. A Pakistani policeman stood at the gangway. Abdus Salam managed to dodge the policeman, but Saeed was stopped.

I came down to collect my small suitcase, and was going to carry it, when Saeed took it off me and placed it on his head pretending to be my porter, thus managing to come aboard. Salam, Saeed and I toured the ship.

Mudassir with Saeed in 1950
Photo taken following their Matric exams in Hyderabad

I wasn't at all familiar with the procedure of going through immigration and other channels. At about 4:30pm I stood in the queue on the first deck with my passport ready to go through all the formalities of both Immigration and Customs, after which it was time to bid "Goodbye" to the family.

I embraced my friends and cousins first, then Muzammil Bhai and Mubashir. As soon as I hugged my sisters Aapi and Beeda Baji, I started crying with them. But when I hugged my mother and father I sobbed uncontrollably.

I had never previously been away from my family; I was taking a big step into the unknown. My family were making great sacrifices to help me fulfil my ambitions, and perhaps improve the standard of living for many. Already I could feel the weight of this heavy burden on my shoulders.

By now almost everyone was crying, except my cousin Faiz-ul-Ghani, who was busy consoling my mother and father.

It was about six o'clock in the evening when my family and friends finally left, and I boarded the ship properly.

The whole ship was first class; it had almost everything on its four or five decks. There were two large swimming pools on the top deck, a chemist and barber's shop, a doctor's surgery, two or three bars, a smoke room, lounge, library, and a children's playroom. Then there was a washing and ironing room, and of course a huge dining hall.

The crew were mainly South Indians. Each cabin had a steward assigned to look after the occupants. The chefs, headwaiters, and other officers, were all either British or European.

I learnt that I was to share a cabin for the whole voyage with two other students, Malik and Rizvi. After formal introductions with my cabin-fellows, there was small talk in the cabin when we discussed our meal times and seating arrangements, then moved onto asking each other where we would be staying in England? It soon became obvious that I was not the only one away from home for the first time.

Our cabin steward told us that the three of us were on the second sitting at the same table for our breakfast, lunch and dinner.

It was almost 8:00pm when the three of us went to the dining hall led by our cabin steward. A very smart head-waiter received us with full English courtesy. He beckoned a well dressed Indian waiter then handed us over to the table-waiter who showed us to our table.

Although I was quite familiar with table manners and etiquette, I was still a little nervous, as I had never had a chance to sit with so many Europeans. More than 50% of the diners in the dining hall were Europeans.

There were four people to each table. Besides us three on that table there was an Indian Bengali student called B. D. Ghosh; he was a very chatty and outgoing person so very soon we all became friends.

None of us had any real idea of the menu, or its contents. Ghosh and Rizvi were the chatty ones, whilst Malik and I kept a lower profile. Later on we all found out to our delight that all the meals on offer were always superb.

We would order two starters, two main meals or sometimes even three, because sometimes the main meal wasn't very filling. As it is in Asian customs, we could always ask for more. In the same manner we would have two sweets, for example cake with custard followed by ice-cream.

We were told that the ship would sail some time the next morning. After supper we settled down in our cabin before getting ready for bed.

I tried to sleep, but feeling homesick and in a strange environment this was difficult. I don't remember when I finally did manage to fall asleep. At about five o'clock the next morning we were all woken up by the movements of our beds, and realised that the ship was actually leaving Karachi. We rushed out of our cabin still dressed in our pyjamas to have a last look at Karachi. Again I had tears in my eyes, but Rizvi was worse than me because he was actually from Karachi. Tears were rolling down his cheeks. Malik's face showed no emotion as he came from Lahore, and had left home ten days earlier.

Every now and then while the ship was at sea, something was announced over the loudspeaker, but mostly I couldn't understand it. Apart from going for meals we spent the whole time exploring the ship.

The next morning while I was fast sleep, a knock sounded on my bedside, and a loud voice greeted me, "Good morning, your bed tea Sir."

It woke me up with a shock to see our cabin steward smiling and putting a tray on my bedside table. I couldn't believe my eyes when I saw a shiny silver teapot, a little milk jug, a sugar bowl, and two slices of toast. I wasn't used to eating or drinking anything unless I had first properly cleaned my teeth, rinsed my mouth and had a good wash.

I thought to myself, 'If this is the usual English way of starting the day, I can't cope with it.'

I decided to visit the toilet first before using the wash basin to brush my teeth, and have a wash and shave. After having a cup of tea we went for breakfast.

The same thing happened at breakfast. We ordered cornflakes, shredded wheat, then porridge and lastly an egg on toast followed by marmalade on toast. No wonder the waiters were giving us funny looks and smiling at each other. I had never tasted Silver or Golden Shred marmalade; the taste of Silver Shred was so appetising to me, that even to this day I use it with great fondness.

After breakfast, while Malik, Rizvi and Ghosh went to the smoke room, I ventured onto the top deck. As far as I could see there was nothing but sea. The movement of the waves mesmerised me; I just stood there holding the barrier rails on the deck. Other ships could be seen in the distance; it all felt so special and mysterious.

I loved the scenery of the Indian Ocean from the top deck. I could understand why poets have written so much about waves and sea breezes. I tried to remember all the Urdu verses and couplets by famous poets about boats, storms, waves, and seashores. The scenery was so magical and romantic, that somehow I just felt like reciting poetry.

By the time I had finished admiring the sea, there was an announcement. I went down to the second or third deck smoke room, where I was amazed to find Rizvi having an ice-cream.

He told me that ice-cream, tea and coffee would be served every day between 9:30 and 10:30am, along with sandwiches, cakes, biscuits, and cold drinks.

'It is going to be such a wonderful and enjoyable voyage for us all,' I thought to myself.

At that moment I didn't know what the next day had in store for us. It started just like the previous day, the only change that I noticed was either the ship had increased speed, or there was something wrong somewhere. I didn't pay much attention to it, and as usual we all went for breakfast.

I was becoming more familiar with the environment and my fellow passengers, so I thought, 'I'll have something different for my breakfast this morning.'

Rizvi and Malik had also felt the difference in the ship's speed.

When we enquired, the waiter told us, "The ship has started rolling. It might get worse!"

That morning on the breakfast menu, I read that there was honey on toast. I had never tasted English honey, so after cornflakes, followed by egg and tomatoes, I asked the waiter to bring me toast and honey.

The waiter smiled broadly at me, looked at his fellow-waiter, then left to get my order.

He brought the toast on a beautiful china plate and the honey in a silver jar with a matching knife. With fond anticipation I spread the butter on the toast and put some honey on top.

Just as I was going to take a bite, the ship rolled. As the rolling movement threw me forward my stomach turned over. I felt really sick and wanted to throw up. Luckily I pressed my left hand to my mouth, and ran towards our cabin. It was too late, I was terribly sick, throwing up everything I had just eaten.

CHAPTER FOUR

Without getting changed I slipped into my bed. Malik and Rizvi followed, wanting to talk to me.

I said, "Shut up and leave me alone," as I truly thought at that moment that I was going to die.

A knock came at the door.

"Enter," I whimpered.

The cabin steward appeared. "Would you like to have your lunch in the cabin?" he asked me.

I felt like throwing a pillow at him; I most certainly didn't want to hear anything related to food or drink.

For two days I was continuously sick; I couldn't bring myself to get out of bed. The only time I left it, was when I wanted to go to the toilet, or to be sick.

Once I got over the seasickness I started enjoying myself again. In front of the Purser's office in the foyer was a large notice board, where different daily events were displayed for the attention of the passengers. There could be a film show, a deck tennis match, a variety show or some other form of entertainment.

One evening a dance was publicised and Rizvi was very enthusiastic about it. I had never been to a dancehall in my life. Although I had seen couples dancing in English style in lots of films, to see them live was quite an experience for me. I felt terribly embarrassed when a young English girl approached me for a dance. I wasn't ready for that, I made some sort of excuse and left the room.

My favourite pastimes were playing deck tennis or games of cards with the other passengers. The majority of them were English, and some were with their families. There were young children, teenagers, and others.

The teenagers were mostly girls; except for one or two, they were all good looking and beautiful. According to our Asian custom at that time, these girls were far too advanced for me. If any of them stood next to me, I would move away immediately. This was perhaps odd behaviour on my part, but this was mostly due to my upbringing regarding persons of the opposite sex.

Some Indian Navy Officers were going to England for training. They were mostly all Sikhs. There was one English Army Officer I can never forget. He was very well-built, and almost 6 feet 4 inches tall, with I am sure, a huge 60 inch chest. I always saw him with a pint of beer in his right hand, his arm raised just above his stomach. I found out that he was a high ranking Indian Army Officer who was returning to England for his retirement. Although he used to drink a lot, I never actually saw him drunk.

Sometimes with a pint in his hand, he would sit next to us and talk about his time in the Army. I could understand him, but it was difficult for me to hold a fast conversation with him in English.

After a week at sea we eventually reached Aden and were allowed to go into Aden city. It was just like any Pakistani town except for the language. There were the same crowded bazaars, dirty cafés, and people spitting on the road. I recall having my last paan for a very long time there. I noticed there were a lot of English soldiers in Aden who I believe were doing their National Service.

After a day and half there the ship sailed towards Port Sudan. Now the weather started getting hotter. Englishmen on the ship were walking about only in shorts, while English women wore lightweight cotton dresses, and teenage girls were dressed in shorts and tops.

One afternoon I was in the lounge resting with Malik when Rizvi came rushing towards us saying, “Hey, the swimming pools are open on the top deck. Do you two want to come for a swim with me?”

Malik and I didn't know how to swim, but we thought Rizvi was so enthusiastic that perhaps we should both go and watch him.

When we reached the swimming pool, I couldn't believe my eyes. Men, women, teenage girls and boys were swimming and splashing about in the same pool.

I had never seen women or girls in swimsuits or bikinis before. They were diving from the board, splashing in the water, and running after each other. It was all just too embarrassing for me, so I left and went down to the lounge and wrote a letter to a friend about what I had just seen.

Throughout the voyage we had lots of entertainment on the ship. There were dances, fancy dress balls, films, bingo, and so many different types of competitions.

During the voyage on the 14th and 15th August we celebrated the independence days of Pakistan and India. On both occasions the ship's captain was the chief guest.

After a few days sailing we reached Port Sudan, where it was extremely hot. I am sure the temperature was well above 100 degrees F.

Malik, Rizvi and I went into the town, where we met an Indian shopkeeper. He spoke to us in broken Hindi. We were sweating a lot, so we thought of going to a café. As we entered, an African sailor greeted us in a deep voice. He thought we three were Indians. I am not sure that he knew where Pakistan was. He started talking to us in broken English and Urdu.

He pointed to me and said something like, "He is the only pure Indian; you two are from mixed races."

Possibly he said this because my complexion was the darkest.

We sailed from Port Sudan in the evening. It was still hot when supper was served on the middle deck. It comprised of assorted sandwiches, cakes, biscuits, tea, coffee, and cold drinks.

I had never tasted coffee in my life, but had a kind of craving to try it. 'At last my wish is coming true,' I thought.

I stood in the queue, collected a sandwich without even checking the filling, and picked up a cup of black coffee.

I walked over to the side near the railings. Looking down over them at the sea, I took a bite of my sandwich and was just about to take a long awaited sip of my coffee, when Rizvi came behind me.

"Ah, there you are; what are you eating?" he asked.

"A sandwich and my favourite coffee," I replied with pleasure. I took another bite of my sandwich.

Rizvi asked, "What sort of sandwich do you have?"

While I was showing him the sandwich, I was about to take my first ever sip of coffee.

Rizvi said, "It's pig's meat in your sandwich."

Rizvi's words and the black coffee's aroma joined together. The smell of the coffee seemed horrible, and I related it to a pig's odour. I threw both the sandwich and coffee overboard, then leaned over the railings and threw up instantly.

In Islam any meat from a pig is strictly forbidden. Muslims don't even like to look at its meat, let alone touch or eat it. I had had a strict Muslim upbringing; I didn't even want to look at this meat.

Although Rizvi kept assuring me that he had played a joke on me, I went off coffee for a very long time after that.

****

On our way to England the ship had to sail through the Suez Canal. At that time the Suez crisis was at its full height and Col. Nasser was in power in Egypt. The warships and gunboats were hovering round on the open sea. Our ship was stopped at Port Suez on the east side of the canal. After a day and a half of negotiations, our Captain was finally allowed to proceed, and our ship entered the famous Suez Canal at Port Suez.

RMS Circasia was the last ship to sail through the canal before it was blocked for all ships, and a couple of weeks after that the Suez War broke out.

Rizvi suggested that the three of us got off at Port Suez to visit the Egyptian town, and travel by taxi or other means to Port Saeed. As our ship was going to berth there for two days, we would be able to join it at the other end. But when we tried to get off, we were told to get back onto the ship. They told us that due to political reasons, Indian nationals could be allowed off, but not Pakistanis. I was terribly disappointed.

It was so wonderful sailing through the Suez Canal, the scenery on both sides of the ship was breathtaking and the ship was moving very slowly. The top deck was filled with passengers as everybody wanted to enjoy the beautiful views. Some people had their cameras clicking away, whilst others held binoculars.

On one side of the Suez Canal, there was nothing but desert, but on the other side everything looked much greener with residential districts and beautiful houses and bungalows.

It was late evening when we reached the famous Port Saeed. It was quite frightening because the Egyptian Authorities seemed to be in a very hostile mood. We didn't dare ask to go ashore and visit the town.

A rumour was going round the ship that the Egyptians might not allow our ship to proceed to England, and that we might be held in Port Saeed for a long time. Luckily however at the end of day we were allowed to continue with our voyage.

As soon as we reached the Mediterranean I started feeling cold, at the same time the ship started rolling, but it wasn't as bad as it had been in the Indian Ocean. I managed to keep myself active. On our way through the Mediterranean we watched the *Queen Mary* liner sailing past us looking very majestic.

Everyone was very excited that we would soon be in England. It was late evening when we finally docked at Liverpool Port.

The first thing I noticed was the Liver Bird building with its two birds. Liverpool's bright lights presented such a beautiful scene. These buildings looked so familiar, as I had seen their photos so many times in our college library books and magazines. Temporarily public phone kiosks were installed on the decks; people were soon busy phoning their families and loved ones.

We were told that disembarking would start early the next day. The following morning we rushed to the dining hall to have our last breakfast, but there was chaos. This time there were no reserved seats, no headwaiter or even waiters.

Before leaving the ship we all tipped our steward for looking after us. The three of us shook hands, embraced and promised to keep in touch with each other, then parted. **Sadly we never did get in touch!**

****

Going through British Immigration and Customs was a pleasure. The officer checked my passport, looked at my face, smiled and let me through.

I had already booked a railway ticket on the ship to Blackburn, so I got on the train at Lime Street Railway Station in Liverpool, for my onward journey.

CHAPTER FIVE

My first day and evening at Alexandra Road will always stay in my mind. After talking to my landlady Mrs T, and settling the lodging arrangements, I brought my luggage home in a taxi from the railway station. Mrs T. showed me to my room, which was on the top floor overlooking Corporation Park.

The landlady informed me, “Tea will be served between 5:30 and 6:00pm.each day.”

This confused me a little, as I was expecting 'dinner' in the evening. She explained to me the proper dining times. I didn't understand fully, but I accepted what she said.

I told the landlady that I was a Muslim, so did not eat any meat unless it was halal. However I had to explain to her what halal meant. The only suitable food for me seemed to be fish and chips.

My next disappointment was when I came down from my room to the dining room for my tea. Besides me, there were six or seven English people seated round the dining table.

‘This is the right time and place to put into practice the training I had received from the British Council’ I thought. So nervously I began to speak, “Do you have table talk?” I asked in my strong Asian accent.

They all looked at each other with blank expressions, then one of the girls asked me, “What is table talk?”

I felt terribly embarrassed, but the landlady came to my rescue explaining to them, “He is a student and has just arrived from Pakistan.”

One of the boys asked me, “Where is Pakistan?”

Before I could answer, the middle-aged man seated next to him, told him, “India has been divided into India and Pakistan.”

Then he turned to me, “Which part of Pakistan do you come from?”

To be truthful I didn't understand what he had asked me. “I beg your pardon,” I said very slowly, carefully pronouncing each word distinctly.

The gentleman repeated what he'd said, but this time, he too spoke more clearly and slowly.

This time I understood him. I wanted to tell him that I was from Hyderabad, but I thought he might not know Hyderabad itself, so I said, “I come from Karachi.”

Upon hearing this he almost jumped out of his seat saying, “Oh! I was in Karachi in 1943 and 1944.” He said a few words and sentences in Urdu, but in an English accent, “Pankha-waala, jaldi-jaldi,” and “Chaa-wala, Chaa laao.”

It is very difficult for me to describe my happiness and excitement at that moment, because at last I felt there was someone else here who had also seen Karachi.

His name was John, and although he told me his surname, I didn't fully understand it. It turned out that John had been a Captain in the army and was stationed in Karachi cantonment for almost a year; he had travelled all over India with his regiment. He had been stationed in Delhi, Puna, Karachi, Rawalpindi, and other famous places in India. I thoroughly enjoyed talking to him because he started talking to me slowly, and in a much clearer accent.

By this time it was about 6:45pm, and I had nearly run out of cigarettes. I was quite desperate to get some more, so I asked the landlady where I could buy cigarettes? What she told me came as a great shock.

“All the shops are closed now, but you can buy cigarettes in a pub.”

“What is a pub?” I enquired of her.

She wasn't a bit surprised at my question. She simply explained to me, “Oh, it is a place where people drink alcohol.”

I was horrified at the thought of going to a pub; “Oh God! What a place I've come to; in Hyderabad one could buy anything even at 2:00am.”

I went to my room feeling very disappointed. I sat on my bed thinking about home, and the wonders of that town. I couldn't go out here, because I felt so very cold. I couldn't amuse myself, as there was no radio or television in the room. TV's were actually quite a rare sight in ordinary houses at that time.

I started getting depressed, and homesick, till eventually I started crying. I must have cried for half an hour, and when I came round to thinking straight, I thought to myself, 'I am going back. I can't live here. It is too cold, too miserable, and the town closes at 5:00pm. How am I ever going to survive in this place? I have made a huge mistake in coming to this country.'

Luckily there was a small table and a chair in my room. I got my writing-pad out and started writing a letter to my father, giving him all the reasons for me **not** wanting to stay in England. "It is too cold here. There is no outdoor entertainment, and the town closes at 5:00pm. The food has no taste, and I can't understand the local accent. Also I am feeling ill as I have caught a severe cold."

It was a lengthy letter, and I wrote down all the arguments for my misery. In the end I finished off by begging my father to send me a ticket to return home. I felt so much lighter and better after writing home.

When I went downstairs for my supper; the landlady asked, "How are you feeling?"

"I feel very cold in the bedroom," I told her through chattering teeth.

"I'll put a hot water bottle in your bed before you go to bed," she said gently.

I didn't know what she meant by hot water bottle, but when I entered my bed I could feel a rubber bottle full of hot water. It felt really good and I fell asleep quickly and started dreaming of back home. I woke up a few times during the night. By about 5:00am I was fully awake, but I didn't dare get out of bed, because to me it was freezing in the room.

However, I managed to pull myself out of bed, and after going to the bathroom with my 'Lotta' (the pot for water to wash oneself after toileting) and having had a shave, I got changed and headed downstairs for breakfast.

I had already told the landlady that I would only have cornflakes and an egg on toast for breakfast. Therefore I didn't have any problem, for besides an egg on toast, I also had two more slices of toast with jam and marmalade.

It was Saturday morning, and the landlady told me, "An Indian student has just come back from his holidays on the Continent. Would you like to meet him, he is staying in Holland Street?"

I was overjoyed to hear this statement, as I was dying to meet somebody from India, Pakistan or even Sri Lanka, as I was quickly running out of my English vocabulary, and was desperate to speak to someone in Urdu.

I ventured out and walked down Alexandra Road. Whilst walking down the street I spotted a letterbox, which reminded me to post the letter I had written to my father begging him to send me a ticket to return home. I felt so much better after posting that letter and hoped that I would soon receive a ticket.

As the weather was better, I thought of walking to the student's address, but my landlady advised me to take the bus.

This time the bus conductor dropped me off at Sudell Cross, advising me to go up Limbrick, which lead onto Shear Brow, at the top I would see Holland Street on my left, and London Road on my right.

Without any difficulty I spotted Holland Street opposite London Road, but I still couldn't understand why they had numbered the houses in odds and evens. I reached the house and rang the bell.

I was expecting the same language problem, so I was repeating a few rehearsed sentences in English in my head, when a little, round, middle-aged woman opened the door, and looked at me with a question mark expression on her face.

After a few repetitions, I was able to make her understand what I meant. Later on I came to know that her English was actually worse than mine, because she and her husband were both Ukrainian, so they spoke only their own language in the house. They had no children, so they took in lodgers for company and to supplement their income.

"Have you an Indian student lodging with you?" I asked politely.

Again she looked at me strangely, but fortunately the student had heard my accent, and being curious had come to the door.

He turned out to be Basant Layalka. After we had introduced ourselves he invited me into his room. He was more or less of my age, but in height he was smaller. For the first few minutes he spoke to me in English. I was managing well, but as soon as we realised we were the only two people in the room, we started speaking in Urdu, which he spoke really well.

Basant was a Maarwaari Indian, so his understanding and speaking of Urdu were wonderful.

After formal talks he asked me, "Have you brought a raincoat with you?"

When I told him I hadn't, he advised me to buy one, as it was very important to own one in England.

Basant got ready and we walked down Shear Brow and Limbrick, passing Richmond Terrace, then went on to Sudell Cross before turning left into King William Street. As we reached the junction of Library Street and King William Street, I noticed the town hall of Blackburn, with the Assembly Hall and fish market next to it. There was a wide area between these buildings on the left, and the Essoldo Cinema, with Marks & Spencer, and Burtons on the right.

In front of us stood the clock tower, and being Saturday it was a market day. There were stalls selling different household things. At one of these stalls I bought a plastic raincoat for fifteen shillings (75p) and had to put it on because it was raining.

After looking around the stalls, Basant and I moved on to Victoria Street. I was so thrilled to see a big sign saying 'BOMBAY STORE'. For a few seconds I felt homesick. We walked towards Church Street and as we reached the end of Victoria Street, Basant told me that the pub at the junction of Church Street and Victoria Street was the centre of Blackburn; I'm not certain if this is true!

We turned left and I could see a F. W. Woolworth store. I had heard of this store when I was in Hyderabad. I went in enthusiastically, and found Woolworths to be exactly as I had been told; one could buy *anything* in that store. We went round the counters, and I noticed beautifully smiling young sales girls behind each one, who were more than willing to help customers choose their items.

It started to rain again and we felt cold, Basant and I rushed back to his lodgings. I discovered that Basant Layalka was the son of a Bombay-based multi-millionaire industrialist. Besides other business interests in African countries, his father owned two vertical Textile Mills in the Kolaba district of Bombay. Basant was the only son, so his father wanted him to take charge of the mills. Basant was doing a two-year diploma course in textiles. He had completed one year, so now he was in his final year of the course.

****

In the 50's and 60's, the cost of living in Lancashire wasn't very high, and a single person could live quite decently and comfortably on £7.00 to £8.00 per week.

Students under the Columbo-plan scholarships got £60.00 to £80.00 per month, while other students who were sponsored by their fathers or family members could get up to £100.00 or more each month.

Basant and a few more rich people's sons used to get more than £100.00, while students like me from middle class families, received £40.00 to £50.00 per month.

Although Basant was a multi-millionaire's son, he was a very ordinary and down-to-earth person. During our two years friendship he never showed off, or made me feel that he had more money than I did.

Basant told me, "Your landlady on Alexandra Road is charging you too much at four guineas." He suggested to me, "Why don't we rent a flat on Preston New Road, and share the expenses?"

The idea greatly appealed to me because I had promised myself not to burden my father financially; I would try to economise in every way I could. Taking care of myself hadn't turned out to be that easy, because I had absolutely no idea about cooking or anything.

I had lived a sheltered life right up to finishing my University education. I had never been away from my family. According to our family tradition I should have spent a few years with my grandparents, like my elder brother Muzammil Hussain and my two elder sisters Asghari and Akhtari had done. Living with my grandparents would have taught me how to look after myself, but this tradition was altered when my sister Anwari and I reached that age, which was unfortunate.

At home there was always someone else available to do things for me. There was mother, my two sisters, and my sister-in-law, who were always more than willing to help me. In school I had a big brother to look after and protect me. Even when I was in High School, College and University I had no idea of even polishing my shoes, or washing and ironing my shirts.

Like most mothers, my mother was very kind and soft in her nature, particularly towards her sons. I remember her telling off my sisters, but she never raised her voice to her sons. Our father was quite the opposite of our mother, as he would always side with the girls. He would even argue with mother when defending his daughters, but never showed any softness towards us boys. He never worked in the army, but he liked army discipline in the house for his boys. I suppose it was because for most of his life he had worked on the railways.

Until 1947 the Indian railways were under British control. Indians were employed only up to the rank of station master, but above this rank they were all British or Europeans. On important stations like Delhi, Karachi or Lahore, only the British were appointed as station masters.

I enjoyed my childhood and adolescence thoroughly because I was the middle one amongst my brothers and sisters, so managed to get away with doing very little work around the house. According to family customs and traditions, the eldest son of the family represents the family at birthday parties, engagements, weddings and funerals.

Our elder brother Muzammil Hussain used to try to pass this responsibility on to me. However if it didn't suit me, I would pass it on to my younger brother Mubashir Hussain.

I never needed to learn money management, as there were enough people already in the family to deal with that. This meant that the pocket money that my father gave me every month was purely for spending; there was no need for me to save anything. Almost every month I used to run out of funds in the third week. I dare not ask father for more money, so my first port of call was always my mother. Like any son in need of money, I would start by praising her.

After a minute or so she would say, "How much do you want?"

I think she always knew that if I started praising her I was in need of something; I always managed to get some money from my sisters too. I used the same tactics of praising them, but always maintained that I was only 'borrowing' money, and would pay it all back with interest when I finished my studies and got a 'top job'.

That top job was supposed to come my way if and when I finished my studies.

****

Due to the high rent of Alexandra Road, Basant and I moved into a house on Preston New Road, but after just a week of looking after ourselves, we both realised that we were hopeless at even making a cup of tea or boiling an egg. We therefore decided to move back with another landlady.

By this time the old students who were on holiday were returning, and some new students from India, China, Pakistan, Combodia, Brazil, Nigeria and other countries started to arrive to join the college courses.

****

It was now three weeks since I had posted that first letter to my father, and his reply had finally arrived. In a way I was disappointed that he hadn't enclosed a ticket home for me, but just to have his letter actually in my hand comforted me a lot.

He wrote,

"In the past, most of our ancestors have travelled to many foreign countries. You too are one of the descendants of those people. There is no need for you to despair at all, as you are in a country where people are caring and trustworthy. I should know, because I have worked with, and for them until 1947. Keep your spirits high and be a courageous man. You shouldn't give up so easily."

Then to console me even more he wrote,

"Give yourself at least three months to get used to the way of life there. Pay careful attention to your studies, and if after that time you still feel you can't settle, and would like to come back home, then I will most definitely send you a ticket."

He told me that my mother and my two sisters missed me a lot. He said that my mother was always talking about me and most of the time she was wondering how I was coping with living on my own? In fact if it had been up to my mother, she would never have let me travel to England in the first place.

Likewise my sisters wondered if I was capable enough of getting myself ready, and going out in a proper way. I had always been the spoilt one in the family. They counted the days off, so that only so many hundred days were left before their brother would return home.

Although I was disappointed at not receiving the ticket in father's letter, I felt very consoled by his letter. I therefore made up my mind to follow his instructions and take up his advice. As time went by I slowly began to settle down.

****

One morning, although it was too cold for me, but as the sun was shining and there was no wind, it felt quite pleasant, so with my two jumpers, jacket and mackintosh on (and still feeling cold) I began walking up Preston New Road. I was on my way to see a student called Mia Abdullah who lived a little further up the road.

It was at the junction of Preston New Road and Montague Street that I saw an Asian-looking, plump man coming down Preston New Road. He was smartly dressed in a three-piece suit, tie, polished shoes, and was holding a mackintosh over his left arm.

As we came face to face he said in English, "Hello, are you from Pakistan?"

"Yes," I replied.

He told me he was from Pakistan too introducing himself as Khalil Ashraf and informed me that he was staying at the Red Scar Hotel on Preston New Road.

I thought he would talk to me in Urdu, but he answered all my questions in English. I struggled a little speaking to him in English, but managed to tell him that I was on my way to see a Pakistani student called Mia Abdullah who lived on this road. Ashraf joined me and we continued walking on together.

Mia Abdullah welcomed us both into his accommodation. Actually it was a three bedroomed house, which he had rented and now shared with two other students, Zahoor and Yaar Mohammed Khan, who were both sons of big landlords in Punjab.

Khalil Ashraf was still speaking in English. No doubt his fluency and vocabulary in English were a lot better than that of the rest of us, as we were all struggling to keep up with him.

At last Zahoor said, “Look, there is nobody English amongst us, so why don't we speak in our own language.”

This did the trick, and we had a very long and interesting talk between the five of us. While we were conversing, the doorbell rang.

Yaar Khan jumped up from his seat saying, “It will be my girlfriend.”

Ashraf and I looked at each other, because this terminology was new to us. However it turned out to be another student's friend.

Yaar Mohammed Khan, Mia Abdullah, Zahoor and Basant Layalka had already completed the first year of their course; they were more familiar with the British way of life than new students. These students were from very rich families, particularly Yaar Mohammed Khan who loved inviting friends to his flat for something to cat. This time too he asked us all to stay and have something to eat with him. He had prepared Okra curry.

During the conversation he asked me, “Are you from Hyderabad Sind?”

“Yes, I am from there,” I replied with a beaming smile.

“A new student called Mohammed Hassan Khan has arrived from your town, and is looking for you,” he informed me.

CHAPTER SIX

Hassan was temporarily staying at the Adelphi Hotel near Blackburn Railway Station.

Without wasting any time I left to go and see him. When I met him in the Adelphi Hotel he looked shattered; he was even worse than I was with his English conversation.

He told me that he didn't even know how to use a knife or fork. As it was time for his evening meal, I asked him to ask his landlord to bring his food to his room. When his meal was served and we were on our own, I explained to him about good table manners, and taught him how to use his cutlery. I had become some sort of expert due to my training in the Ritz Hotel in Hyderabad, and practise on *HMS Circasia.*

In the Adelphi Hotel Hassan was paying too much. A week later he wanted to move in with me to my lodgings, but I had already arranged with Ashraf to go to Preston and live there. Ashraf and I wanted to find some sort of work so that we would not burden our parents too much financially, so we both decided to take a year out from our full-time studies in Blackburn College.

I had no idea as to where to go to find a job, but Ashraf told me that I stood a good chance of getting a job in a textile mill in Preston. Ashraf himself had already found a job in Tulketh Spinning Mill.

The next day I caught a Ribble bus to Preston. The return fare to Preston at that time was one shilling & eleven pence (almost 10p). I got off the bus in Preston, and walked down the very narrow ginnel. Once again I felt very lonely and a stranger in this new town.

Preston bus station was totally different in those days than it is today. I don't know how I came out of the bus station, but I found myself on Lancaster Road. I was at the point where today the Guild Hall is located. After a few moments I looked around, before starting to walk towards Church Street.

Luckily I spotted a police officer at the junction of Church Street and Lancaster Road; again this policeman looked huge to me. He directed me to Horrocks's in Stanley Street. By then I was starting to get used to the Lancashire accent, so my communication was slowly beginning to improve.

I walked down the very lively Church Street to go to Stanley Street. I noticed the famous Parish Church on my right, the TSB bank building, the Empire and Palladium cinemas, and other shops were on my left. Then I walked past the brightly lit up Ritz cinema, and the Old Dog pub, moving past the row of shops on both sides of Church Street right up to The Lamb. Church Street ended where Stanley Street, Ribbleton Lane and Deepdale Road all started.

Just after Manchester Road there was a busy shopping area. Walking down Stanley Street I reached the front gates of the famous Horrocks's and Crewdson's main office, where I informed the commissionaire that I was enquiring about a job. He directed me to the personnel office.

The personnel officer was a middle-aged gentleman and was quite a pleasant person. It was no wonder he was nice and kind to me, as afterwards I learnt that he had been in Delhi cantonment for three years during the Second World War.

After asking me different questions, he gave me a slip for the manager of Centenary Mill, New Hall Lane, and a second slip for the manager of the DSS in Miller Arcade. At that time I didn't know the purpose of the second slip, but later on I found out it was to obtain a National Insurance Number.

First I reached Centenary Mill in New Hall Lane, and knocked at the reception window.

A pretty girl opened the window saying, "Yes!"

I didn't know how to reply, so I simply pushed the personnel officer's slip to her.

After reading this, she instructed me, "Wait there for a few minutes."

After a while she came back with the manager Mr Cowell. He seemed to be in a hurry, but looked at me and said something that I didn't understand at all, but I knew he was willing to give me a job.

Mr Cowell was always a very busy man, so didn't have much time to talk to anyone.

The girl who had brought the manager must have noticed that I didn't understand what he had told me, so she explained to me slowly, “The manager has given you a job, and your wages will be £6.14 shillings a week. Your job will be cleaning the spinning machines. You will be in a team of five people.”

The girl who I first met at reception was called Olive Sloane. She was married to Eddie Sloane; they had a little girl of eighteen months. Olive and Eddie were lovely people who became very good friends to me. Later on I used to visit their house in Brockhalls View. They always welcomed me into their home. Their daughter Judith became quite attached to me as I saw her almost every evening during the week. After work I used to walk with Olive to the nursery, where she picked Judith up. At Horrocks's nursery, as soon as Judith used to see me, she would put her little arms out towards me and I would pick her up to take her to the sweet shop, where I would buy her some chocolate or toffees. It was not just Olive and Eddie who took to me; Olive's mother also became very fond of me. She used to bring cakes or sandwiches for me during our lunch breaks.

****

After finding jobs in Preston, Ashraf and I needed somewhere to live, so the following weekend we went to Preston Police Station, off Lancaster Road and got the address of a Mr & Mrs Spencer. We both walked down to see the Spencers on Hudson Street off Avenham Lane, Preston.

We found them both to be very reasonable people. We looked at their living room, front room, yard, toilet at the other end of the yard, and our bedrooms. At that time neither Ashraf nor I even thought about a bathroom.

We agreed to stay on a full board basis. Rent and board were fixed at 3 guineas (£3.15) per week. It might not sound very much these days, but in 1956 it was half of an ordinary worker's weekly wage.

Mr Spencer wasn't a big man, he was about 5 feet tall, weighing only about 8 stone, while Mrs Spencer was as tall as Mr Spencer, but she was a little too heavy for her height. She used to have difficulty walking because of her weight; I felt sorry for her when I saw her sweating while ironing or cooking.

They had a set routine of work for the whole week. Mrs Spencer would cook, wash, make the beds and do her weekly ironing, while Mr Spencer's jobs were to go to town to do the shopping, pay all the bills, do the hoovering, clean up, plus he always did all the outdoor jobs.

On Sunday mornings at about 10:00am, it was Mr Spencer's job to clean the whole house, which consisted of hoovering, dusting, and sweeping the yard.

Hudson Street was off Avenham lane just five minute's walk from the town centre through the churchyard. During the 50's and 60's, like in any other Lancashire town, Hudson Street was a typical community based cobbled street. From one end of the street to the other, almost everyone knew each other. People were very friendly, helpful, and concerned about their neighbours' welfare.

The majority of people in the street worked in the local textile mills. Five or six spinning and weaving mills were within walking distance from Hudson Street and its neighbouring streets. The mills in that area were mostly on day work, with working hours from 7:30am to 5:30pm, with a one hour dinner break.

When we first moved into this street people were a bit wary of us, but after a few days they took to us and treated us just like one of them. Sometimes I would accompany Mrs Spencer to the corner shop. This shop was just like the shops we see in *Coronation Street* on television, as it was a good source of daily gossip.

In the shop I would stand behind Mrs Spencer and listen to them all. Though I didn't understand everything, I knew they talked about young people's behaviour, affairs amongst married people, or the girls running away with somebody.

My English was very limited and bookish, but Ashraf was very fluent, so when we were together he used to do all the talking. As previously mentioned, at the time of viewing the house, we forgot altogether to ask about the bathroom. I took it for granted that there would be a bathroom in the house. I only realised there wasn't one, when on the third day of moving into the house I wanted to have a bath.

I therefore approached our landlady, “Mrs Spencer, I would like to have a bath today please.”

“Right, I'll get the bath into the living room tonight after tea,” she responded.

I couldn't understand what she meant by, ‘I'll bring the bath in.’ I asked myself, ‘Why? Was there no bathroom in the house, and why was Mrs Spencer going to bring in the tin bath hanging outside into the living room?’

She carried on saying, “I'll fill it with hot water and you can then have a bath in the living room in front of the fire.”

“But what about Ashraf, and you and Mr Spencer?” I asked.

What she said in response I couldn't believe.

She said, “Oh, we'll be around. You just carry on.”

I was dumbfounded and shocked to even imagine myself sitting naked in a tin bath in her living room. To us Asians to have a bath really meant to have a shower, or at least to throw clean water all over the body in complete privacy. I had encountered no bathing problems at all on the ship, or even at Alexandra Road, as there were proper bathrooms there.

I was now facing the first problem of my stay in that house. On no account was I going to sit in the same water that I had already used once to wash my body with soap. The other alternative Mrs Spencer told me was to go to the public baths.

When I heard the words ‘public baths’, I thought that it would be a big bathtub, and members of the public would all be sitting in it. That thought totally horrified me as well, so I rejected it.

I had seen two medium sized buckets in Mr Spencer's greenhouse, so I asked Mrs Spencer if I could use them to help with my shower.

Mrs Spencer looked very confused, but in my own Pakistani accent I assured her that I would manage with those two buckets. She was wondering as to where I was going to have this shower?

I took her to the greenhouse in the yard, and told her via some sign language how I was planning to bathe myself. Just as I was explaining this to Mrs Spencer I looked around the greenhouse, and to my horror I saw that three sides of it were glass panelled.

“Could I please borrow three bed sheets to put across the panels?” I requested.

Although this seemed very strange to Mrs Spencer, she went along with my arrangement.

I filled the two buckets with hot water and carried them to the greenhouse. I was shivering like a leaf with the cold after I had this wash down in the greenhouse, but at least it left me fully satisfied that I was perfectly clean.

****

The roads in those streets were cobbled, and the footpaths were all flagged. One could always hear the clunk, clunk of clogs, and the clip-clop noise of the horse's hooves as it pulled the milk cart behind it early each morning. Ashraf and I used to wake up to these sounds.

Mrs Spencer was always up before us, busily preparing our breakfast. She served us with cornflakes, egg, tomatoes and toast. We didn't eat our dinner at home, so Mrs Spencer always gave us each a packed lunch to take with us. She made wonderful evening meals, and for supper we had biscuits and cakes, and I had a beaker of hot milk.

By now I had become quite used to English breakfast and meals, the only thing that confused me again, was when on our first day with her, Mrs Spencer told us that dinner would be served at midday, and tea at about 5:30pm, with supper being available at about 10:00pm.

I found out later that in Lancashire they didn't use the posh system, like bed-tea, breakfast, lunch, tea, dinner and supper. In the industrial towns of Lancashire the system is totally different.

During the week Mrs Spencer kept talking about our first Sunday tea. She had invited some friends over on Sunday. I thought it would be a big feast, with some wonderful dishes, like English kebabs, samosas, pulao, and zarda. I was really looking forward to this meal.

On Sunday Mr & Mrs Spencer's guests arrived in the afternoon at about 3:00pm. Actually there were only two couples. We were formally introduced to them and found them to be wonderful people.

At about 5:30pm we sat around the dining table ready for our Sunday tea whilst Mr & Mrs Spencer served us all. It consisted of our usual soup as a starter, and then the main dish with two slices of tomatoes, a boiled egg, lettuce leaves, grated cabbage, cress, (which I later called grass) and cold tinned fish. We finished off with a sweet dish, followed later by a cup of tea, which completed our Sunday meal.

I kept looking at Ashraf, hoping that he would tell me that other wonderful and tasty dishes were to follow, but I was terribly disappointed, and had to be content with this meal.

The other thing that I detested was the toilet being outside of the house. If I needed to use it during the night, I had to put my dressing-gown on, go downstairs, walk through the living room and kitchen, unlock the kitchen door, then go out across the yard to reach the loo, as it was situated right at the far end.

By the time I came back shivering to bed, I was always fully awake, so it took me a long time to drop back to sleep. At times like these I used to curse myself for ever coming to England. When I grumbled about it to Mrs Spencer, she wanted to put a bucket for me under my bed, but I couldn't agree to that.

After settling down in jobs and digs, Ashraf and I started on part-time courses in textiles at Harris College, Preston, where I met Mr Ainsworth, who was the head of the textile department. He was already a knowledgeable person, but he liked to talk, and partake in discussions with me in order to find out more about Islam. Although my fluency in the English language wasn't good, I somehow managed to express myself.

Most of the time Ashraf and I were together. Wherever we went, he would always take over talking to the people, so this meant that I hardly had a chance to talk or learn how to speak the English language, or pick up the local accent.

I spoke to Ashraf about it, and we agreed that whilst going to and coming from college we could be together, but socially we would start to go our separate ways.

Whenever I was alone I loved asking people for directions to certain places, as the instructions they gave me were wonderful. The other thing that fascinated me was that they always made sure that I understood their instructions perfectly. Some would ask me to repeat what they had told me. In that way I had a chance to speak and practice my spoken English.

On a cold, but sunny and bright Wednesday evening when I was going to college I spotted two police officers near the Bull & Royal

Hotel (presently the Old Bull), at the junction of Lancaster Road and Church Street.

I approached one of the officers saying, "Excuse me officer!"

"Yes, lad," one of them turned towards me.

Gathering all my English vocabulary together carefully, I asked, "Could you direct me to Harris College, please?"

Holding my shoulder, the policeman turned me around instructing me, "Right, if you go through this Miller Arcade, you will reach an open place, which is Market square. On your right then is the Harris Library, on your left, the black building is the Town Hall, and facing you is the Cenotaph and General Post Office. In front you will see three roads. The right hand one will lead you to the covered market, the middle one leads to the same market. You must take the left one, which is Friargate. Go down this road, and after six or seven minutes walk you will come to a little hill. Go up that hill, down to the bottom, and just before you come to the end of Friargate, you will see the Adelphi Hotel in front and a narrow street on your left. You turn into this street on your left; when you come out of this street, Harris College building will then be facing you."

It wasn't that I didn't know how to reach Harris College; I did! Actually I simply loved the way the officers used to explain it all to me. In the end they would ask me to repeat it all back to them, which was only to make sure that I had fully understood their instructions.

After a while, particularly amongst my fellow students in Blackburn, I became well known for this method of learning and practising my spoken English, as well as learning to speak and understand the Lancashire accent.

The other method I used was that I would stand somewhere near Woolworths in Fishergate, Preston, then when I spotted a very good looking young girl going in or coming out of Woolworths, I would approach her saying, "Excuse me."

"Yes," the girl would stop with a pleasant smile.

"Could you direct me to Harris College please," I'd ask.

"Yes, of course," she would reply, and patiently explain the route to me.

Quite often after this the girls would ask me, "Are you a student? Which country do you come from?"

Sometimes this would lead to several minutes of conversation.

At one time there was a well-known saying amongst English people that all Chinese folk look alike, so the English can't tell the difference between individuals. I believe that this same idea was also later applied to Asians, as I have been told this once or twice.

Not many people seem to believe me when I tell them that when I first arrived in Blackburn in 1956, then moved to Preston, all the English boys and girls looked the same to me, and I personally found it hard to tell the difference between any two; in fact I thought that they must all be related to each other.

My classes at Harris College were twice a week on Mondays and Wednesdays from 7-9pm. At approximately 6.45pm, I sometimes used to walk down Friargate to the college with a girl and we would talk. With my limited spoken English I would speak slowly, and she would listen very patiently, conversing with me all the way to college. After classes had ended we would walk back to the town centre via the same route at about 9.15pm.

I always thought that it was the *same* girl who walked beside me each time. **I was wrong!** Both girls had white faces, each one was more or less of the same height, and both wore shoulder-length blonde hair, so I really had no reason to suppose that they weren't indeed the same person.

However one evening whilst we were returning from our classes I noticed that she seemed to have a different handbag, then I noticed that her coat seemed new also, so I asked her about these. Then I went on to enquire if we had already spoken together on certain topics? Her reply really shocked me.

She answered, "I don't know what you are talking about at all!"

I asked, "Aren't you the young lady who usually walks to and from College with me?"

I was left terribly embarrassed when she told me that I was mistaken. I had to apologise to her and told her quite frankly, "I'm very sorry, but to be perfectly honest all English people look the same to me."

Luckily she took this well, and we both laughed at my silly remark and ignorance. When I told Mr & Mrs Spencer about this incident, they too had a good laugh.

****

In Centenary Mill, Preston, I quickly became some sort of a novelty for the workers. Though I worked in the draw frames room; during my spare time and at lunch times, I would wander around going into the doubling room, spinning room or the mule room. The operatives in those rooms were females, and they all liked talking to me.

Once I remember Mr Cowell the manager saw me talking to one of the doffers in the spinning room.

He said, "This lad has only been here for three weeks, but already everybody knows him. I have worked in this mill for ten years, and nobody knows or talks to me like they do with him."

****

Ashraf and I were very happy and contented living with Mr & Mrs Spencer in Hudson Street, but we both got fed up with eating fish and chips every day; we missed our spicy food very much. Although we saw Hassan and Basant almost every weekend, they too lived with landladies in Blackburn and missed their curries and chapatties.

In order to fulfil our wishes, and taste our own kinds of food, we had to make special arrangements to go to Manchester, where we only knew of one Indian Restaurant on Oxford Road; this was situated in front of the Gaumont Cinema. We all thoroughly enjoyed the food so much, but knew that we could not afford to eat there on a regular basis.

Ashraf knew how to cook curry, so we made a plan that we would ask Mrs Spencer if we could cook egg and potato curry in her kitchen?

So often nowadays I hear young English people praising curry, but the incident of us cooking curry in the Spencer's house, and Mrs Spencer's reaction to that, gave me a lot to write home about to my family and friends in Pakistan. While my father and his friends were amused to read about it, my mother almost cried. She wished she could come to England to look after me.

CHAPTER SEVEN

On Saturday afternoons Ashraf and I used to go to Preston town centre. Our favourite route was from Hudson Street to Church Street, via Lancaster Road, the covered market, Friargate and Fishergate.

In Fishergate, whether we wanted to buy anything or not, we always called in at Woolworths, Marks & Spencer, and British Home Stores. At the junction of Church Street, Fishergate, Cheapside and Glover Road, there was an E.H. Booth store where one could buy continental foodstuff and spices.

In Booths, two young sales girls, who we soon discovered were called Pat and Irene, were very friendly towards us. We always bought something from there, like a tin of mangoes, lychees, or other tins of tropical fruits.

Although Mrs Spencer had heard of curry and rice being the main meal for Indian people, she had no idea as to what it really consisted of. She told us that she and Mr Spencer were going to visit some family friends on the following Saturday, and would return late in the evening. Ashraf asked her if he could cook curry in her kitchen while she was out.

Willingly she gave him her permission to make curry.

As soon as Mrs Spencer agreed to our request, we became very excited and looked forward to Saturday.

When that day finally arrived, Ashraf and I went to Booths. Ashraf told Pat and Irene that he was going to cook curry, so he needed some spices. Both girls were more than willing to get us the ingredients. We bought butter, eggs, bread, tinned tomatoes, some red pepper, onions, and cloves.

There was no question of us making chapatties, because the flour was not available, nor were there any facilities to do so. Besides neither one of us knew how to make chapatties anyway, so we agreed on toasted bread, as the best substitute for them.

To me Pat was a very beautiful and pleasant girl and I always enjoyed talking to her. She was about 5 feet 4 inches tall, with blue eyes, and shoulder length blonde hair. She was a very sweet girl. Because she used to talk to me more than Ashraf, I think he got a bit jealous.

A few years later I met Pat again in Preston library. She had married a Preston North End football player. Pat also told me about Irene who had got married and gone to live in Australia with her husband. Pat did invite me to meet her husband at her house, but somehow we never did manage to get together after that.

To prepare the curry, Ashraf asked me to peel the onion and chop it into thin, fine slices, while he boiled the eggs. He then opened a tin of tomatoes and put the spices together. I had no idea about peeling or chopping onions properly, so Ashraf had to teach me almost everything about cooking.

We started preparing and cooking at about 2:00pm; the spicy flavour and smell were making me more and more hungry, but Ashraf wanted to stick to our usual tea time of the 5:30pm ruling.

Anyway at approximately 5:30pm, Ashraf dished out the egg and potato curry for us both, whilst I made toast out of almost three quarters of the whole loaf.

For me it was the tastiest of curries. In fact we both thoroughly enjoyed this wonderfully tasty, spicy meal, and after eating we settled down to listen to the BBC Home Service.

At about 8:00pm we heard the front door open, and almost a scream with the words, "Ashraf! What the heck have you been cooking? Open up all the doors and windows; I am not coming in till all this horrible smell has gone out of the house. It is suffocating me!"

While Mrs Spencer was shouting, I pushed Ashraf in front to appease her.

Standing at the front door poor Ashraf tried to explain it all, but Mrs Spencer wouldn't hear of anything, insisting that all the doors and windows *must* be kept open. She went to stay at the next door neighbour's house until the smell had completely disappeared.

We were both worried and concerned about Mrs Spencer's behaviour, but luckily Mr Spencer came in after a while; he apologised for his wife's behaviour, but Ashraf and I agreed that the smell was very strong, and perhaps it could be unpleasant for people who were not used to it.

We had no choice but to open all the doors and windows of the house, although we were all shivering. It was almost midnight before Mr Spencer finally persuaded Mrs Spencer to come back into the house.

The next day was Sunday, and Mrs Spencer told us, "All my neighbours have also complained about the curry smell."

Nowadays though I often hear young English people praising curries, chicken tikka masala, naans, biryanis and such food, and I smile, but I always remember Mrs Spencer's strong reaction. After that experience we never dared cook any more spicy food there.

****

As usual one Saturday afternoon, Ashraf and I were in Preston town centre near Miller Arcade, when I said to him, "I need to visit the public toilets."

"So do I" he replied.

The public toilets were situated underground between Miller Arcade and the Gaumont Cinema; we therefore went down the steps.

****

Before my departure to England the staff at the British Council in Karachi were very helpful to me; amongst many other things they informed me that English people have a very good sense of humour. They often even make a joke of their own mishaps. They told me that if for instance, an English person bumped into somebody, or someone bumped into them, they would most likely say "sorry!" But if one says "sorry" first, then the other one would probably make a joke of it, laugh, then reply, "It's all right, do it again!" In this way both parties have a laugh together.

****

There were quite a few men in the toilets; four or five of them were elderly. It was very quiet as no one was talking to anyone, just busily attending to their personal toiletries.

All of a sudden there was what we call a rude noise, as an elderly gentleman had broken wind.

In order to hide his embarrassment he said in a loud voice, "Sorry!"

Instantly I remembered the advice given to me by the British Council in Karachi, and clearly recalled the English sense of humour. I thought that this was a very good chance for me to show my own sense of humour off, so in my proper Asian accent, and in a rather loud voice I said, "It's all right, do it again!"

It makes me smile even today to recall how much laughter there was in response to my words echoing round in those toilets.

****

My first Christmas in England was a most wonderful and memorable event for me. I had seen British people celebrating Christmas when they were in power in India. We children in those days called it the 'Big Day'.

On important stations or junctions, British officers' bungalows were specially built, and located away from Indian quarters. Actually that area used to be known as 'Little Britain'.

There used to be many celebrations around Christmas in those bungalows. Almost every night there were parties, songs and dances. The bungalows were decorated not just inside, but outside too. The fronts of all these dwellings were full of little coloured flags, and in the evening the whole British residential area was lit up with small coloured electric bulbs, whilst music played on gramophones.

The British residents of those bungalows never did any manual work. Poor Indian servants did all the Christmas decorations and trimmings. They laid out drinks, food and other things for the party. The Sahibs and Mem Sahibs only entertained the guests. Even the children of English couples were looked after by Indian nannies.

On Christmas Day the railway engines of passenger trains and the guards' compartments were fully decorated with little coloured flags. This was because the engine driver and the guard on the main passenger trains were English. To please their English bosses the Indian station masters of even small stations decorated their station. This practice continued right up to 1945 or 1946.

English families would hold some special events in the evening on Christmas Day for both grown-ups and children. Sometimes they would include some well-to-do Indian families and children, and they would have a big celebration.

****

At my workplace in Centenary Mill Preston the workforce started talking about Christmas in the middle of November. Young people were making plans to go to pubs, dances, parties, and other places. Quite a few times I was asked where I would be spending my Christmas.

A week before Christmas Mr & Mrs Spencer had a Christmas party at their house. Ashraf and I helped Mr Spencer to decorate the living room. In one corner he put a Christmas tree, and Ashraf and I pinned the paper ribbons onto the walls, and hung paper bells from the ceiling. Over the fireplace on the chimney breast in golden letters, we proudly placed a banner which read:-

'A VERY MERRY CHRISTMAS
AND A HAPPY NEW YEAR.'

For the party the guests started to arrive at about 2:00pm; Ashraf and I had got ready well before, and were wearing our best suits and ties because we wanted to give a good impression of ourselves to the guests. We were introduced to everyone.

As usual Ashraf was very chatty and joined in the conversation without any problem. I was a little hesitant, as I was still having some problems with understanding the Lancashire accent, but I still managed to join in.

We all sat round the extended table for dinner. Mrs Spencer already knew that we didn't have meat with *our* meals, so she had kindly prepared two plates in vegetarian style. There were crackers on everybody's side, which I enjoyed pulling with the guest next to me.

The Spencers and their guests were teetotallers, so there was no question of any alcohol on the table. After the meal the table was cleared and party games commenced. One was of general knowledge, where the host had made sure that there were some questions on the Indian Sub-continent, so that we could take part. Then there was a game where one had to pick a card from a hat, and had to act according to the instruction written on the card. The last game was Bingo.

Each time the winner received a prize from Mrs Spencer. The party only went on till 10:00pm, because the guests had to leave in order to catch their buses.

During the same week a party was held at the mill. I wasn't ready or prepared for this type of party. I think it was on the last day of work in the mill before Christmas.

I had been informed by Olive the reception girl that some girls and women were going to buy a Christmas present for me, so if I wished to do so, I could buy something for them.

We exchanged gifts in the morning whilst working. After dinner nobody started work as all the machines were stopped.

Only then was I told that the workers were going to have a Christmas party in their own departmental rooms, such as the cardroom, blowroom, spinning room, mule room, the office and reception.

I noticed that because all the machines were stopped, the male workers were missing from their departments, and the female workers were drinking alcohol sitting round their machines. I found out later that all the men had gone to the pub across the road in New Hall Lane, in front of Centenary Mill.

Some younger female workers in the spinning room started to sing and began a rock 'n' roll dance. At that time it was a newly imported craze from America. They called it a dance, but to me it seemed to be just people jumping about on the floor. All this was very new to me, and I watched it with a bit of amazement.

At about 2:30pm Olive came to me with a little parcel saying, "Happy Christmas." She placed the parcel in my hand.

I then gave her the presents I had bought for her and her daughter Judith.

By this time it was 5:30pm, the time that we all usually finished work. Some of the workers were drunk and staggering all over the road on their way home. It was a good job that there weren't so many cars on the roads in those days.

The following week I arranged to see Hassan and Basant on Christmas Eve, inviting them to come to Preston. They arranged to come by Ribble bus; I had suggested meeting them at the bus station. I was there early waiting for their bus to arrive from Blackburn.

It was terribly cold all that day. I met my friends off the bus as arranged, then all of a sudden we saw white flakes coming down, and realised that it was snow falling. Basant had experienced snow before, but this was the very first sighting of it for Hassan and me.

The snow looked so beautiful to me that I didn't want to go home, so I suggested to Hassan and Basant that we should walk to the park and enjoy this beautiful scene. Surprisingly the weather had become a little bit warmer, making us all feel a lot better.

The snow started to stick; soon all the roads and paths were covered with this beautiful whiteness. We stood at the top of Avenham Park. It looked like somebody had spread a pure white sheet over everything. The snow was all over the park, the buildings, the trees and the lawns in Avenham Park. It all looked so magically white. After a stroll in Avenham Park, Miller Park and a walk on the banks of the Ribble we reached our house.

Mr Spencer almost shouted at me saying, "Have you gone crazy, you'll catch cold, and maybe even pneumonia if you walk like that in the snow."

In the past few weeks Mrs Spencer had been busy buying presents and food for Christmas. She asked Hassan and Basant, "How do you both plan to spend your Christmas?"

They each told her that they had some plans for Christmas, and left for Blackburn in the evening.

CHAPTER EIGHT

At last it was Christmas Day. I woke up at about 8:00am and looked out of my bedroom window. I was so pleased to see that the snow was still there. I tiptoed downstairs and very quietly had a shave and wash, got dressed with two pullovers and a double pair of socks, donned my thick trousers, jacket, overcoat, scarf and gloves, then opened the front door and ventured straight out into the street.

In Hudson Street the road and paths were all covered with snow. It all looked so very beautiful, just as if I was looking at a painted picture. I walked down the street onto Avenham Lane, and reached Winckley Square at the top of Avenham Park. I stood there with my hands in my pockets simply admiring this wonderful and breathtaking scene. Once more it looked as if somebody had spread a pure white sheet right across the park's lawns. The trees and bushes were the same, all covered with snow. Once again I couldn't resist going down to the banks of the River Ribble.

I was the only person in the park at that time of day. To me it was such a romantic atmosphere, that I couldn't understand why *all* the people weren't outside admiring it. After going round Miller Park and walking on the River Ribble's banks, I walked through Winckley Square to Fishergate. I was shocked to see that not even a single shop was open. Next I went to the railway station. I was surprised to see that the station was also closed; I felt so very disappointed!

I was completely devastated knowing that this was actually Christmas Day, yet nobody was out in the streets. In India and Pakistan on Eid, Divali and Christmas, right from early morning, there is always some hustle and bustle. Men would get dressed in their new Shalwar, Qameez and Sherwani to go for prayers, whilst the children in their bright new costumes would be in the streets going to meet relatives or friends.

I walked back down Fishergate, past Miller Arcade, and reached Church Street. Passing the Parish Churchyard I noticed the lights on in the church. I thought they would be getting ready for their morning service.

Throughout all of this crazy exhilarating walkabout I didn't see anybody in the whole town. When I reached home I was freezing and shivering with cold; luckily Mr Spencer was up and busy making the fire in the living room.

During the 1950's, almost all the houses had open coal fires. It was cosy and wonderful when it was alight and roaring, but it used to take time to start the fire, because one had to take out the ashes and cinders from the previous night, clean the fireplace, bring some coal in from the yard or cellar then arrange firewood or firelighters to light it. It was quite a task and a fairly skilful job. The first gas fire that I saw was in Doctor Saxena's Surgery in London Road Preston.

Mr Spencer couldn't stop laughing when I told him about my adventure. A few minutes later Mrs Spencer and Ashraf came down.

Mrs Spencer thought that I was really crazy when she heard what I'd been up to, "Nobody in their proper mind and senses would go out in this weather," she told me.

"But it is absolutely glorious and after all it is Christmas Day. You can't possibly spend such an important day just sitting at home," I said.

Then it was explained to me that in England, Christmas Day is a family day. All the fun takes place at home. A lot of families drink alcohol and have a large Christmas dinner. They exchange gifts with their family members and friends and often they enjoy playing party games later on.

Only then did I understand the true meaning of the saying, "Eat, drink and be merry."

We all exchanged our presents and Mrs Spencer got busy with preparing the Christmas dinner while Mr Spencer took some gifts to his neighbours. Later on some of their neighbours called at the Spencer's house. I was surprised that one of them brought presents for Ashraf and me also. Everyone had thoroughly enjoyed their Christmas meal, especially me, as it was my very first one ever!

****

Television sets weren't so common in those days. The most common source of entertainment in ordinary working class families was BBC Radio, the Home Service, or Radio Luxembourg. In some better off families they had pianos or gramophones in their front rooms.

Eating our Christmas dinner at the Spencer's was a wonderful experience. It was a four or five course meal. Ashraf was as bubbly and chatty as ever over the Christmas dinner. He explained to Mr and Mrs Spencer the Eid celebrations in India and Pakistan, and compared it in detail with Christmas celebrations in England.

In the evening I went out hoping that there might be some life in the town after all, but to my disappointment there was nothing, even the cinemas were closed. After Boxing Day people went back to work and talked about the festivities they had enjoyed so much over Christmas.

New Year's Eve of 1956 was a memorable evening for me. At the mill I was told that a large crowd of people would gather in the open market place, in between the town hall and the GPO building, to welcome in the New Year.

Ashraf and I had worked all day till 5:30pm on New Year's Eve. After our evening meal we had a little rest before getting ready to head for the town centre at about 10:30pm.

As we were just about to leave for the Market Square, Mrs Spencer gave a lump of coal to Ashraf saying, "When you come back and enter the house, will you please bring this in with you?"

I couldn't understand why she wanted us to do this, but then it all became clear to us as Mr Spencer explained, "It's supposed to bring good luck for the rest of the year, if you bring in the New Year with something dark."

In later years at college, I used to say to English boys and girls, "If your parents want some good luck bringing in, then I'll be more than willing to do so, as I myself am dark enough."

Initially I said this as a joke, but in the following years, I was requested a few times to visit English families at midnight on New Year's Eve. I always willingly obliged them!

CHAPTER NINE

After working for a few months in New Hall Lane Mill, I got to know a lot of the workers, and sometimes during our dinner hour I would go upstairs to the spinning rooms to talk to the spinners or doffers. Most of them were young girls, but a few were married women.

One dinner time I walked down to the waste room, which was in the basement of the mill. In that room two men filled large bags with cotton waste. One of them was about 6ft 3inches tall and was always covered with dust and cotton fibres.

After our usual "Hello" and greetings, he got talking to me. When I told him I came from Hyderabad Sind, he was most enthusiastic to speak to me. He told me that he had been stationed in Hyderabad Sind cantonment in 1943. His name was Tom and in 1943 he had been a sergeant in the Military Police.

After a while he was transferred from Hyderabad to Delhi, where he and another MP used to patrol the platforms of Delhi City Station, including Queen's Road Station. Their job was to see if there were any deserters or soldiers who were not supposed to be there.

It was very interesting talking to him, because around the time when Tom was in Delhi, I would have been about ten-years old. At that age I used to go to Delhi regularly. While waiting for the train at Delhi's Queen's Road Station to go back to Pataudi, I used to watch these British MPs on the platform with envy.

They were always in twos, walking majestically on the platform. They were very impressive due to their good height, broad shoulders, and impeccable starched uniforms with peak caps. Most striking of all were their white armbands, with red letters stating 'MP', and their white revolver holsters.

They wouldn't usually talk to ordinary Indian people. If they did speak to an Indian, he had to be either a very well-to-do one, or a high-ranking Government official.

I remember one occasion very clearly when I was with my elder brother Muzammil Hussain and his friend Ghulam on Delhi Station platform. We were having a cup of tea at a tea stall when Ghulam's face suddenly changed, and he went almost white. Actually a year earlier he had joined the Royal Indian Air Force and was now on leave, but he was a day or two late in joining the air base. When he saw these two MPs coming towards us, he thought they were coming for him. Luckily they didn't spot him, but Ghulam was terribly shaken up that day.

****

Tom told me about his stay in different parts of India and he recalled what an enjoyable experience it had all been for him. He had so many pleasant memories of his stay in India. I couldn't believe my eyes when I compared Tom's *present* condition to the smartness of his uniform in those days. Now he wore a dirty blue bib and brace overall, covered with dust and cotton fibres and was wearing an old pair of shoes on his feet.

I thought back to those days when I had been a ten-year old boy, and had seen the MPs with their immaculate appearance, long ago when Tom had been in India. The memory of those shiny boots, starched uniform and peak cap kept flashing before me.

I asked him if he remembered two restaurants that used to be situated on Queen's Road Railway Station Delhi; one was used for Indians and the other solely for Europeans.

"I remember them both very well," he replied. "It was extremely rare indeed for us to see any Indian in the European restaurant, as it was reserved exclusively for whites only."

I recalled once I had looked into that European restaurant. It was very clean, its tables were all laid out with perfectly white tablecloths, and beautifully polished silver cutlery. On each table was placed a bouquet of freshly cut flowers, exquisitely arranged. I seem to think that there was one waiter to each table. Each waiter was smartly dressed in spotless white trousers, tunic and turban with a crest. The doorman was always there ready to open the door for the customers.

However the situation in the restaurant for the Indians was totally the opposite.

Tom explained, "I used to visit these restaurants. I didn't agree, and didn't like the way some of the Englishmen in India used to behave towards Indian people, but it was the accepted thing in those days; however it just wasn't right!" He shook his head sadly.

Tom had returned to Lancashire in 1946.

I wondered later on, 'How long would it have taken Tom to adjust himself to Lancashire life as a factory worker? After all he had spent time in India, where he had authority, dignity and pomp. When I saw him that day he was in a blue dust-covered overall, his hands and face were also very grimy, and he seemed to me to be very dirty.'

****

Whilst living with the Spencers in Hudson Street, every Saturday afternoon I used to go to town with Ashraf. On this particular Saturday afternoon, Ashraf was busy writing a few letters, so I ventured into town on my own.

I was approaching Woolworths in Fishergate when behind me I heard a very sweet female voice saying, "Hello."

At first I didn't pay much attention to this voice, because I didn't expect anybody to be speaking to me. After a few seconds I heard the same voice again. Looking back I saw a young girl just behind me smiling.

I slowed down a bit, and responded with a greeting back to her. I didn't know who she was at first, but all of a sudden I remembered that every Saturday whilst walking with Ashraf, I had noticed this particular girl near Woolworths or the Miller Arcade. She always gave us both a friendly smile.

I had never previously paid any particular attention to this young girl, because I always thought that young English boys and girls looked upon us as something strange, and she might have the same idea about us. In appearance she didn't look to be much more than fourteen or fifteen-years old. She was about five feet four inches tall, of medium build, with blonde hair; she was rather smartly dressed.

I slowed down and she walked up alongside me.

"Are you going to Woolworth's?" she asked.

"Yes I am," I replied. "Are you going there too?"

"Yes," she said, and we walked on before entering Woolworth's together.

I was so nervous at that time that I couldn't talk to her properly, so I made some feeble excuse and left.

When I reached home I told Mr & Mrs Spencer and Ashraf about this experience. They all had a good laugh at my expense.

Mr Spencer said laughing, "Mudassir, she just wants to be your friend. You should talk to her, but do make sure that she is not thirteen or fourteen-years old."

Mr Spencer kept asking me different questions, and teasing me about it all day, but at last Mrs Spencer came to my rescue and told him to leave me alone.

I didn't really understand what Mr Spencer meant when he warned me about thirteen or fourteen-year old girls.

For a few weeks after that I didn't see her in town, but every Saturday whenever I was in town near Woolworths, I thought of her, and decided that if I saw her again I would definitely ask what she was called.

One Saturday at about 11:00am, I was in town and I came out of the gents toilets. The toilets were situated right in the middle of the road on Church Street, in front of the Miller Arcade. I was just about to cross the road, when I spotted this same girl standing underneath the verandah of the Gaumount cinema, (which sadly is now all boarded up). I plucked up a little courage and went across to her.

"Hello again," she came forward with a big smile.

After our initial greetings she asked, "Where are you from?"

When I told her I came from Pakistan she didn't fully understand. So I explained to her that it used to be part of India.

She smiled and said, "Oh, one of my uncles was in the North West Frontier in 1940. Is that in Pakistan?"

"Yes, that is in Pakistan," I agreed, "but I come from the South of Pakistan. Have you heard of Karachi?" I asked her.

She seemed quite good with her geography saying, "Of course I know where Karachi is."

"Well I come from Hyderabad just one-hundred miles away from Karachi," I explained to her.

First of all I wasn't that fluent in English, and I was still very nervous of speaking to any girl, so I couldn't ask her any questions about herself, but I thought that she was in the mood for talking to me.

She asked, “What is your name?”

I thought, ‘If I tell her that my first name is Mudassir, she will never understand it, and also it would be difficult for her to remember.’

So to make it easier for her I asked her, “Have you ever heard of the Aga Khan?”

“Yes, do you mean t*he* Aga Khan,” she asked.

“Well yes, you see my name is Khan too.”

Then she asked me a lot of other things, to which I could only answer “Yes,” or “No.”

I was still so nervous, that although I asked her name, which she gave me, I couldn't quite catch it properly. I didn't like to ask her to repeat it, because I felt too embarrassed.

This was my first experience at having an acquaintance with any English girl socially.

In the evening I told Ashraf and Mr and Mrs Spencer about my chance meeting with her. Obviously Mr Spencer wanted to know her name, and more about her, but when I said I forgot to ask her, they all had a good laugh.

Two or three weeks passed by, then one Saturday at about 10:00am whilst I was walking down Lancaster Road to go to the Harris Library, I saw her standing under Miller Arcade. I thought she was waiting for somebody, so for a moment I hesitated before approaching her.

She had spotted me too and she walked towards me with a smile.

This time I had made my mind up to ask her name and age. After our initial greetings I asked her, “What are you called?”

The way she pronounced her name it sounded like Pearl, or something similar.

Though this time too I didn't understand properly, but once more, I was too embarrassed to ask her again. “Are you waiting for your boyfriend?” I asked her.

“No, I am waiting for my sister,” she laughed. “Where are you going?”

“I am going to the library,” I replied.

By the time her sister came we had begun to tell each other a little about ourselves. I told her, "I came to England as a full-time student at Blackburn College, but I am now studying textiles in Harris College."

In return she told me, "I work in the town hall as a Secretary for the Primary Schools. I live with my parents in Albert Road, Preston. I have one younger sister and a younger brother."

After a few minutes her younger sister Barbara came along. Beryl introduced me to her. Before we parted, and as I was still not sure of her name, I asked her for her name again.

This time she pronounced it very clearly, telling me slowly, "My name is Beryl."

****

British Home Stores, Marks & Spencer, and Woolworths were my favourite stores to visit on Saturdays. On Sunday afternoons if the weather was good, Ashraf and I would go to Avenham Park and Miller Park. I always loved having a stroll on the banks of the famous River Ribble. As we were the only two Asians in Preston at that time, we were some sort of novelty for people, particularly for the younger children. Whether they were walking with their parents or on their own, they would turn around a few times just to have another look at us.

Sometimes some elderly ladies would greet us with big smiles, and ask us directly, "How do you like England?"

One Sunday it was quite sunny and warm, so after our Sunday dinner Ashraf and I decided to go for a stroll in the park. Whilst we were passing the bandstand in the middle of Avenham Park I spotted Beryl with her parents and younger brother David. In those days I wasn't bold enough to approach people. I hoped that Beryl or her parents hadn't seen us.

However Beryl came over to us. I introduced her to Ashraf saying, "This is Beryl, the young lady who I was telling you about."

"Oh yes, how do you do?" Ashraf and Beryl shook hands.

Looking towards her family Beryl said, "Would you like to meet my parents?"

I was a bit reluctant to do so, but as usual Ashraf was enthusiastic and said, "Yes of course, we would both love to."

We approached her family, and shook hands with her mother and father. Her parents were wonderful people, particularly her mother. They showed a lot of interest in us.

"How do you like our country?" her mother asked us.

Ashraf was very good at expressing himself, particularly in praising England.

"What do you think of our English weather?" Beryl's father asked me.

The only answer I could give was, "It is very cold here."

At this they all laughed.

As usual Ashraf was really chatty. "We aren't used to a cold and damp climate, otherwise we are very happy, and are enjoying being in Preston very much."

Beryl's mother must have noticed that I looked a lot younger than Ashraf, and wasn't saying very much. She turned to me and asked, "Do you miss your family?"

"Yes, very much indeed," I replied. I was sure that they all felt very sorry for me.

"They are students at Harris College," Beryl told her family.

We were just about to leave when Beryl's mother invited us, "Why don't you two come over to our house sometimes?"

"Thank you very much, yes we would love to," Ashraf replied.

Leaving this family, Ashraf and I started to walk away.

Beryl looked at me and said, "I'll see you next Saturday morning."

She sounded very cheerful, and as the saying goes, full of beans.

I don't remember what I said to her, but when we got near the fountain in Miller Park, Ashraf, with some cheeky tone in his voice asked, "What does she mean, she will see you next Saturday?"

"I don't know," I said, "I don't see her regularly, just by chance we sort of bump into each other on Saturdays."

Beryl was seventeen-years old, and a pleasant looking, cheerful and well-mannered girl, filled with a lot of self-confidence. Since meeting me she had become very interested in Indian history. She borrowed some books from Harris Library to read about India and its Independence, its division into India and Pakistan, its religions, languages and cultures. Although she was almost eighteen-years old, she still didn't look to be more than fifteen.

As she had told me previously, she was working in the town hall as a school secretary, and was also completing a shorthand and typing course at Alston Hall, Grimshargh, near Longridge.

A few weeks later I visited Beryl's parents. I took with me a bunch of flowers for Beryl's mother, and a box of chocolates for her family. The family were very hospitable.

It was after 6.00pm when I reached their house. Beryl's mother told me that some of their neighbours wanted to meet me. At about seven o'clock four ladies walked into Beryl's house. One of them had lived in India for five or six years when she was very young. The lady's father was a Major in the British Indian Army. I was pleased to hear that at one time her father had been stationed at Delhi cantonment.

Since the British had taken over India in 1857 they had kept the British Army away from the Indian public, hence the railway stations of Delhi cantonment, Lahore cantonment, Karachi cantonment and suchlike places were exclusive to British Army personnel only. The Indian public were not allowed onto the station unless they were attached to the British Army.

Beryl's neighbours wanted to meet me because they were curious about me as to whether or not I could speak English, and if so what I sounded like? I could actually speak much better English when Ashraf wasn't around. I stayed at Beryl's house for supper, leaving at about 10:30pm.

When I reached home, Mr & Mrs Spencer and Ashraf were all waiting for me. Ashraf and Mr Spencer started teasing me with all sorts of questions, but in the end Mrs Spencer once again came to my rescue by telling them both to stop annoying me.

****

Although Ashraf and I were very happy, comfortable and contented staying with Mr & Mrs Spencer, three things made us think about moving. Firstly there was that incident regarding the curry cooking; secondly was the fact that I realised that I was paying exactly half of my weekly wage for my board, so it was no wonder I couldn't save as I had originally intended to do. The third thing was that there was no bathroom at Hudson Street.

I couldn't have an Indian shower all the time in the Spencer's greenhouse, so twice a week I had to go to the public baths. There I had to pay for two baths, as I could never wash my hair in the same water that I had bathed in. So I used to fill a large tumbler with clean water and saved this until the end of my bath, in order to wash my head.

It was the end of February or early March of 1957 when Ashraf told me he'd heard about a Polish couple in Deepdale Road. Apparently they owned a house that was too big for them, so they had a couple of empty rooms.

"Would you be interested in coming along with me?" Ashraf asked.

I agreed to do so.

One evening Ashraf and I went to this house on Deepdale Road. The husband could speak a little English, but his wife could barely understand English. The rooms were on the first floor, comprising of one large one at the front of the house, and another small one at the back. Naturally this time I asked if there was a bathroom in the house. Luckily there was a proper three-piece bathroom, which meant an awful lot to me.

As Ashraf was the negotiator, I gave him the first choice of the rooms. Naturally he took the larger front room, leaving me to settle for the back room.

Now the question was, "Who was going to tell the Spencers about our move?"

In the end it was Ashraf who told Mrs Spencer first, but at the same time I told her about my intentions too. Mr & Mrs Spencer were sorry to hear that we were both leaving them, but they understood exactly why we were, so they both kindly wished us luck in our new lodgings.

****

The main advantage we got in Deepdale Road was that we could cook fast curry. As they were Polish, this couple were used to spicy food themselves. The area was quite respectable. In front of our house was a big Ribble bus depot, next door to us was Damar Dry

Cleaners, a hardware shop, and a corner shop for groceries. At about a two-hundred yard distance stood the famous North End Football Ground.

From the end of March summertime started, and the weather began improving as the days became longer. By this time I had become much more familiar with the English way of life, and I truly started enjoying my stay in England.

One evening I finished work at the mill and walked with Olive to the nursery; her husband Eddie was at the gates of the nursery with Judith.

He asked me, "How would you like to visit us at our house in Brockhalls View one evening?"

On the following Friday arrangements were made and I went to see them. Olive and Eddie were lovely people. I took a bunch of flowers and a box of chocolates for the couple and a toy for their daughter Judith. Eddie and Olive welcomed me wholeheartedly. It did not take very long before I felt totally at home with them.

Judith was always pleased to see me at their house. It was about 8:00pm, which meant it was time for Judith to go to bed. First she kissed Olive, then Eddie, then she spread out her little arms as she came towards me.

Hugging me tightly, she gave me a kiss saying, "Night, night."

****

One evening while I was at their house, Eddie asked, "Are you at all interested in football?"

"Oh yes indeed I am really interested in the game," I replied.

He then suggested that I should go to Preston North End ground to watch the team play.

The following Saturday Preston North End was playing at home, as I had nothing planned for that afternoon, I thought, 'I might as well go to the football match.'

I remember I paid half a crown for entry. I was surprised to see that thousands of people had come to watch the match. It started exactly at 3:00pm. The spectators were making a lot of noise; some had rattles in their hands and were spinning them round.

Two elderly gentlemen behind me were the worst. They were swearing at the referee, asking in very loud voices if he was blind.

I had read somewhere the definition of an English football game. It said, *"The English football game is a game played between two teams of eleven players each, and 25,000 referees."* I found this to be quite literally true in that match.

During the match I didn't know who the Preston North End players were, but I noticed one player in particular. He took the ball from his penalty area, then dribbling, weaving, and dodging every player on the opposite team he took it all the way across to the other side. Nobody could stop him. He went all the way to the other end of the ground with the ball and scored.

The goalkeeper looked at the spectators and shrugged his shoulders, as if he was asking, "How the heck do you stop him?"

The spectators went wild; there were huge roars and cheers and much clapping and shouting.

At that time I couldn't understand what the cheering was all about, because I didn't know any player then. But later on I found out that the player with such great skill, was none other than the famous, international and legendary one and only Tom Finney.

I had the pleasure of saying "Hello," to this great person in 1961. I was passing through Byrom Street in Preston when I saw this somewhat familiar face standing at the door of a shop. As I was just reaching him it came to me that it was Tom Finney.

"Hello, Mr Finney," I greeted him politely.

"Hello there, please call me Tom," he answered.

I was very surprised at his response, because I was under the impression that the English were very reserved and pompous, and hardly ever spoke to strangers. I talked to him for a few more minutes, but I was so nervous, that now I don't even remember what I said to him. I found him in the truest sense to be a down to earth and perfectly proper Lancashire gentleman.

CHAPTER TEN

Living in Deepdale Road independently was wonderful for both Ashraf and me. By now I had learnt how to cook potato curry and pea curry. I wrote to my mother and sisters begging them to send me some recipes and methods of cooking different types of curry. In reply my father sent me recipes for other curries, such as egg and potato, pea and potato, tinned fish, spinach and potatoes and a lot more.

We could buy red peppers, tomato powder and one or two more spices from the Polish and Hungarian shops, but we couldn't get turmeric, coriander, cumin, bay leaves and other such items locally. To obtain these spices we had to travel to Manchester.

It amuses me as to how many things have changed in England even in my lifetime. At one time the English people used to pull their faces at the smell of curries, but now these same people take a deep breath in saying with pleasure, "Oh what a beautiful smell; it is making me feel hungry."

I have seen so many alterations in Blackburn, Bolton, Preston and Accrington, not only regarding food, but the fashions, buildings, social outings, neighbours, the community feeling and understanding have altered also. Some changes were for the better, but others we could have done without.

The time that I spent with the Spencers in Hudson Street in 1956 and '57, was typically Lancastrian. Neighbours cared for one another. They talked to each other almost every day, if not in the street they would talk in the corner shop. During summer, if they didn't go to the park, most housewives would camp in front of somebody's front door and speak to each other on different subjects.

While these discussions with each other were taking place, they always kept an eye on their young ones. If they noticed some children behaving badly they would tell them off, regardless of whether the young one was their own or someone else's.

Lancashire was well known for its old and black buildings. It is refreshing now to see new developments in the towns. Almost all of the Lancashire towns have moved with the times. At least there is now no danger of getting wet when it rains, as it is a pleasure to shop in indoor modern shopping centres.

Whilst one is pleased to see these modern developments, one cannot help but miss the character of Lancashire, that sadly in some towns, and with the exceptions of just a few, many old buildings of character have now been demolished.

Some of these memorable structures were pulled down to make way for new roads and housing estates. The side streets in towns were easy to direct a stranger in town to. Now the new estates are often a bit like mazes, a new person visiting them might well have to ask many times for directions before reaching their destination. I still recall how the odd and even way of numbering houses confused me when I first looked for the correct house in Alexandra Road way back on my very first day in Blackburn.

****

I thoroughly enjoyed working in Horrocks's New Hall Lane Mill. It wasn't just at New Hall Lane Mill that I was well known though, as a few people from Stanley Street Mill also used to come to talk to me. Once or twice the personnel officer also came to see me, as he had spent quite a few years in India during the war.

In April 1957, Mr Cowell the manager of New Hall Lane Mill told me that he would like me to work on the Scutcher machines in the blowroom. Before I could answer him he told me that I would get £1.18 shillings per week more in my wages if I accepted this job.

As that sum was quite a lot of money in those days, I didn't know whether Mr Cowell was genuinely giving me that job, or if he wanted to keep me away from his doffers and spinners, as most of them loved talking to me, which could quite easily have disrupted production.

Although the wages were good in the blowroom, the work was very heavy and hard. I enjoyed working there, but I missed going to all the different departments and talking to the workers. I had to look after four Scutchers. These machines were constantly producing cotton laps one after the other. The Scutchers used to run non-stop; if

I wanted to go to the toilet, or for a wash, perhaps just to make a cup of tea, whatever the reason, I had to always ask another operative to look after my machines whilst I was away.

****

In April and May the weather was getting better, it was sometimes really nice at weekends, so we started going out in the evenings. We would perhaps go to Avenham Park, or at other times we visited Farrington Park.

My favourite place for a walk was always on the banks of the River Ribble. Standing near the iron bridge over the Ribble I could watch the steam trains passing over the bridge. I have always had a soft spot for steam trains and loved going to Preston Railway Station just to watch the trains going to London or Glasgow.

As the weather started getting better, Ashraf and I started going away at weekends. We usually travelled by train, but for a change we sometimes used the Ribble buses. Ashraf loved going to Blackpool, he couldn't wait to get off the train or bus to make his way to the Pleasure Beach. He would go on almost every ride, but the dodgem cars and playing penny games were always his favourites.

Sometimes Basant, Hassan and Giddy came to visit us at Preston, and all five of us would either go to Blackpool, Southport or Morecambe.

All of a sudden during that period, I realised that the days were a lot longer. I was so amazed at this that I even wrote to my father and friends in Pakistan saying, "In England it is proper daylight at 4:00am and stays light until 10:00pm."

I thought, 'It is no wonder that they used to say, t*he sun doesn't set on the British Empire.'*

Staying in Deepdale Road was a pleasure. Ashraf and I were both very happy living independently. I had now got quite used to cooking our fast curry dishes of peas, beans, eggs, Okra and other delicious items.

It was then that the landlord on Deepdale Road told us that he was selling the house, so we would have to look for some other accommodation.

This news really upset us both. Once again we went to the police station to see if they could help us? They gave us a name, Mr Orepuck, of Frenchwood Street off Avenham Lane.

CHAPTER ELEVEN

Mr Orepuck was a Polish gentleman who had came to Preston during the war. Once again Ashraf was the negotiator; he made sure that Mr Orepuck didn't object to us cooking curries. My main concerns were an inside toilet and bathroom. Fortunately both of these facilities were available at the house on Frenchwood Street.

The arrangement was that the rent would be £1.00 a week per head. We would have to use our own pans, crockery and cutlery, washing up liquid and the rest. Mr Orepeck had to be informed at least two hours before we could have a bath, as he had to open some sort of shutter on the coal fire in order to heat the water in the bathroom tank.

During the 1950's Frenchwood Street was full of European immigrants; there were Polish, Ukrainians, Italians, Hungarians, and some Greek people. It was the beginning of June 1957 when Ashraf and I finally moved there.

This street was like most other ordinary typical industrial town streets. Some terraced houses were with three bedrooms, whilst others had just two. Most houses had a three piece bathroom upstairs and the kitchens were reasonably large. Besides Ashraf and me, a young Ukrainian couple occupied the next bedroom to mine.

The summer of 1957 was very good as most days were warm, sunny and beautiful. Ashraf usually felt tired after his work so he would stay in, but I always went out in the evening. The greenery around Avenham Park, Miller Park and across the River Ribble always appeared quite breathtaking to me. It looked as if somebody has spread green velvet all over. I hadn't seen so much greenery before in my whole life. Some evenings I would spend hours writing home about 'Pretty Preston' and the beautiful scenery around it.

At one time, Church Street between Manchester Road and Lancaster Road, was very lively. Coming down onto Church Street from Miller Arcade and Lancaster Road on one's right-hand side was the brightly lit Bull & Royal Hotel, almost facing it across the road was Dunn's the famous gent's shop. Facing the cinemas and next to the Parish Church, was Atkinson's, the famous bedding shop, a photo studio, the Horseshoe café and many shops.

Whilst the shops closed at 5:30pm the cinemas remained open till the last show ended at 10:30pm, then people rushed out for their last bus home.

Sometimes Ashraf and I walked down to the Ritz Cinema to watch a film; if we didn't want to see that particular picture, there was a choice of going to three other cinemas, all within easy walking distance.

As we walked away from the Ritz, we used to notice a cameraman standing somewhere in that area; he would dash across the road in front of us then quickly snap a few shots. The cameraman always managed to catch us quite unaware of his presence and took some photographs. He would give us a ticket and the next day we would send off a half-crown postal order so that we would get our photos delivered in return.

Khalil Ashraf and the author in Church St. Preston.

Mudassir Khan with his former landlady, enjoying the most usual form of entertainment in those days.

Originally I used to wonder about some young people standing under the canopies of the Ritz, Palladium and Empire cinemas, and in the Miller Arcade. I asked Mr Spencer about them; he told me that they would most likely be waiting for their dates. I didn't fully understand this, so Mr Spencer explained to me about British culture relating to courting couples.

While living in Frenchwood Street I started going out on my own to parks, the railway station, or to the pictures, and once or twice I was a little late in arriving home. Ashraf didn't approve of this and told me so. I didn't like him telling me off in this way, as in my opinion I was an adult, a fully grown-up man. I know he meant well, but I didn't like the tone of his voice when he was not pleased with me. After these episodes there was always an atmosphere, so we both thought it best to find separate accommodation.

Ashraf told me that he had found lodgings with a couple on Blackpool Road, near Tulketh Mill, and was going to move there the following weekend.

It was the end of July 1957 when I decided to move from Preston and look for a fresh job in another town. In the late 50's it wasn't really difficult to get a job anywhere, particularly in the textile mills. To this day I don't know why I decided to go to Bolton for a job, as there were hundreds of jobs in Preston and Blackburn.

Anyhow for whatever reason I caught the Ribble bus to Bolton. It was a beautiful sunny and warm July day. I sat on the front seat of the top deck thoroughly enjoying the scenery during my journey. As the bus entered Bolton's boundary I started taking notice of the mill chimneys. I noticed a huge mill chimney at Astley Bridge on Blackburn Road.

I got off the bus at the next stop and walked down to the mill. It was North End Spinning Mill; when I arrived there I asked for the foreman. Luckily for me he had three vacancies; one of them was on a Scutcher in the blowroom. I accepted this job because the wage of £8.5s was better than what I was getting in Preston.

Now I was facing the problem of lodgings. I had no idea of Bolton town at all, so I asked the foreman if he knew of any landlady who might take in lodgers. He wasn't sure, but he told me that there were some foreign families on Seymour Road who did take in lodgers.

Seymour Road was off Blackburn Road, which was only a few minutes walk from the mill. I called at that address, a woman aged about fifty-five answered the door. She spoke perfect English, but with an accent, I later realised she was either Russian or Hungarian. She lived with her elderly father and older sister in this large house. I learnt later that the family had been forced to leave Hungary during the uprising against the Russians in 1956.

We agreed on terms of £1.00 a week rent for the room, but I had to share the kitchen and bathroom with the family. I told her that I preferred to cook curry rather than live on fish and chips. She had no objection to curry, but at the same time she seemed very interested in understanding what curry was.

My room was upstairs; it was a lovely room, with a comfortable single bed, wardrobe, dressing-table, writing-desk and a small chair as well as an easy chair.

The next day I collected my belongings from Frenchwood Street, Preston, and moved them all into Seymour Road, Bolton. This was the best room I had lived in since I came to England.

On the weekend before I started work at North End Mill, I told my landlady that I was going to cook some curry. Although she didn't know anything about this type of food she was very enthusiastic to learn about curry, chapatties and other Indian dishes.

I had already bought fresh onions, garlic, ginger and other Indian spices from Manchester. All three members of the family wanted to watch and help me make the curry, so one was cutting the garlic, whilst the other was slicing onions. As I mixed the spices I explained to them how to blend the other spices for making into different curries.

That day I was going to make pea and potato curry with some boiled rice, as in those days this was the only way I knew how to cook rice. Initially I was going to cook for myself, but when I noticed the family's interest in the curry, I invited them all to taste the curry and rice with me. They gladly accepted my invitation; when the food was cooked and ready, one of the sisters set the table, while their father laid out the cutlery.

I did my best to set the table out in Eastern fashion. We put the rice in a tray and the curry into a casserole dish. Then I explained the combination of curry and rice and other Indian dishes. At the same time I informed them about Asian manners and etiquette. To my surprise they all enjoyed the curry and rice very much.

****

North End Spinning Mill was just like any other Lancashire mill as most workers there were female. I liked the work and settled down very quickly. It didn't take me long to get to know some of the other workers.

It was the end of September when one afternoon I felt like I had a bit of a sore throat. I didn't pay much attention to it at first, but by the time I went to bed I was feeling really down. However I thought that perhaps a good night's sleep would get rid of it, as I didn't feel like troubling my landladies.

During the night I must have built up quite a high temperature, and when I have a temperature, I always suffer with Lumbago. My back was killing me and the pain was unbearable. I didn't know what to do except moan and groan.

The following day my landladies thought that I was having a lie in, so they didn't want to disturb me. But when the younger sister came home after shopping at about 10:00am, she noticed that I wasn't up, and became rather concerned.

She knocked at my door and when there was no reply, she came in asking if I was feeling all right?

When I told her that I wasn't, she touched my forehead and almost screamed, "Oh you poor boy, you are burning up with a high temperature. Have you got a doctor?"

I was registered as a patient with Dr. Saksena in Preston.

The landlady told me, "You will have to change your doctor now. Can you manage to walk to the doctor's surgery on Blackburn Road?"

"I really feel too ill to walk," I said weakly.

She must have gone to the surgery for me, because within two hours a Dr Jack visited me at the house.

He examined me thoroughly, assuring me, "There is nothing serious for you to worry about; it is only a common flu." (Asian flu came later).

The doctor prescribed some tablets and a bottle of medicine, which the landlady kindly purchased from the chemist at a cost of one shilling.

Once again I felt really homesick, because during the previous night when I had such a high temperature, I had tried to shout out to attract somebody's attention, but there was nobody to answer my cries. Perhaps I hadn't shouted loud enough. At that moment I really missed my mother, my sisters and my sister-in-law.

As mentioned previously I was the spoilt one in the family; if I had been in this condition in Hyderabad, there would have been somebody running around for me until I got better.

****

I remember the time in 1954 when I was off ill. The first day that I had a bit of a temperature a doctor was sent for. He examined me and prescribed some medicine. However my temperature kept going up and down. This rather worried my elder brother Muzammil Hussain. The next day he took me to one of the famous TB specialists in Hyderabad, Dr Abdul Majeed Memon.

After a thorough examination he suspected something more serious than just a temperature. This was because four years earlier one of my elder sisters had actually died from TB.

Dr Memon's suspicion shattered the family. My family didn't want me to be admitted into hospital, so the treatment had started right away at home. It was arranged that an assistant from Dr Memon's clinic would call at our house each morning and evening to give me two injections. The table in my room was filled with pills, tablets and medicines. Everyone was anxious to do things for me.

Thankfully Dr Memon's treatment was successful, so I was allowed to go to Larkana where my father was the Railway Station Master. I was pampered there too; if I was going to the town's library in the evening, one of my father's orderlies would accompany me to carry my books.

****

Now I was feeling sorry for myself in Seymour Road and was so homesick that I started crying. At that time I only had two friends, Hassan and Ashraf. Hassan was in Blackburn and Ashraf was still working at Tulketh Spinning Mill in Preston.

Not many homes had the luxury of telephones in those days, so I had to write to Hassan and Ashraf telling them about my illness. The following weekend they both came to see me.

I was worried about work as it was only a week since I had started at North End Mill, naturally I feared that I might lose my job. As the mill wasn't too far away from the house, my landlady very kindly went over to the mill with my sick-note and informed the foreman about my illness.

Fortunately I recovered within two weeks and the following Monday when I went back to work, I was asked by the foreman to give him my fit note.

I didn't know then that I had to have a note proving that I was well enough to go back to work from the doctor before starting again. Luckily the foreman was a very understanding person, and he allowed me to go to Dr Jack's surgery to get the required document.

CHAPTER TWELVE

It was October 1957 and I was very worried about my studies, because all the courses had started in September, I really didn't want to lose out on another year.

At the same time I received a few letters from father and my brother and sisters. They too were missing me very much and insisting that I should do one final course before returning home.

At one stage I even thought of taking up a course in Bolton College. I saw the head of the chemistry department; who suggested that I could do my M.Sc. or Associateship of the Royal Institute of Chemistry.

I almost decided to do A.R.I.C. but one weekend Hassan came to see me in Bolton. He told me that Mr D. L. King, the head of the textile department at Blackburn College was concerned about me and would like to see me.

I took a day off from work and went to see Mr King. He was a six feet three inch tall giant, but was a very kind person, particularly so to the overseas students; he would always go out of his way to help them.

Although Mr King had all my documents, I needed to convince him that the science subjects I had already been taught in my degree course should be sufficient to do textile related subjects, and therefore I should already be on target to complete the Associateship course in two years. Mr King promised to look into my case saying that he would let me know within a week.

I was very worried at this stage because if I didn't get the exemption of one year, I would have to stay in England for another three years, which would be far too much for me as I wanted to return home as soon as I possibly could.

Luckily Mr King informed me that he was prepared to exempt me from the first year of the Textiles Associateship Course provided that

I joined the course as soon as possible. By now it was already almost the middle of October.

I was very happy with this news. I wrote to my father straight away saying that I would like to complete this course on a full-time basis. Father was pleased too, because he didn't approve at all of me taking a year out.

While working in Preston and Bolton I had managed to save some money, which now came in very handy for paying my college fees. Father wanted to know the monthly expenses that I would need during my full-time course.

I didn't want to overburden him with many expenses, so I told him that although I would have a sanction of £100.00 per month from the Pakistani High Commission in London, he didn't need to send this amount of money, but like a very good, considerate and kind father, he regularly sent me £50.00 each month.

Hassan, Ashraf and Giddy were pleased with me for joining the full-time course in Blackburn.

My next task was to find some accommodation closer to college. Hassan and Giddy were already staying in May House Cottage at Lancaster Place. Giddy had already completed his Textile Diploma at Blackburn College, but was going through some training with Platt Bros. the spinning machinery manufacturers. This training was only for a further few weeks then Giddy was heading back to India. It was therefore agreed that I could move into May House Cottage with Giddy and Hassan.

Khalil, Basant, Mudassir, Gidwani and Hassan as college students.

May House Cottage was a detached building, situated at the rear of Lancaster Place which belonged to two butchers known as the Cowburn brothers. They used the downstairs halls of the cottage as a warehouse for their meat and let the upstairs self-contained flat to overseas students.

Jack and Bob, two of the Cowburn brothers, also owned a couple of retail shops on New Bank Road. So Hassan and I went to see one of the brothers to let him know about the new arrangements. Luckily he had no objection to this at all.

I brought my belongings from Seymour Road, but I was so sorry to leave that family in Bolton as they had all been so kind to me.

The rent for the whole of May House Cottage was £3.00 a week, which worked out at £1.50 each for me and Hassan. Our accommodation was upstairs where there were two large bedrooms, one good sized living room, a three-piece modern bathroom, and a modern kitchen. May House Cottage was one of the very few places in those days with all the modern facilities such as inside toilets, a fitted kitchen, wall to wall carpeting on the stairs, landing, bedrooms, and the living room.

This was the first house where I found a modern gas fire in the living room, which was a real luxury indeed in those days, which I found only in the better off residential areas. It took me a few days to settle in.

After a few weeks Giddy left for India. The arrangement between Hassan and me was that we would share the weekly expenses such as gas, electric, newspapers, and groceries.

I joined the second year textile classes; by the end of November through working hard, I had managed to catch up with the rest of the class. I met some newly arrived students from India, East Pakistan, West Pakistan, Egypt, Turkey, Nigeria, Hong Kong, China and Ghana.

The students were either on Government Scholarships, Colombo Plan, or were from mega-rich families, such as mill owners, landlords, Army Generals or high Government officials. Most students received £100.00 per month and lived a life of luxury, whilst other people like me were very careful about their weekly expenses.

My father was quite willing to send as much money as I needed, but I didn't want to overburden him. I asked him to send me £50.00 in the first week of each month.

****

Besides Mr D. L. King, the head of the textile department, I got to know the subject lecturers namely Mr Wilkinson, Mr Poynton, Mr Riley, Mr Newton, Mr Clayton, Mr Weaver, Mr Pava, Mr Massarvi, Mr Daimler, and Mr Bencroft. All these lecturers were well qualified in their subjects and I thoroughly enjoyed their lectures.

Then there was Miss Crank, the colour and design lecturer. She was a very young looking lady, with a charming personality and a beautiful smile. She was very popular amongst the overseas students and hardly any of them missed her classes. Some of the students attended her evening classes also. She was engaged to Mr Burgess who lectured at Alston Hall Preston.

Once I was terribly surprised and shocked when Miss Crank asked me, "Do you know any student in Alston Hall, Preston?"

"No, I don't think so Miss," I replied.

She smiled broadly saying, “Are you sure, you don't know anybody there?”

“Yes, I'm sure,” I said confidently.

But then all of a sudden, a thought flashed through my mind, ‘Beryl! She is a student at Alston Hall.’

“Oh yes, I do know someone there, but how do you know about it?” I enquired.

It appeared that Beryl had been talking to Mr Burgess about an overseas student in Blackburn, and since Miss Crank was engaged to Mr Burgess, he had told her about Beryl’s conversation with him. Miss Crank couldn't think of anybody else but me who it could be, but to this day it still remains a mystery as to why she should think of me at all.

****

Mr Gammul, a lecturer at College, used to take the students to Blackpool, Southport, Morecambe, the Lake District and other places of interest in Lancashire. Somehow he always arranged meetings to introduce overseas students to British culture.

Our classes were held in the old Victoria Building as the new wing was not yet complete and the spinning and weaving machines were in the process of being moved from the old building shed to the new one, which was very modern and well equipped.

The canteen was situated at the back of Victoria Building, where most students went for a cup of tea or coffee during their breaks. Many of the female students were on part-time secretarial, hairdressing, nursing and other similar courses. I got to know a few of these girls; namely Carole, Marjorie, Marian and Jean.

Instead of chairs there were long benches at the tables in that canteen. Hassan and I always seemed to manage to find room on a table where a group of these girls were gathered.

Amongst the older overseas students I can still remember were Hassan, Dada Bhai, Ghosh, Goha, Jabbar, Khan Lum, Munir, David Hindle, Lee, Montinegro, Qureshi, Rauf, Ghafoor and others. The newcomers in the first year who I recall are Riaz Chaudry, Ajmal Hassan, Javed Khan and Atta Mohiuddin.

Jabbar, Mudassir, Hassan and Dada Bhai in St. Andrews Street, Blackburn in 1957, when they were all students

Living in May House Cottage was wonderful. The cottage was detached and the distance between the other houses and the cottage was so great, that nobody was disturbed by any music or noise. At weekends most of our friends would come over to May House Cottage, purely because there we could cook spicy curry, listen to Indian music and converse freely in our own Urdu language.

Actually our weekends would always start on Friday nights with going to the pictures. Hassan and I frequently went to the cinema in town as the Rialto on Penny Street was our favourite picture place. A few years later it was named the Odeon Cinema, but eventually it was demolished in the late 60's.

Between 6:30 and 7:15pm teenagers would stand patiently under the Rialto cinema verandah waiting for their dates. To see these young people standing quietly and patiently always used to amuse me.

In the late 50's not many people had cars, so they mostly travelled on local or Ribble buses as hiring a taxi in those days was also quite rare.

We used to look forward to our Saturday nights. Giddy was very keen and fond of going to dances, particularly to King George's Hall. There were two more dancehalls, Tony's and Court ballroom.

****

By the time I settled down in May House Cottage and Blackburn town I had made quite a few friends both in and out of college. My college studies were in full swing and we were now getting ready for the holidays, as Christmas was now quite near.

From the last week or so of November, we had Christmas festivities organised by different people. There were many parties, such as the one at college, the Student's Union, the Textiles and the Overseas Student's party, along with many fringe events. The parties were held on Friday evenings in the Windsor Suite of King George's Hall or alternatively at Tony's Ballroom.

People were kind to us students in those days, particularly so over the Christmas period. I am sure that most English families felt sorry for us young overseas students. Quite a few English families invited us to their homes over the Christmas holidays.

Often the students were invited by local clubs, such as the Conservative, Labour and Rotary Club to join in their Christmas parties. These invitations were sent out through the British Council.

Once I attended a Rotary Club's Christmas Party. There were a few members there who had spent some time in India during the war. Two or three of them had been stationed in Delhi cantonment and were pleased to meet me, as they hadn't previously met an Indian from Delhi.

One of the members who I got talking to was Sydney Harwood. During our conversation he told me that he was the general manager at Palatine Dairies. Somehow we got talking about student's financial situations. When I told him that I didn't want to burden my father financially and therefore received limited money from him, Mr Sydney Harwood was very sympathetic towards me.

A few minutes later he approached me again and asked, “How would you like some part-time work at my dairy on Saturdays and Sundays?”

I was more than willing to take up his offer.

He gave me his card and asked me to visit him the following Monday.

Palatine Dairies was situated on St. Clements Street, which is off Furthergate in Blackburn. I went to see Mr Harwood. He collected my insurance card and took me on a tour round the dairy, showing me all the different departments and explaining certain jobs. I noticed that the floor was wet through because of the water running constantly.

"This is due to us spilling milk from the churns collected from the farms," I was informed. "It has to be washed off the floor right away."

The foreman told me that he would supply me with a pair of wellingtons, but I should bring some *old* clothes with me, such as trousers, shirt and pullover or a cardigan. This was because the work was mostly rather wet and dirty.

In the dairy they had both sterilised and pasteurised milk, as well as cheese and orange juice. For the workers all these things were free, also we could drink as much milk or orange juice as we wanted.

Furthergate is between Copy Nook and Accrington Road which at one time was a good shopping centre. I can distinctly recall there being a row of shops at the very spot where we have Jan's Petrol Station now. One of those shops sold pies, biscuits, shortbread and other refreshments; I think it was called Coopers. Now there is no sign of the community spirit we used to experience, as so many shops have been replaced by superstores.

On my first Saturday at the dairy I started at 8:00am. I hadn't brought anything with me for my dinner, so at lunch time I took a short walk to Furthergate to see if I could buy something to eat from a shop. I saw Coopers across the road and as there were no customers in the shop I entered.

Within seconds a young girl aged about seventeen or eighteen appeared from the back room. She was charming and attractive; for a moment I was so mesmerised that I even forgot what I went in for, and what I needed to buy.

She started talking and was very chatty. Our conversation started in the usual manner.

"Where do you come from? Do you like England, the English weather and English people in general?"

Eventually I think I bought some biscuits and shortbread.

On the following Saturday I visited the shop again, this time the girl told me that her name was Sandra. I continued visiting the shop every Saturday and learnt that it belonged to her mother. During my Saturday lunch breaks, if there were no customers in the shop we would chat for fifteen or twenty minutes.

Sandra has a married sister called Norma who sometimes came to the shop, once or twice I met their mother. Sandra's mother greatly reminded me of Mrs Spencer, my former landlady in Preston.

It was around Christmas when Hassan also wanted to do some part-time work. He asked Syd, "Is there any chance of me working at Palatine Dairies?"

Luckily Syd agreed to employ Hassan temporarily.

Once when Hassan and I were at Sandra's shop her mother came into the shop and joined in our conversation.

She asked us both, "Are you going anywhere on Christmas Day?"

I replied, "We have no plans, except that one or two other students might come to our flat and spend the day with us."

Sandra's mother looked at Sandra then turned to us and offered, "Why don't you two boys come to our house on Boxing Day?"

We were very thrilled at receiving this wonderful but totally unexpected invitation, so we accepted her kind offer there and then.

On Boxing Day we took some presents for Norma and Sandra and were surprised to discover that Sandra's mother, Sandra and Norma had each bought us some presents too.

Looking back we shouldn't have been so surprised with a wonderful culture of receiving and giving. However we really enjoyed the whole day at their house, where we met many of their other relations. The time flew by so fast, and it was almost 11:00pm when we left their house.

As usual we were in great demand on New Year's Eve. I was already booked by the Spencer's in Preston, to bring the New Year into their house. It was great to spend New Year's Eve of 1957 in Preston.

At approximately 8.00pm Ashraf came to the Spencer's house. He wanted them to accompany us to Preston town centre, where people gathered to welcome in the New Year at the open market place. Unfortunately Mrs Spencer was unable to walk that distance, so in the end it was just me and Ashraf who went to the open market. It was brightly lit up; the music was playing loudly making the atmosphere seem very exciting.

Hundreds of people, young, middle-aged and the elderly were all gathered in the market place. It was mostly the young people who were dancing all over to the beat of the loud music.

Ashraf and I were standing in front of the old town hall watching these young people dancing when suddenly I felt somebody tapping my shoulder.

"Hello," a very familiar voice greeted me as I turned round to look.

It was Beryl with her sister Barbara and their brother David, all smiling as usual.

"Oh hello, how are you all?" I quickly responded.

Ashraf and I thoroughly enjoyed talking to them. It was now almost midnight and everyone was getting ready to welcome in the New Year of 1958. Exactly at midnight the town hall clock started to strike the first of its twelve chimes ready to bring in the midnight hour.

A big cheer rose up from the crowd and the church bells rang out loudly. We could even hear the ship's loud hooters from Preston docks, as everyone heralded the arrival of 1958.

Friends and strangers kissed each other and wished everyone, "Happy New Year."

Ashraf and I wished Beryl, Barbara, and David a Happy New Year; in the spirit of the occasion we greeted a few strangers as well. We stayed there till 12:30am then left as we had a job to do.

Mr & Mrs Spencer never drank alcohol. When we brought the New Year into their house they offered us soft drinks, then in turn we wished one another a very "Happy New Year."

****

After two weeks at the dairy, for two days work I got £3.00, which was good money in those days. Although our hours of work were eight hours a day, we sometimes used to finish at about 3:00 or 3:30 in the afternoon, as the foreman would let us go a little earlier if everything was done.

Palatine Dairies was a family firm, which was run entirely by the four Harwood brothers. I never came across the eldest brother, but came to know the other three brothers quite well. Besides Syd, there were Tom and Gerald too.

As I was only a casual part-time worker, I worked wherever the foreman required my services. Sometimes I would load the truck with crates filled with bottles of milk ready to be delivered to the Milk Marketing Board, East Lancs Dairies; at other times we took the traditional method of distribution, which was door-to-door deliveries in and around Blackburn.

Occasionally I would accompany one of the drivers to go to the farms to collect the churns ready filled with milk; a few times I would go with the milkman to deliver milk door-to-door. I really loved working at Palatine Dairies for it was a family firm in the truest sense. From the top management down to the ordinary worker, every single person was very friendly and helpful towards each other. During the summer I enjoyed delivering milk on Sunday mornings, and riding with the milkman on his horse and cart.

Once on a summer Sunday morning in 1958, the foreman asked me if I would like to accompany Jack on the horse-driven cart to deliver milk in another area. It was such a beautiful, bright, warm and fresh morning that I would never have dreamed of refusing. More than willing I joined Jack the milkman and sat next to him. The sound of the horse's hooves trotting on cobbled streets was like music to me. I'm not very sure now, but I think it was the Lammack or Pleckgate area that we were driving along.

Whilst Jack was driving the horse and cart, I jumped down from the cart, rushed forward and back again putting full bottles of milk at the front doors and collecting the empties. It was tough trying to keep up with Jack, but I was doing my best to deliver and collect the bottles as fast as I could.

I collected some empty bottles from a doorstep and was just crossing the driveway when I heard a voice calling out.

"Hey, come here."

I turned around to have a look and saw an elderly lady dressed in her dressing-gown and slippers. I stood at the gate of her drive, wondering what to say or do?

She shouted again, this time beckoning me with her hand, "Come here."

I walked towards her rather hesitantly.

She gazed at me, rubbed her eyes and said, "What have you been doing, you weren't of this colour yesterday."

"I am not your *regular* milkman Missus," I said, quickly walking away without any further explanation to her.

She stood at her doorstep looking quite puzzled and confused. I think it was the first time she had ever seen a coloured man. We had a good laugh later on when I told Syd and my friends about this incident.

The wages I got from the dairy helped me a lot, as my father didn't need to send me the full amount of money sanctioned to me by the State Bank of Pakistan; even if he did send me the money I always tried to save it. Most students had their accounts in Lloyds Bank. Our money was always directly deposited into our accounts on the first of the month. Some students, who got hundreds of pounds every month, would spend it so lavishly that they were always broke by the last week of every month.

****

The ground floor of May House Cottage was used by the Cowburn Brothers for the storage of their frozen meat. Our two bedrooms were situated directly above these freezers, which consequently made the bedrooms feel very cold.

All four or five of us boys used to go out on Saturday evenings for a boys' night out, then we would return to the cottage quite late in the evening. Instead of going back to their own digs, the other boys would come back to the cottage with us. The bedrooms were so freezing cold, that we would bring pillows, blankets and mattresses from our bedrooms into the sitting-room, where it was always a lot warmer and bed down on the floor.

The arrangement for the next morning used to be that whoever got up first in the morning would make cups of tea or coffee for everyone.

The first time Ashraf stayed with us over the weekend, I explained this arrangement to him. Ashraf always had a problem in the morning, for as soon as he woke up, he couldn't hold on, he had to go to the toilet immediately.

That Sunday morning as soon as Ashraf came out of the bathroom someone shouted, “Mine is coffee Ashraf,” or “I will have tea with one sugar.”

In fact we all used to be awake at that time, but didn't like making five teas or coffees in that freezing kitchen, so mostly poor Ashraf was the victim, then there would be a race to go to the bathroom. Yelling at each other was the usual practice if anyone took too long in the bathroom.

We always had a very lazy Sunday morning. Before too long it used to be afternoon and everyone would be busy making curry with eggs and potatoes. Everyone had a chore to do and brought something with them for the curry, such as eggs, or a tin of tomatoes, potatoes, onions, garlic, or loaves of bread.

Someone would peel and slice the onions, whilst one of the others would be busy slicing the garlic and ginger, or washing and peeling potatoes, or boiling the eggs then shelling them after they had cooled a little.

In the beginning Ashraf used to be the ‘head chef’, but later on I took over this responsibility. I would start cooking the curry at about 2:00 in the afternoon. Some Pakistani or Indian students who were with landladies and hadn't tasted spicy food for a whole week, would start arriving at the flat at about 5:00pm. By this time the curry would be almost ready.

There would be a knock at the front door downstairs, somebody would look through the living room or kitchen window and shout, “Hey, Sattar is here.”

With each additional name, an extra glass of water would be added to the pan instantly creating very watery gravy.

At the cottage we had created a purely Asian atmosphere and hospitality, in that whoever came to May House Cottage was always invited to join us in the feast.

This meant that by 5:00pm there would be Jabbar, Dada Bhai, Baqi, Salim, Giddy, Hassan, Ashraf, Sattar, Rauf and me.

In that big pan there were only one or two eggs, the cut pieces of two or three potatoes, whilst the rest was gravy. But this thin gravy was always spicy, so to us all it tasted extremely tasty.

Ashraf used to open three loaves of bread and dish out the curry in individual bowls. We would fight over the halves of eggs or pieces of potatoes, but Ashraf's decision always used to be final. After finishing off all this wonderful curry we would all walk down Preston New Road to go to the town centre cinema.

We had such a good choice of cinemas in those days. These were the Essoldo, Royal, Rialto, Palace, Roxy, Alexandra and others. Once we reached the town centre we split into separate groups, because we wouldn't all choose to view the same film.

When the films finished we always used to catch the last bus heading towards Preston New Road; after getting off the bus we literally used to run to reach the cottage as we didn't want to miss the top twenty pop songs that were played each Sunday night on Radio Luxembourg.

For a long time the number one hit of 1958 was Joe-Mr- Piano-Henderson's instrumental *Trudy.* Rock 'n' roll soon dominated the music scene. Bill Hailey, Fats Domino, the Kingston Trio, Lonnie Donigan, Acker Bilk and others were well known in those days. Elvis Presley was just beginning to make his name, with songs like *Hound Dog*, and *All Shook up,* Cliff Richard was also just coming onto the pop scene.

****

Lodging with Mr & Mrs Spencer had turned out to be very useful for me, as I had learnt to live in a systematic way organising myself very well. Like Mrs Spencer, I divided my week for certain jobs on particular days. I never wasted my evenings during the week; if I washed my shirts by hand one evening, then I would cook the next evening, or iron my washed shirts.

I had brought six or seven white shirts with me from Pakistan. I had thought that these shirts would last me for three years, but I soon realised that white shirts in Blackburn get dirty very quickly, particularly around the collars, I always liked to wear a clean shirt with a stiff collar.

Since joining my classes in October 1957 I had made quite a lot of friends at college. I had also made a few friends in Blackburn outside of college, like Sandra and her family, Jean and family, and Carol and family.

Local English families used to regularly invite overseas students to spend an evening with them. It was done through our very sociable Mr Gammul. Jean and Sandra's family took to me so much, that my fellow students thought these two families had really adopted me. I think there was a small element of jealousy there.

Jean's parents, Mr and Mrs Blackburn lived on Whalley Old Road. In those days if someone was in the house, the front door would be left wide open, only the vestibule door would be closed, but it was not locked.

Sometimes after 2:00pm, if I didn't have any class, I would walk down on my own to Whalley Old Road to Jean's house. That part of Whalley Old Road is demolished now. Mrs Blackburn was always at home in the afternoon. She used to finish all her shopping in the morning.

I started addressing Jean's mother as 'mum', and often as soon as I went in her house I would say, "Oh mum, I am starving."

"Go on then, have a look if there is something in the kitchen," she always said.

I usually found my favourite home-baked sponge cake in the cupboard.

"Make a cup of tea for me too while you are there," she would state, and I would gladly oblige.

****

One Sunday afternoon the weather was very pleasant. Mr and Mrs Blackburn asked me. "Would you like to accompany us on a visit to some of our relations in Skipton?"

Naturally I agreed to do so as I had never been there before. The family we visited insisted on us having an evening meal with them. Jean had a married sister called Marjorie who was married to Alan Sergeant.

In order to return Mr and Mrs Blackburn's kindness and favours, I often took Jean to the pictures or to college functions. Jean and I had very good understanding, that we were just good friends, and as such we treated each other with respect. She turned out to be a very true and sincere friend.

Jean's father Mr Blackburn was a very kind man. He was always humorous, telling jokes continuously. Marjorie and Alan were devoted to each other. Most weekends they visited Mr and Mrs Blackburn.

Mudassir with Jean, Marjorie and Mrs Blackburn

I was told in Hyderabad and Karachi that I would find English people very reserved and not as hospitable as Pakistanis or Asians, but in truth I personally found that perception to be totally baseless. Within the first eighteen months of being in England I had found most English people to be very kind, helpful, reliable, generous, sociable and thoroughly hospitable.

Almost every month I was invited to spend an evening with English families in Whalley New Road. Whenever I was invited I would take a bunch of flowers or a box of chocolates with me, as this helped a lot to please the 'lady of the house' and the children.

Once I went to visit a family on a Friday evening in Whalley New Road. The front room of this house where we sat seemed enormous to me; there were some elderly ladies, the host and some young people were already in the room. They were all very nice to me. We talked about different things like Asian food, Asian dress and discussed the way of life in Pakistan.

The elderly ladies were more interested in finding out about our joint and extended family system, while the young people in the room wanted to know about our education and transport systems, not to mention our sports facilities.

One of the young boys had already done his homework. He had learnt about the major cities of Pakistan, namely Karachi, Hyderabad, Lahore, Rawalpindi, and Peshawar. He asked me various questions regarding these cities. He sounded very interested in visiting India and Pakistan when he got older.

****

Buses were the usual means of transport around Lancashire in those days. Returning from these visits I always tried to catch the last Preston New Road bus. Sometimes though I would miss the last bus home, which meant I had to walk from Whalley New Road all the way to Lancaster Place. There was no fear in those days though when walking through the town centre, even at midnight.

CHAPTER THIRTEEN

During the late 50's, Pakistan's fast bowling legend Fazal Mahmood, played for Lancashire Cricket Club. A huge photograph of him was displayed in the *Lancashire Evening Telegraph's* reception area.

When the Pakistan cricket team defeated the English team in 1954 at the Oval, Fazal was named the man of the match and gained a band of English fans too. He became a big hero in Pakistan. Fazal was such an important person throughout his native country that it was impossible for people like me to contact or get in touch with him at all. However in Blackburn it turned out to be exactly the opposite.

It was the end of June 1958, when one afternoon just as Hassan and I were walking past Marks & Spencer's we saw a tall, handsome Pakistani-looking gentleman walking along with another man heading straight towards us.

I said to Hassan in a confused voice, "Look who's there!"

Before Hassan could answer me these two men came right to us.

Fazal said, "I take it that you two are from India or Pakistan?"

We were both dumbstruck. The only words we could manage to utter were, "Yes, we are from Pakistan."

I am sure Fazal and his friend could see that we were a bit nervous, so he started speaking to us in Urdu, asking us about our courses and how long we had been in England? After a few minutes of conversation he asked us to come to Alexandra Meadows Cricket Ground to watch him play the following Saturday.

When I wrote to my brother Muzammil, my cousins and some friends in Pakistan about our conversation and meeting with, '**The Fazal Mahmood'**, they couldn't believe me, because as I said earlier, it was impossible to meet or talk to stars like him back home in Pakistan. For Hassan and me this was such a wonderful and extraordinary experience.

Fazal Mahmood
Pakistan Cricket Legend

In our lessons, Mr Newton our textile testing lecturer used to tell us about the beautiful Lancashire countryside and places like Clitheroe Castle and Pendle Hill. He talked about these places so much, that I developed a yearning to go and see them for myself and spend some time there.

The college closed after our yearly exams in the middle of June 1958. From June to September most students went on holiday to Scotland, Ireland or the continent. One or two like me couldn't afford to go away, so we just stayed in Blackburn and had a few days out.

Palatine Dairies manager Sydney Harwood, allowed me to work full-time during my three month holiday period in his dairy. I worked during the week but had the weekends off. Some of the other students who stayed in Blackburn during college holidays were Rauf, Riaz, Hassan and Ashraf.

In the first week of July, on a glorious, warm, sunny and bright morning, not even one little cloud could be seen throughout the whole perfectly blue sky, it felt just too nice to stay in and waste such a delightful day, so after having a shave, wash and breakfast I decided to go out.

While walking down Preston New Road to the town centre I met Rauf at the junction of Sudell Cross and Limberick. He too had the same idea about this beautiful morning and didn't want to waste it by sitting in at home.

"Why don't we go to those places that we have heard so much about?" I suggested.

Rauf was in full agreement with me, "That's a good idea, how about visiting Clitheroe Castle?"

Together we walked through the town centre to the bus station and asked a bus inspector about the service to Clitheroe?

"Take a Ribble bus, a double-decker," he told us, "as these are mainly used on this route."

There was enough room on the top deck, so Rauf and I went upstairs and sat on the front seats, as these gave us a full panoramic outside view. As soon as the bus left Blackburn boundary in Wilpshire, the scenery became both breathtaking and magical.

There was greenery everywhere we looked. The whole journey was so beautiful and refreshing, that I wished we could have stayed on that bus for a very long time, but as we had now arrived we both alighted.

In Clitheroe we first looked around the town. It wasn't difficult for us to find the castle, for it stands very proudly high up on a hill overlooking the town. As soon as we reached it a man at the main gate greeted us. We toured around and both thoroughly enjoyed ourselves.

By now it was almost one o'clock; we were both feeling a little tired, so we went to a café to have something to eat and rest a while. It was far too early for us to return to Blackburn on such a wonderful day, so we decided to take a stroll away from Clitheroe town centre.

We were passing through a residential area when we noticed rows of semi-detached houses. All these houses had front gardens with their lawns all beautifully maintained and wonderfully displayed flowers.

Rauf and I were walking along leisurely, admiring the cleanliness on the roads, houses and gardens when we noticed a young boy of about seven or eight-years of age, coming running at full speed towards us sweating and panting.

For the first few seconds he could hardly speak, but recovering a little he said, "Hey Mister, hey Mister, could you stop for a moment, and stay here for just a few minutes?"

"Why do you want us to stay here?" asked Rauf.

The boy gasped and very enthusiastically said, "My friends have never seen coloured people, I want to show them what you look like?" He said this very seriously then ran off out of sight to get his friends.

I was a bit amused, but it worried Rauf. He said, "Mudassir, let us make a run for it, otherwise there will be hordes of children following us."

So before the young boy could bring his friends, we hurriedly disappeared. I still wonder if the little boy's friends ever believed him about his discovery.

****

In my childhood in the 1930's whoever had a white face was thought of by us as English (Engraiz). Some could have been French,

Scottish, Irish, Dutch or any other Europeans, but to us they would all appear as English.

I first attended my primary school in 1938. My father was then the station master at a railway station called Satroad, which was situated between the famous stations of Hissar and Hansi in Haryana India. As it was a roadside station, amongst the staff were the station master (my father), one assistant station master, two pointsmen, one waterman, and a sweeper.

Before World War II, about six passenger trains used to pass through Satroad station daily, but when the war started these were reduced to just two trains per day.

****

The incident in Clitheroe with the young boy reminded me of *my* first reaction upon seeing an Englishman at Satroad Station. Including other staff's children, we numbered about ten in total. Most of us were under ten-years of age. Whenever a train arrived we children would rush onto the platform to have a look at the train and its passengers. Sometimes we spotted some English people on the train. Now I realise those English people weren't ordinary passengers, they were either railway officials or high ranking Government officials.

As usual that particular winter morning, we children were on the platform when a train arrived. We noticed an Englishman getting off the train; he walked past us towards our father's office. His servant, an elderly Indian, followed him carrying his briefcase.

This was the first time I had ever seen an English person so close up. He was a traffic inspector and it was his scheduled visit to Satroad for inspection. He spent most of the morning and afternoon in the office with our father, but in the evening before his train arrived, he came out of the office. The Englishman, my father and his assistant were on the platform discussing some work related matter.

All the children were playing on the spare ground behind the station building. As soon as I saw the three of them together, I drifted away from the other children. I noticed that the Englishman had a wonderful smile. I don't know about the other children, but I was mesmerised by his white face, blond hair and his spoken English. Without realising it I started following my father and this

Englishman. I kept looking at his face and wanted to get nearer to him.

The Englishman must have noticed that a child was following them. He stopped, looked down at me with a big smile he said something that I didn't understand, but father kept talking to him.

I ran to the back of the station to tell the other children about the inspector. We all went running to the platform to have another look at the Englishman, but my father didn't like it and told us off. However the Englishman himself was very nice and kind; he tried to talk to us, but none of us, except for our father and his assistant, could understand English, and I think the Englishman's Urdu was very limited, which meant that we couldn't really communicate.

****

Not many of the present generation know of the wonderful life that British people led during the time they ruled India. Most English officers were in a true sense very nice; they loved India and its people, but a few were really very pompous. They often regarded Indians as third class citizens, and wouldn't consider them as responsible people. One particular inspector I remember well, as whenever he visited Satroad our father stopped us coming near the station, because this gentleman didn't like any noise. His servant was always sitting outside our father's office, just in case this gentleman wished to have a drink or something.

Sometimes married British officers would be on an official tour of railway stations with their wives. No matter how low ranked the officer was he would always be accompanied by a male orderly for the 'Sahib', himself, and a female servant for the 'Maim Sahib'. If they had children there would be a nanny. Whichever station they visited the railway always bore their full expenses.

****

In Blackburn the young people were as curious of us as we were in India of the English people. In Blackburn we used to have a good laugh about the young children's reactions when they saw us for the first time. I can never forget a pretty young girl aged about three or four, who was on the Preston New Road bus with her young mother. Rauf and I were sitting behind them.

As soon as she spotted us, the young girl turned round once or twice, looked at Rauf and me then looked again. She did this a few times during the journey.

Then she nudged her mother and whispered, “Mummy, mummy, look black men.”

The young mother heard the child, but ignored her, probably hoping that no one else had heard her. But for the innocent little girl we were some sort of novelty which she wanted her mother to see.

Later the child pulled her mother’s sleeve to attract her attention, and said in a little louder voice, “Mummy look black men.”

“Be quiet,” the lady said in a whisper to her child.

But the child was even more determined to show her mother what she had seen. This time she said in a very loud voice, “Have a look Mummy, two black men.”

By this time her poor mother was clearly so embarrassed that she didn't know what to say.

Rauf whispered to me in Urdu, “Mudassir, we’d better get off at the next stop.”

****

I continued to enjoy working at Palatine Dairies. Sometimes I would be in the booking cabin, where I had to book the churns of milk brought in from the farms. This was the only job where one could keep their clothes dry and clean.

To roll a churn full of milk from truck to the milk tank wasn't easy, it was big, heavy and awkward to handle. The churn had to be rolled in a certain way. Actually it was quite an art, it took me a couple of days to master this skill.

I had now to revert back to weekend work as college had opened in the first week of September 1958. Some more new students had arrived from India, Pakistan, Iran, Egypt, Jordan and other countries.

One of our old second year students was an Indian Bengali called Ghosh. He was aged thirty plus, small, very slim, and thinning on top. He spoke very good English in a typical Indian accent. He was very keen to have an English girlfriend, but unfortunately he wasn't successful in fulfilling his wish for the whole year.

His luck changed in October 1958 when he managed to have a few dates with a really lovely looking girl. After that he became rather a pain in our necks, as he just wouldn't stop talking about her. He would go on and on about her all the time wherever we were, and no matter what we were doing. Whether we were going to college, or in the class, even if we were in a café, he would speak about her. We were all getting rather fed up with him.

In our class there was a South-Indian student. Venkatarama. Venkata as we used to call him was 6 foot 3 inches tall, with a muscular body, and very broad shoulders. He was almost a picture of the perfect man.

One afternoon Mr Riley's class was full. Hassan and Dada Bhai were sitting in front of Jabbar and me. Ghosh was in the middle row in front of Hassan and Dada Bhai and was annoying everybody with his silly remarks. Mr Riley tried to quieten him, but Ghosh would stop for only a little while before starting again.

Hassan turned back to me and whispered, "Mudassir, can you do something to stop him?"

I didn't know what to say to Hassan, but an evil thought flashed through my mind. I leaned over to Hassan and whispered back to him, "Tell him that I have seen his girlfriend sitting in the Royal cinema with Vankata."

Hassan leaned over his desk and passed my message to Ghosh, who just sank down in his seat and went dead quiet and never said a word till the class ended.

As soon as the class finished, I tried to escape from there quickly, but Ghosh caught up with me in the corridor.

"Are you in a hurry Mudassir, can I talk to you? By the way I have cooked aubergine curry Bengali-style. I would like you to have lunch with me."

I tried to get away from him, but aubergine curry and rice were my weakness too, so I accompanied him to his lodgings in Limbrick. He made me feel at home in his house. Then he asked me to excuse him as he went to his kitchen to warm up the food. After just a few minutes he brought out two plates of rice and curry.

As we settled down to eat round the table, Ghosh said, "Please Mudassir, tell me the truth, did you *really* see my girl out with Vankata?"

Poor Ghosh, he looked really depressed and filled up with emotion. There were tears in his eyes.

I felt sorry for him and said, "Well I am sure about Vankata, it was him all right, but I could only see the back of this girl's head, though I am pretty sure it was her."

Ghosh almost broke down. He reached for his hanky, wiped his eyes and chokingly said, "I am going to see that so and so Vankata about this."

At that point I thought, 'This is now getting too serious, if Ghosh approaches Vankata with this kind of attitude, Vankata will make mincemeat out of him. I'd better cool the matter down.' So I said, "Look Ghosh, I might be wrong about your girl, because it was very dark in the hall, they were far away. It might have been a different girl. All English girls look the same to me."

Then explaining the situation to Ghosh again I said, "After all you are in a free country; people here do what they please. Anyway neither you nor anybody else have any rights on any girl here, they can go with anybody they wish to. Why not just ask her in a round about way about it. Don't go accusing her of anything."

Luckily Ghosh didn't take up the matter with his girl and they finished fairly soon afterwards.

****

During my first year in college Riaz Ahmed Chaudhry and I became close friends. Riaz lived in Preston New Road, which was only a two minute walk away from May House Cottage. During exam time we studied together, if we got tired of studying we would go for a walk along Preston New Road, or go down Buncer Lane to Witton Park.

Once while we were walking down Buncer Lane we noticed it was a well off region, as all the houses there were semi- detached. At that time there were no brown faces at all in that area.

Riaz came from Bahalpur in Pakistan. His father, Dr Niaz Ahmed, was a successful physician there. Riaz had completed his college education in Bahalpur, then proceeded to England for further education in textiles.

Riaz was an expert at making curries. If ever I was at his flat around teatime, Riaz would cook curry and I would get a loaf of white bread. The students who lived in flats and did their own cooking used bread instead of chapatties. Mostly we toasted the slices to eat with our curry.

Later on in 1958 Riaz bought a house in Shear Brow; after some time he sold it and purchased a house in London Road where he lived for a long time.

One evening I was trying to iron a shirt in my flat, when I noticed there was something wrong with my iron. As I needed an ironed shirt urgently, I took it over to Riaz's on Preston New Road. I got talking to him, and it was almost 3:00am before I left.

Instead of going onto Granville Road, I started walking down Preston New Road with my unfolded pressed shirt over my arm. I saw two police officers coming up from the opposite side. As they reached me, both stopped, and one of them shone his torch at my shirt.

In a very deep voice he asked, "Where are you going to son?"

I was surprised to hear the word 'son' because nobody had ever addressed me as son in England. "To my flat," I replied.

"So where have you been?" he asked again, eyeing up my shirt.

At this stage I explained to them about my iron, saying that I was a student and the shirt was mine. At that point they believed me and let me go.

****

In the late 50's there was a sub-police station at the junction of Preston New Road, Revidge Road and Billinge End. The police officers used to patrol the street in pairs.

In those days the standard height for a police officer seemed to me at least, to be six feet, and they had to have broad shoulders. The majority of police officers used to have a moustache. Their helmets and the cape over their shoulders served to make them look even more impressive.

****

It was in 1958 that we noticed one or two other 'brown' faces in Blackburn. These people didn't appear to be doctors or students. I discovered later that they were from Bangladesh.

****

Once Riaz and I were in town when I wanted to catch a bus to get to our flat, but on Riaz's insistence we started walking up Preston New Road. At Sudell Cross, we noticed some Asians who looked like newcomers to Blackburn. At that time we referred to them as Dessi's (from our country).

I said, "Riaz, I think there will be a lot of Dessi's in Blackburn in the next few years."

"What are you talking about there aren't even twenty in Blackburn now. Where will they come from?" Riaz retorted.

I thought for a minute, but with confidence I said, "I don't know where they'll all come from, but I quite honestly feel that there will be a lot more Dessi's coming here."

CHAPTER FOURTEEN

At that time nobody could ever have imagined that after a few years there would be thousands of Asians in a small town like Blackburn. I am not exactly sure what made me think that a lot more would come; perhaps it was just some sort of hunch.

May House Cottage was still a weekly gathering place for Asian students. I received a letter from my father that Eid was on a particular date and as every one of us wished to celebrate Eid on that day, we tried our best to book a room in town to offer up our prayers; but because we were small in number we were unsuccessful in our efforts.

In the end we agreed that in order to celebrate Eid all our Muslim friends, whether Pakistani, Egyptian, Turkish or Nigerian boys would offer their Eid prayers in the cottage and partake of something to eat later on, in order to celebrate this special occasion.

Although we agreed to perform our Eid prayers in the cottage, this raised the question of who would be the Imam for that morning and lead the prayers. Most of us were not well versed in this requirement, but we all decided and agreed on one person, who was called Salim Farooqi. Though unwilling at first, Salim eventually agreed to be the Imam; for an hour or so our May House Cottage was turned into a make-shift mosque; perhaps the very first one in Lancashire.

After prayers we greeted and embraced each other as is the proper Islamic way by saying, "Eid Mubarak."

Keeping with our customs, prayers were followed by a tasty feast. Jabbar prepared a rice pudding, while Hassan and I prepared Pulao, rice and meat cooked together. Javaid, Riaz, Rauf, Sabri, and Qureshi had each brought different edible items with them. Everyone was dressed up in their national costumes and as it was such a lovely day we decided to go into town. Naturally the unusual costumes we wore caused many heads to turn that day.

****

Regularly the overseas students were invited out by the local societies and clubs such as the Rotary Club, Lions club, YMCA and YWCA. Most of these clubs were situated in the town centre.

Once we got an invitation from the YWCA to join them in a social evening with an International flavour. We were asked to attend the event in our national dress. Most Pakistanis had a black Sherwani, which is a knee-length jacket, and white Shalwar, or baggy trousers. I had brought with me from Pakistan a black Sherwani, a white Shalwar, white Aligarh-style trousers, a colourful pair of Salim-Shahi shoes and a Jinnah-Cap. There were Nigerians, Ghanayans, Jordanians, Indians Chinese and Turkish students too, all proudly kitted out in their national dress outfits.

The stage secretary for the event was a very pleasant, chatty and sociable American girl, who had travelled through most of the European countries and was very interested in Eastern countries, their people and their cultures.

Halfway through the proceedings she announced that we should sing the national anthems of our countries. In order to do this we were invited up onto the stage.

We Pakistanis started whispering to each other as to who could sing our national anthem? To my horror nobody knew even the first verse except *Pak Surzameen Shaad Baad.*

Rauf and Hassan came to me saying, "Mudassir, it is going to be an insult if nobody sings our national anthem."

"What can I do, I don't remember even one line of the Anthem," I was ashamed to admit.

Hassan couldn't keep quiet, he said, "I have heard you singing in the college hostel in Hyderabad."

"But that was just a joke and humorous poetry," I tried to explain.

Rauf came to my rescue, but dropped me into even deeper problems by saying, "Except for us, who is going to understand what you sing?"

The American girl came over to us saying, "I am sure your national anthem is as beautiful as your national costumes."

The trouble was she was directly addressing me, and holding out a pen and paper she asked, "Right, can you spell your name out for me?"

I was trapped and as there seemed to be no escape for me, I gave her my name. I don't remember when and how my name was announced; the only thing I remember was receiving a nudge from Rauf. At that time I was still wondering what I was going to sing?

By now everyone in the room was standing. I moved to the front of the stage and placed my right hand on my chest as a sign of respect. The audience looked very far away from me, which gave me a little courage.

I started to sing reminding myself, "As it is all in Urdu, nobody except Pakistani boys would be able to understand the meaning."

It went like this:-

Why did you hit my buffalo with a stick?
It could have killed my buffalo's calf.
Your buffalo had entered my farm to graze,
So that is why I hit your buffalo.
I would have paid you for that,
But why did you hit my buffalo with a stick?

I repeated these lines in my singing voice a few times. In the end the audience applauded. I was certainly sweating when I came off the stage, but somehow I managed to keep my cool. The audience appeared to be really impressed and full of praise. The Pakistani boys were pleased too that we had managed to get out of that sticky situation nicely.

Some time later I wrote about this episode to my younger sister.

She wrote back to me saying, "You have not changed a bit."

****

My time as a student in Blackburn passed beautifully. I had no worries at all except about my studies and passing all the exams. Working full time at Horrocks's had given me a lot of experience to study the full process of spinning and all the preparation of yarn. With Mr Cowell's permission I often visited the weaving shed.

As the last year of my course was final and crucial, I had to work hard in 1959; this meant that I had to finish my part-time job at the dairy in order to devote most of my time to my studies.

I was regularly getting money from my father on the first of each month, but one week when I went to draw some money from the bank, I was horrified when the cashier told me that there wasn't enough money in my account for me to draw anything out.

I was shocked, but I thought I might just possibly have overdrawn. Luckily I still had one pound in my pocket, so I thought, ‘I can at least manage for a day or two.’ (Thankfully a pound in the 50’s still had some value).

The bank manager told me that my money from Pakistan hadn't been received. In fact none of the other Pakistani students had received any money either. A few days later we were told that it was due to some dispute between the State Bank of Pakistan and the Pakistani High Commissioner in London.

As weekend neared we got even more worried, as we didn't like the thought of telling anyone about our situation and we most certainly didn't want to get anything on credit. Hassan and I had enough money between us to buy a sack of potatoes, which would last us for a few days.

We managed on just those potatoes for a little while, but we realised that very soon we were going to run out of them. In the end, we were forced to ask Dada Bhai to go to Birmingham to get some cash from his contacts. He came back the next day with some money which we all shared. This was indeed a low point for everyone.

****

Two of my class fellows, Salim Farooqi and Abdul Baqi from the Government College Hyderabad arrived in Blackburn in 1957. Salim Farooqi basically came to England to study Mechanical Engineering at Burnley College, while Abdul Baqi had no real educational plans.

Salim changed his mind and completed the College Associateship in Blackburn in 1960. Abdul Baqi took a job at the National Coal Board in Burnley, so he moved to live there rather than travelling so far each day. Baqi and Salim used to stay with us at May House Cottage most weekends.

One beautiful summer afternoon, Hassan, Ashraf and I were walking down towards Corporation Park. As we were going down West Park Road we noticed Dr Tyler, the principal of Blackburn College, cutting the hedges in front of his house.

We were all quite shocked to see the Principal doing this job himself and compared him with Dr Duart, the Principal of Government College Hyderabad Sind, who had two gardeners and other servants to do these sorts of jobs for him.

On completion of my course I took my exams in June 1959, hoping to gain my College diploma. After a week's rest I started to look for work. The idea of working in a textile mill was for me to gain some practical experience and also to help me to save some money to buy things for home. Father didn't approve of this, he was going to send me a ticket to return home, but I explained that gaining experience in England would be a lot better for my future career in Pakistan. In the end I was able to persuade father to agree to me staying in England for a little while longer.

By the end of August 1959 the exam results were out. It was very good news for me as I had passed all of my exams and gained my Textile Diploma.

Photo taken at the Pakistan Student's Social (1957-58) in Blackburn.

Preston had always been my favourite town, so naturally I chose to go there and look for work. Without any difficulty I obtained a job in Tulketh Mill. I was happy working there, but the weekly wages were very poor. I was still living at May House Cottage and travelling to Preston every morning. All this was rather costly, inconvenient and made it difficult for me to reach the mill on time.

Courtaulds, Red Scar Works, Preston, the Rayon manufacturers was a newly established firm, with a modern brand new plant and buildings for different departments. Red Scar Works was situated on the main road to Longridge. It worked on a three shift, continental system, without any difficulty I found employment there.

This system suited me fine, as I could go to town after finishing work at 2:00pm and above all the wages were almost double compared to Tulketh's. I therefore decided to leave May House Cottage and move to Preston.

I found a room with a Polish couple in Miller Road. I was very happy to learn that they didn't mind me cooking curry, as they were both quite used to spices.

I started my job at Red Scar Works on September 10th 1959 in the continuous spinning process department (CSP). It was smelly, dirty, and full of acid fumes. After just three weeks of training the foreman informed me that I was going to be transferred to their coning department.

The following week I started in their coning department. Some other 'coloured' workers were transferred there too. *(This term was in common use in those days for all Asians).* Most of them could hardly speak English; I was one of the very few who could speak English fluently.

There were ten new male Asians who had all been sent from the CSP or the box spinning department. There were eight Pakistanis and two Indians but none of them spoke good English. An Irish girl called Margaret was our instructor; she started training us for the work. Straightaway my job became two-fold; I was still learning, but at the same time I was also interpreting for Margaret.

There were three or four other English male workers in the large coning department. After four weeks or so I was put on the inspection of packaging section. This work involved the thorough inspection of cones, packaging and keeping a strict record of the rejected cones.

****

Soon it was Christmas time 1959. None of us realised that before finishing for Christmas, the afternoon shift would hold a Christmas party in the department. That particular week we were on the afternoon shift. We all worked till five o'clock, then when we came back after our meal-break, our foreman told us to carry on working until all the English workers were in a party mood. They were eating, drinking and dancing on the shop floor already.

After a while we were invited to the party too and eventually we joined them. The partying lasted right through till ten o'clock.

****

Somehow I felt I wasn't so free in Miller Road, so I started to look for a better place to live. An Indian called Haroon had just bought a house in South Meadow Street, Preston. It was a very small, typical Lancashire terraced house. It had just two bedrooms, one a good sized room and the second much smaller. There was a sitting room downstairs and a little kitchen. There was no bathroom and the toilets were outside at the other end of the yard. By now I didn't mind this at all, as I had got used to outside toilets and using the public baths.

I rented the downstairs sitting room for £1.10s per week, under the understanding that the room would be entirely at my personal disposal, and nobody, not even landlord Haroon, would have access to my room. There was another lodger called Jabbar in the house, but in order to go to their rooms both Jabbar and Haroon had to use the back door.

By the end of 1959 my prediction to Riaz was becoming true, as we were starting to see a much larger number of Asians in Blackburn, Bolton and Preston.

The majority of the shop floor workers in Courtaulds were foreigners, such as Italians, Polish, Ukrainians, Jamaicans, Indians and Pakistanis.

A few weeks later, some new Pakistani boys started in the coning department. One of these boys was Khalid Wasim. He was a Pathan from Peshawar. Khalid was almost six feet tall, well educated, cultured, and fluent in Urdu, English, Punjabi and Pushto. As he had studied Urdu literature and worked in Radio Pakistan for a long time, his knowledge in Urdu was wonderful. As I was very interested in Urdu poetry we became very good friends.

Often either I invited him over to my house, or I visited him at his home. We soon found out that we had quite a lot of interests in common. On our day off we would go into town, or in the evenings we would go to a cinema, or attend any other point of interest in Preston.

CHAPTER FIFTEEN

During the late 50's and early 60's there was a workforce shortage all over the United Kingdom. They needed nurses in the hospitals, workers on their railways, conductors and drivers for the buses, but above all they needed people for the cotton industry in Lancashire, and the wool industry in Yorkshire.

The Indians and Pakistanis (including the present Bangladeshis) who came here during that period were all very hard-working people. Their main aim and object at that time was to make as much money as they could, so that they could send some money to their families back home. The majority of these people were not very familiar with the English language, customs or cultures. They liked to live either in the same house, or at least to be near each other. It was quite common to see eight or ten men living in a two-up, two-down ordinary terraced house in Preston or Blackburn.

They worked all the hours, as they say, that God sent. Mostly they liked to work on the night shift, because the rate of pay on that shift was usually 25% higher than on the others. They were also quite keen on working overtime.

At that time Courtaulds was the best paying firm in the area, so most of the young single people liked to work at that factory. Abdul Baqi from Burnley, and Sattar Mahmood and a young man from Pakistan, came to Preston and got employment at Courtaulds.

In our circle of friends, all were well educated and had a good standard of living. Within weeks of working in the coning department I had made quite a few friends. I got to know the staff in the office too, where there were a few young female clerks and typists, as an inspector of cones and cheeses I had to be in touch with the staff for paperwork.

Barbara, an Irish girl, was the instructor for inspection and packing of the first quality cones. She was a very sociable girl, who was engaged to a joiner called Bernard, who worked in the maintenance department at Courtaulds. They were going to get married in a few months time. Barbara told me about Bernard, saying that he was fond of spicy food and would like to try Indian spicy food.

One Saturday when I had a day off work, I arranged to cook curry and rice for Bernard for his evening meal. Barbara had persuaded me to cook this meal at her flat in Bairstow Street, off Avenham Lane, so that she could watch and learn how to cook the curry herself next time.

I was happy to oblige her.

By early 1960 there were one or two Pakistani grocery shops in towns like Preston, Blackburn and Bolton, from which we could buy halal meat, and halal chickens.

On this particular Saturday afternoon, I bought a chicken and a few spices from a Pakistani shop belonging to Maliks, reaching Barbara's flat at about 3:30pm. Barbara and Bernard were already there.

I got them both working on the preparation of the curry. Peeling and slicing onions, garlic and ginger was fun for all three of us. Although Barbara didn't have curry and rice when it was finally ready, Bernard and I thoroughly enjoyed it.

A few months later Bernard and Barbara got married and I was invited to their wedding. It was my first opportunity to attend a British wedding.

I was a little nervous about my invitation to this wedding, so I sought advice from some of the girls in the office. They briefed me about English weddings, so I confidently went to this event.

It was the first time I'd entered or sat inside a church. It turned out to be a wonderful experience for me, because I was welcomed by Bernard's brother at the Church and he introduced me to the Priest, who was very pleasant and genuinely pleased to see me along with the other guests.

Bernard looked very smart in his suit. The guests were coming in and taking their seats in the church. Bernard was sitting at the front with his best man. All of a sudden the Church organ started playing a different tune and all the guests stood up. I followed everybody else, as all eyes looked towards the door.

Barbara was standing at the back in her white bridal dress, holding tightly onto her father's arm. They walked down the aisle right to the front where Bernard was waiting. Barbara looked very beautiful.

The Priest read some verses from the Bible and after their vows were said Barbara and Bernard were pronounced husband and wife. The whole ceremony was very quiet and dignified.

After the wedding all the guests went to a hall where they held their reception. Barbara and Bernard's families were really nice to me; everyone welcomed me wholeheartedly. I could say that I was the only coloured person in that crowd, but nobody made me feel that I was any different than any of them. Actually they all spoke to me as if they had known me for a long time.

CHAPTER SIXTEEN

There were some girls from Longridge working in the coning department. Amongst them were two sisters, Barbara and Lilian. Barbara was aged about nineteen, whilst Lilian was approximately two years younger. Lilian was a real chatterbox, whereas Barbara was a rather quiet girl. I used to talk to them both.

One afternoon Barbara informed me, "My mother and father would like to meet you. Would you like to visit our house and meet them?"

This was a little surprising to me, but later on I found out that Barbara and Lilian had been talking about me to their parents. I visited them a few times. Barbara's parents were very kind and wonderfully hospitable. Every time I visited them I always stayed till late in the evening. They were so keen to learn about India and Pakistan and extremely interested to know more about someone who was willing to leave his family and travel thousands of miles in order to gain a better education and work experience for himself.

****

Our foreman in coning was a Scot called Andy MacLaren. At one time Andy had played football for Preston North End. He was a successful player and a big name in the football world, but unfortunately an injury had ruined his football career, so he ended up working for Courtaulds. I clearly remember him being a very down-to-earth man who was always friendly.

****

Almost every week the number of Indian and Pakistanis was increasing in Preston. I met two Kumar brothers, as well as Raj Passi and Roy. These four boys were from Indian Punjab; their families had to leave Lahore because of the division of India. Raj Passi and Roy had received their high school education in Urdu. Due to Khalid and I both being Urdu speakers, the four of us loved to converse at every opportunity.

As mentioned before, although politically and religiously we Pakistani boys differed from the Indian boys, we still became very good friends as we were all more or less from similar cultures and had a common language for communication.

Perhaps I should mention a little about the division of India here.

****

It is a well-known fact that between 1712 and 1757 the great Moghul Empire started to crumble and disintegrate. The Maharajas of large and small states throughout India started to detach themselves from the Royal Moghul Courts of Delhi and were declared as independent states.

While the Moghuls were losing control over India, the foreign nations, namely the French, Dutch, Portuguese and the British, who initially went to India as traders, saw their opportunity to take part in Indian politics. They all conspired with Maharajas of different states who were pre-occupied with fighting each other trying to expand their territories.

Under the banner of tradesmen, these Europeans began to employ the natives as guards, build the forts and arm themselves with modern weapons.

An Englishman called Robert Clive who went to India with East India Company as a clerk, made his way into the Indian elite classes. Over a short period he successfully incited Mir Jaffar, one of the trusted ministers to revolt against the ruler of Bengal.

Clive, with the collaboration of Mir Jaffar, fought and succeeded in defeating the ruler of Bengal, thus laying the foundation of the British Empire. For his success in India, Clive was knighted by the British Crown as Lord Clive of India.

Some Indian Rulers tried to regain independence for the whole of India and fought separately against the British, sometimes with the help of the French or Dutch, but they failed every time. They lost the wars because they lacked leadership amongst themselves. The Europeans sought their own interest in helping Indian Maharajas.

Then as a last attempt the Indians declared war against the British in 1857 under the leadership of the very old, frail, helpless and hopeless Moghul Emperor of India, Bahadur Shah Zafar.

The British called that war *The Indian Mutiny,* but in Indian History it is known as *The War of Independence.* The British crushed the mutiny with the help of other Indians.

Eventually the whole of India from the Khyber Pass to the eastern borders of Burma came directly under the British Crown, thus the British Empire was truly established.

In 1885 an Englishman called A.O. Hume retired from the Indian Civil Services. Instead of going home to England he decided to stay in India. He felt that the natives should take an active part in their country's affairs. So in that same year of 1885, after consultation with his friends, he founded a party and named it *The Indian National Congress (I.N.C.).*

In the early part of the 20th century, the leadership of the Indian National Congress came under the influence of Gandhi and Nehru. Eventually in 1947, after much turmoil and loss of many lives, the I.N.C. successfully achieved independence for India from the British.

Before, and during the British Raj, the Muslims were the largest minority in India and ruled the country for almost one thousand years.

During the movement for independence by *The Indian National Congress,* the Muslims felt that their interests were totally ignored by the Congress party, so in 1906 they founded a political party under the name of *The All India Muslim League* to represent the Muslims of India.

Historically since the Hindus and Muslims have always been rivals with each other, the Muslims feared that if the British left and the power switched to the Hindu majority, the Muslims would lose their identity. As a result the Muslim League started a movement demanding separate and independent homeland for those marginalised within greater India.

The movement, under the leadership of Mohammed Ali Jinnah was eventually successful, and the sub-continent was divided into India, East Pakistan and West Pakistan. Thus the independent state of Pakistan came into being in 1947. Gaining independence for India and creating Pakistan was very costly in the loss of human lives, with both countries suffering the loss of millions of people.

There were merciless massacres of innocent people, including young children and women, on both sides of India and Pakistan. Millions of people were forced to leave the places where they themselves and their ancestors were born and brought up. With the overwhelming evidence of ethnic cleansing, the two nations remained in turmoil for a long time.

****

Just a few years later in England, despite our political differences, we got on really well with these Indian students. The Kumar brothers had originally come from Lahore; their family was well off. Roy was working for North Western Railways in Lahore. These boys missed Lahore, Rawalpindi, Lyallpur and other places in Pakistan, in exactly the same way as we missed Delhi, Pataudi, Rewari and other places in India. Sometimes we even joked about our politicians, cultures and communities, but it was always in a light-hearted fashion.

****

Ashraf was still working at Tulketh Mill, but we all met on our day off or sometimes at weekends. By September 1960, I had settled down pretty well in Preston. I regularly visited Mr and Mrs Spencer, Mr and Mrs Sloane, and Mr and Mrs Gent. Mr and Mrs Spencer always wanted me to move back in with them, but I couldn't, because I had lived independently in Blackburn and Preston, so I couldn't start living again under some kind of supervision.

During the time I started in the coning department, the firm was setting up the beaming section. Some new staff started in that section. There were three or four girls who always seemed to be together. They went to the canteen, the toilets and even for a smoke together. One of these girls caught my eye. She looked to be about seventeen or eighteen years of age. She had a very pleasant face, and I wanted to make friends with her. Every time she passed my side I tried to attract her attention.

I'd say, "Hello," or "Good morning," or something like that, but she seemed to take no notice of me.

It was the first time in my life that a young girl had ignored me like that. In many ways it hurt my pride, so I made my mind up to talk to her. I found out that her name was Kathleen. She was always with her friend Joan, who was more daring at speaking to people than Kath was.

It was approaching Christmas and like on previous years, the girls in the coning department were going to have a Christmas Party. It had been scheduled for the last Friday before the Christmas holidays.

It so happened that our shift was on the same afternoon that week. It was about six o'clock when the party began. Somehow I managed to approach Kath and got her away from the other girls.

Straightaway I asked her, "Why have you been ignoring me for the past eight or nine weeks?"

"I haven't been ignoring you," she managed to answer me.

I was determined to obtain a proper explanation from her, so I queried, "Then how come you never returned my greetings."

She had no answer to that, but kept on talking to me.

In the meanwhile Joan came over. I didn't like saying much while Joan was there. However Joan was in a proper party mood. During our conversation I found out that she liked an Indian boy called Kashmir, who had just started in the coning department but was a bit shy.

Once or twice Kashmir, Joan, Kath and I went out together. After a while I thought it best to see Kath alone, before long I managed to start seeing her separately.

After a long time Kath told me the reason why she didn't talk to me; it was because I was quite friendly with the other girls in the department, and this had given a lot of people the wrong impression of me.

The following is Kath's account of how she came to work at Courtauld's and her first impressions of me in her own words.

****

"Before coming to Courtaulds, I was working at Horrocks's in Stanley Street Preston. I worked there with my elder sister June and a family friend called Joan Patterson. I wasn't really settled at Horrocks's, because the weekly wages there were very poor.

One morning Joan told us that a big firm, Courtaulds at Red Scar in Preston, was advertising for workers in their coning department. Joan also told us that their worker's wages were a lot higher than those that we were getting at Horrocks's. This really attracted me, because being very young I was the lowest paid worker in Horrocks's.

Joan had already made her mind up to go for that new job. I spoke to my sister June about the vacancies, but as June was expecting her first child and didn't want to start a new job at that time herself, she advised me to try for the position..

I didn't need any further encouragement, so the next day Joan and I went together to visit the personnel office of Courtaulds. After our formal interviews both Joan and I got offered jobs in the coning department.

The following Monday morning we went to our new department at Courtaulds. There were a few more girls there who were starting work with us. An experienced woman took charge of us and we started our training on the winding frames, as our job was to wind a very fine yarn from a 'cake' to a 'cone'.

Working on those winding frames was clean and wasn't very hard, so I managed to pick it up quickly. Joan and I were always together. Whether it was for a tea break, a smoke, visiting the toilets, or going to the canteen for breakfast or other meals, Joan and I could always be seen together.

In order for us to go to the canteen, we had to pass a section where the workers were all male. Joan told me that these workers were from India. There were about ten workers and every one of them was just a young man. At that time I couldn't tell the difference between Indians and Pakistanis.

Walking down that passage I used to notice these boys, but as I am a shy person by nature, I didn't really pay any serious attention to anybody. However unlike me, Joan was a daring, forward and outgoing sort of girl, she used to talk about one of the boys in particular in that group.

I only took notice of two boys. One was about six feet tall and slimly built. The other was about five feet six inches tall, with a normal build and appeared to be younger than the other. These two were always together. Every time we girls passed them they would look at each other and talk; I felt sure that they were speaking about us.

I found out that the taller one was called Wasim and the younger guy was called Khan. I noticed the younger one liked talking to the other workers, particularly so to the females. In the canteen the other girls talked about him, saying that he was a bit of a good timer, but trustworthy. Though I liked him a lot, with his reputation, naturally I couldn't bring myself to talk to him.

It was customary in the coning department that before Christmas the whole department had a Christmas party. We were told that we could stop work in the afternoon and have a Christmas party. Halfway through the party I was with other girls, when Khan came over to us, and asked me if he could have a word with me?

We moved away from the group and he asked, "Why have you been ignoring me?"

It was the first time that I had heard him speaking in English and I could understand him quite well. I denied his allegation, but he was rather serious.

"Then how come you never returned my greetings?" he enquired.

I had no real answer to his question, but we kept talking. Then he asked me if he could see me sometimes?

Joan told me later on that the boy she liked had already asked her if he could see her, so she was going to see him some time during that week.

That was the start of my association with Khan; the rest becomes clearer later.

****

Amongst the newcomers from Pakistan to Preston were two boys, Mohiuddin Khan and his friend Asad. Mohiuddin called himself Ali Khan. This was due to the fact that his first name was as much a mouthful as mine is for English people. These two boys were educated, cultured, sociable, and because they were from Karachi they instantly became my friends. Ali Khan spoke very good and fluent English, he loved making English friends. He made some friends at Horrocks's where he had previously worked in the spinning room. Actually I met and befriended Ali Khan before I met either Kath or her family.

One evening I was with Ali Khan and his friend near the Bull and Royal in Church Street, Preston. Ali Khan saw an English couple with two young girls in their late teens across the road. They were standing at the corner of Church Street and Lancaster Road, near the

Red Lion Public House. All of a sudden Ali Khan made some excuse and took himself off across the road to see these people.

Asad told me that they were Ali Khan's friends and that Ali Khan has visited the family. When Ali Khan returned to us he was full of praise for the family. He talked that much, that it sounded as if he was the only Asian in Preston who could make friends with English people. He told us about his visits to the family and how they had kindly taken to him.

After some time I found out that Ali Khan was poorly. At that time he lived in Deepdale Road. One weekend I thought I should visit him in the evening, but I had already arranged to see Kath that same evening. When I met Kath I told her about Ali and because she already knew Ali herself, she agreed to accompany me to see him.

I told Kath not to say anything to Ali when we reached his flat. At his Deepdale Road home I knocked at his door. When he answered, he was pleased to see me, but was shattered into pieces when he saw Kath with me.

A few seconds later he turned to me and said in Urdu, “How the hell did you manage to date this girl?”

“So you know each other?” I asked him, pretending to be ignorant.

All of a sudden he came down to earth, and said in English, “This is the family I have been telling you about.”

“Yes I know, they told me about you when I visited them,” I explained.

After that Ali Khan never tried to put on me in any way and we all remained good friends.

For the first few weeks Kath and I didn't tell anybody about our friendship. This was because of the fear Kath had of her parents that they might not approve of our association because I wasn’t English. I don't know what June's reaction was when Kath told her about me, but June and her husband John invited me to their house in Oakley Street, Preston.

I met Kath in Lune Street and we both walked to Oakley Street. I was looking forward to meeting June and John, but just as we entered Oakley Street, Kath spotted her father's car in front of June's house.

She stopped me and walked back saying, “Mum and Dad are at June's; I’m not going in.”

“Whilst I could understand her fear perfectly well, I didn't agree with it.

Having an unexpected visit from her parents, June was terribly nervous too, as she was expecting us at the same time. She came out of her house, making the excuse to her parents that she wanted to get something from the shop.

She spoke to us at the end of the street, saying, “Mum and Dad won't stay long.”

Luckily her parents left soon and we went into her house. I found June and John really wonderful people, with open minds and liberal views. June and John had recently got married and were expecting their first child.

I have always had a very high regard for June, she is a very sociable, cultured, broad minded and confident girl. June and John gave me a proper welcome at their house.

It was due to their hospitality that Kath and I visited June and John regularly during the week, and so many times we would stay at their house in Oakley Street for our evening meal. Our meals used to be mainly soup. My bowl of soup would naturally be covered with white pepper, as that was the only way to make my soup a bit spicy.

Whenever I ran out of money, June was always there to help me out and lend me some. John was equally as good as June to me, as he too always made me feel welcome in his house. At one time June and Kath worked at Horrocks’s in Stanley Street. Ali Khan came to work in the same room and it was there that June and Kath had first come to know him.

****

In the early 1960’s a television in the house was a luxury which not many families could afford. There was no television in June's house, so whenever Kath and I called at her house, playing cards was our usual pastime and we used to chat about all sorts.

I think we played Chinese Rummy, where Kath and John would be partners and June and I ended up as partners. During the game the partners had to score points, and whoever had the most points would be the winners. Nine times out of ten June and I cheated, so we always managed to be the winners. In later years we fondly remembered the Oakley Street house where we used to have such a good laugh.

June has always been a very hard-working girl. When she moved from Preston to Leyland she worked in a chip shop. She ran that chip shop single-handedly. The owner of the shop Barbara, trusted June so much, that she gave June all the responsibilities. Actually the chip shop's sales were boosted because of June's presence on the premises. Customers in the chip shop didn't *just* come in for fish and chips; they actually loved talking to June.

June now has four children, Beverly, Debbie, Carl, and Clare. Beverly married a charming young man called Gary. They have twin daughters Cloe and Olivia. Debbie married a businessman called Steve. They also have two children Gemma and Max. Carl married Ann, and Clare got married to a police officer called Alan.

June and I have great respect for each other. Sometimes we say so many things about each other, but neither one of us takes it seriously or gets offended. We might not see each other for years, but when we do meet at weddings, birthday parties or engagement parties, we talk as if we had seen each other just last week.

Somehow Kath's mother found out about Kath and me. Personally I could never find out as to with what intentions she went to see Dennis Mitchell, the personnel manager of Courtaulds. But I found out later that the personnel officer had spoken very highly of me. He told Kath's mother that I came from a respectable family and had travelled to England in order to achieve a higher education.

Actually a few months earlier Dennis Mitchell had received a letter from my father enquiring about me. Furthermore my father had requested him to try to persuade me to return home to Pakistan. In fact I had already kept in touch with my father promising him that I would return home very soon, possibly in the next few months.

Mr Mitchell summoned me to his office. As I entered I could see a Pakistani airmail letter placed in front of him on his desk. Straightaway I knew that it could only be my father who would take the step of writing to Mr Mitchell.

Mr Mitchell had my full records in front of him. He went through my academic achievements, then after reading my father's letter he said, “I have to write to your father, telling him why you haven't returned home yet. Can you explain why to me?”

I told him the truth that it was purely to gain some practical industrial experience and to save some money up, so that I could take some modern things like a fridge, washing machine and suchlike back with me.

Father continued to exchange a few more letters with Mr Mitchell. I'm sure Mr Mitchell somehow convinced my father that I wasn't an irresponsible person, so he need not worry about me.

Two different photographs showing Kath with her parents and other family members.

CHAPTER SEVENTEEN

Although Kath's mother was satisfied with what she had learnt about me; I heard that when Kath's father found out about us, he was furious.

I was told that he said, “My daughter is certainly NOT going to get mixed up with some coloured man if I have anything to do with it!”

I found out through June and Kath that their mother would like me to meet their father. One evening Kath invited me to their house in Lancaster Lane, Leyland. I had no transport in those days so I had to catch a bus to Leyland, as I had already arranged to meet Kath at a bus stop there.

As I got off the bus on Preston Road, there was Kath with her younger sisters Neva and Eileen and their youngest brother Michael all waiting for me.

Neva was eleven, Eileen nine, and Michael was only about four at that time. The youngsters were shy in the beginning, but just a few minutes later Neva got hold of my hand and we started talking. The five of us chattered all the way from Preston Road to Lancaster Lane.

Kath's mother met us at the door and showed us into the living room. I looked around and noticed that Kath’s father was reading a newspaper, whilst Jimmy, Kath’s eldest brother was having a cup of tea.

After formal introductions I sat down. There was silence for a few minutes, but then I noticed Jimmy's arm was in a sling, which gave me the opportunity of starting the conversation.

“What happened to your hand?” I enquired.

“Oh it's nothing serious; I hurt it at work,” Jimmy answered.

Kath’s father still kept his head buried in the newspaper, though after a while he too started to converse. Kath's younger brothers Ken and Alan came in then and joined us.

I had already spoken to Ken on the phone a few times before this meeting, so it was easier to talk to him. Ken was about fifteen-years old, whilst Alan looked to be about twelve. They chatted for a while, before leaving the room.

Soon Kath's father started talking to me and the conversation flowed. We had a long discussion about India, Pakistan and other countries. It was clear that he had never come across an Asian before, but he remained very polite.

At about 4:00pm Kath's mother came into the room and asked me, "Would you like to stay for tea with us?"

"I would like to, but please don't put yourself to any inconvenience, thank you," I replied.

I stayed at their house for the evening meal. Somehow I felt at home with this family immediately; I found all the family members very down to earth. Kath's father asked me to visit them again, as he too had enjoyed talking to me. I left at about 8:00pm.

Kath's father, Mr Bill Hubberstey, worked at Roach Bridge Paper Mill as a colourist. The management depended on his skills. He himself never talked about either his work or his talents. Years after his death, I met somebody who worked at Roach Bridge Paper Mill. He told me that once on the night shift the colourist had tried his best to match certain shades for the next batch, but couldn't do so. In the end he stopped trying and left it until Bill Hubberstey came into work the next day. Bill just looked at the shade, mixed different dyes, and the shade was matched with very little effort.

Unfortunately Mr Hubberstey had never previously come into contact with any foreigners, so his views were drawn from baseless stories and tall tales about foreigners; otherwise deep down he was really a very liberal minded man, without any prejudices.

I was told that in the beginning he was against our association and marriage, but later on he agreed. I became very close to this family, so much so that I always addressed Kath's mother and father as 'mum and dad'.

Whenever the family went out for the evening, dad always asked me to join them. In fact a few times mum and dad took Kath and me to dad's brother, Uncle Bob's and other relatives.

A few years later when one of Bill Hubberstey's sons was getting married, he asked his son, "Are Kath and Khan invited to your wedding?"

His son and daughter-in-law to be were shocked and said, "Yes of course, but why do you ask Dad?"

Having a sip of his cup of tea he said calmly, "If they are not invited, I don't think I would come to your wedding."

Kath's mother was a proper housewife. Professionally she was a fully qualified nurse, but because of her large family she couldn't return to her profession. She devoted herself to looking after the children and bringing them all up. When all her children were young and there was only her husband's wage coming in, she had a hard task in making ends meet; however she always did her best to provide for all of her children.

She was very good-natured and a generous lady. She always welcomed visitors offering them something to eat along with the usual cup of tea. Sometimes she found it difficult to pay all her bills on time, but somehow she always managed to keep her head above water, but how she managed is quite beyond me!

She was lucky in so many ways that she saw all her children growing up, getting married and settled with their own families. She was extra happy and cheerful all day when one of her granddaughters, Susan, had a son, and mum therefore became a great-grandmother.

The praise goes to both of Kath's parents for bringing up such a large family in a decent manner. In return all their children have always been a credit to them.

It is often said in the Asian community that English people don't have any consideration for their elders and don't look after them. My first-hand experience is rather different in this context. Kath's brothers and sisters got married one by one and set up their homes with their partners and families. But without fail every Saturday afternoon almost all of them would visit their parents. If one of her children and their family couldn't come to mum on the Saturday, they would most definitely go to see her on the Sunday.

In 1968 and 1969 mum and dad were living in Seed Park Cottage, which was situated in the middle of a field in Samlesbury off Preston

New Road. It was a large house surrounded by huge fields and hundreds of trees. There was no gas or electric, the toilets were outside and were the old fashioned type. Thankfully there was a water supply. They used logs in the fireplace and cooked their meals on an Aga cooker. Paraffin lamps were used for light at night.

All of this had its compensations though, as their grandchildren were free to play in the fields around the cottage; if the couples wanted to go for a walk, they could enjoy a lovely leisurely stroll without worrying about traffic or any pollution.

Every Saturday afternoon there used to be a competition between the Hubberstey's offspring as to who would reach the cottage first. There used to be Jimmy and Pauline, Norman and Gwen, Neva and Jim, June and Brian, Ronnie and Maureen and Kath and me. The couples all visited the cottage with their children. There would be about fourteen or fifteen adults, and thirteen or fourteen children. During the summer, on warm and sunny days, we all used to sit outside the cottage. Sometimes we would all picnic together. Mum always made cups of tea for whoever wanted one. We had lots of fun at Seed Park Cottage, particularly in the summer and at Christmas time.

After Dad's death in January 1976, Michael was the last person left with his mother. He looked after her until her final day. Michael got married, but before he did so, he made it clear to his wife-to-be Steph that his mother was the most important person in his life; on no account was he going to leave her. He told Steph that whenever they went out and his mother was with them, his mother would take the passenger seat in the front whilst Steph would have to sit in the back.

Kath came from a big family having five brothers and four sisters. At the time of my introduction to this family one of her brothers Ronnie, and two of her sisters Gwen and June were married, whilst her other brothers and sisters, Jimmy, Ken, Alan, Neva, Eileen and Michael were all still at home.

Ronnie and his wife Maureen lived in Leyland. June lived with her husband in Oakley Street, Preston. At this time Kath's elder brothers Jimmy and Ronnie had completed their National Service with the RAF.

Jimmy was a very intelligent member of the family, but he was extremely modest. He never gave the slightest impression that he was a test pilot in the RAF. After leaving the RAF he joined Preston Borough Council, remaining there until he retired. He was married to Pauline; they have three daughters, Susan, Karen and Beverley, but sadly he passed away in 2003.

One evening, in the early days of our friendship, Kath and I had been to Preston Railway Station and were walking down Fishergate, when I spotted Jimmy getting off a Fishwick bus from Leyland. Kath was a bit reluctant to go over and talk to him, but I went ahead and spoke to Jimmy.

He asked, "Are you two going anywhere particular?"

"No, nowhere particular at all," we both said.

"Come on then, I'll buy us all a drink."

We all went to Rowntrees café in Fishergate and had a pleasant chat. Jimmy had inherited a quality from his father in that he would never tell tales, nor would he do any back-biting, split on anybody or gossip. If anyone ever did start something of that nature, he would either change the subject, or get up and do something else. He just wouldn't be part of that sort of thing at all.

Next to Jimmy, Kath's elder brother is Ronnie. He has always been the opposite of his elder brother and is a very happy-go-lucky person. He has a wonderful sense of humour. Most of time he is cheerful and he always finds some humorous element even in a disaster. Parties are a bit dry without Ronnie as he will liven up any situation. It might be tasting some foreign food for the first time, or perhaps repairing a washing machine or a car engine. He might spray a door panel, decorate a house, or do a bit of furniture removal. Whatever needs doing, Ronnie will always have a go.

****

One of my close friends Riaz Chaudry, who was my classmate in college, later bought his own business called Lancashire Dry Cleaning in Blackburn. I used to visit him almost every week at his shop on my own, or on other occasions I would visit his house with my family.

One evening in April or May 1977 I visited him at his shop. We started talking about the times when we were at Blackburn College.

During our conversation Riaz came up with the idea of us starting a business on a bigger scale in dyeing and finishing. As we had both learnt how to spin, weave, dye and finish during our course, the idea was especially attractive to me.

I agreed with Riaz in principle, but asked him to give me a little more time to think it over. I then discussed the whole thing with Kath. She agreed with me, so the following week Riaz and I met to work out the finances and to discuss obtaining a building somewhere that would be suitable as a dye-house. We also worked out the possible costs of purchasing dyeing machines and dyestuffs.

At that time financially neither one of us was actually very stable, so we decided to approach a bank regarding further finance. Luckily however Riaz had a friend who was financially much stronger than us and was willing to join us in this venture as an equal third partner.

We found a reputable firm of solicitors who agreed to handle our legal affairs. One of their solicitors drew up a contract for us. We agreed on naming the newly formed firm as *Osprey Dyers Ltd.*

Furthermore we agreed that I would work full time as the manager and that we would also employ an experienced colourist. The three of us put up an equal amount of money; then took out a loan from a local bank in order to buy machinery and different dyestuffs.

We managed to rent large premises in Darwen which had already been used as a dye-house, but the previous owner of the firm had left. As it was already laid out more or less as we needed, we didn't need to make many big changes to the building as the required spaces for putting in machinery and drainage were already there.

It was 1977 when Riaz and I worked at Osprey Dyers in Lorne Street Mill, Darwen. Riaz bought some machinery from Yorkshire and also managed to get us some customers. They wanted their tufted bedspreads dyed in different colours.

My wife Kath, and Riaz's wife Ann, also agreed to work for us on a part-time basis, as they both had to take their young children to school and then collect them afterwards.

For the first six months we all worked very hard and soon we had a very good business. Before we knew it the business started growing, and we were employing about twelve people. Osprey Dyers was in full swing and we were doing fine in every way. Our weekly turn over went well into thousands of pounds. However during August 1978 the roof of our premises started to leak and rain poured in from it and spoiled our dyed bedspreads.

One weekend Kath's brother Michael and their mother came to visit us at our house. During our conversation I mentioned about our dye-house and the leakage from its roof, stating that I would have to get somebody in to repair it.

I was really pleased when Kath's mother told us, "Our Ronnie and Mick could repair the roof for you and it wouldn't cost you too much that way."

The following day Ronnie and Michael came to our dye-house and within two or three days they had repaired the whole roof. In fact they did a really good and totally professional job.

Riaz was pleased with their work on the roof. At that time we really needed somebody reliable to be on the premises while Riaz or I were away on business.

As I've already mentioned we had increased the staff greatly over the first six month period. On Riaz's suggestion I asked Ronnie and Michael if they would like to work full-time in the dye-house. I was pleased when they both agreed. There were five or six other workers in the dye-house and Ronnie took charge of them too.

Ronnie is so very versatile that he easily adjusts himself to any task. Whilst he was stationed at the RAF base in Aden, on his day off Ronnie would drift away to some remote village of Bedouins, sit cross-legged with a Bedouin family on the floor and have a meal with them. That's Ronnie!

Unfortunately after a while our third partner couldn't stay with us, so he pulled out of the business. Then in late 1979 Riaz decided to return to Pakistan for good with his family. In 1980 Riaz and I decided to close the dye-house in Darwen as the business was too big to handle for one person; sadly I had to finish with it altogether, so very reluctantly I closed it down.

Riaz's dry-cleaning business and house were both sold; he bought two large vans to take over to Pakistan. He planned to go to Pakistan all the way by road, but he could only drive one van himself and there was nobody to drive his other van to Pakistan.

Ronnie heard about Riaz's problem and offered, “I'll drive his van overland for him with my family, as long as Riaz agrees to pay our air-fares back to England.”

Riaz agreed to do this; so gladly accepting Riaz’s offer, Ronnie, Maureen and Paul went to Pakistan with Riaz, Anne, and Anisa. Ronnie, Maureen and Paul and their family, everyone thoroughly enjoyed their three week stay in Bahalpur, Pakistan.

When I first met Ronnie and his wife Maureen they had five young children; these are twins Susan and Lynn, Stephen, Paul and Mark. Maureen has always been a sensible and friendly girl. She kept the social balance between her own parents and her in-laws and is very well liked in the family.

Ken is younger than Kath; he was only fifteen when I first met him. He has always been a very smart and intelligent person, who is mechanically minded and loves repairing car engines. I always sought his help in emergencies. He helped us out in the maintenance of the boiler at our dye-house. He worked for most of his life in the powerhouse at Accrington and Heysham.

Younger than Ken is Alan. He was still at school when I first met him. He has always been a well-built person. Basically he is a quiet man, but when he is in a party mood he is just as witty as Ronnie. He is a great believer of discipline in the home. He got married to Christine and they have a son Jason and a daughter Sandra. Besides running the house and bringing up the children, Christine has always worked either part or full-time.

Neva and Eileen are Kath's two younger sisters. Neva has always been especially close to Kath. Neva was about eleven when I first met her. Even at that very young age Neva was always active; she had to be doing something all the time, otherwise she would get bored.

I first saw Eileen the youngest girl in the family, at the bus stop with Kath, Neva and Michael. She was then eight or nine-years old. Despite her young age, she gave me the impression of being a sensible girl. She is usually a quiet person, but she can be as witty as anybody else and can hold a conversation on many different subjects.

Eileen is very good at money management. She had a family of four children at a young age, but she brought them up in such a disciplined way, that all four children are a credit to her. Eileen herself runs a printing business, and her husband Colin has been a tower of strength for her. Together they have worked hard to bring up their family. Their very chatty, filled with confidence and sociable daughter Amanda, completed her law degree and married a successful solicitor Kevin Preston. I often heard him in Blackburn Magistrate's courts whilst I was a JP there. Eileen's son Andrew qualified as a joiner at Accrington College and soon set up his own joinery business. Eileen's daughter Vicky qualified as a social worker, whilst her youngest daughter Denise completed an accountancy course.

Michael is the youngest, the 'baby' of the Hubberstey family. He was very close to his mother and father. Likewise his parents thought a lot of him. He got away with a lot more with his parents than his elder brothers and sisters did.

Like his other brothers Michael is very good with his hands and loves working on cars and decorating rooms. Tidying and looking after gardens are his favourite pastimes. He is an interesting and fast talking person. If he had taken up salesmanship, he would have ended up as a sales director in a big firm by now.

Michael was only about four-years old when I first met him at the bus stop in Leyland with his older sisters. He was quite chatty even at that age. Walking with those youngsters on Lancaster Lane, I noticed Michael looking at me continuously.

'Oh, this young man is going to say something,' I thought. I was right. I could see the question mark written all over his face.

He couldn't resist any longer, "Khan, you are an Indian, aren't you?"

Everybody, including me cringed. I had to answer him, so I said, "Yes Michael, I am an Indian."

He paused for a few seconds, looked towards my head and said, "Where are your feathers then?"

Everybody gave a sigh of relief.

I laughed and said, "I lost my head gear and all my feathers were in that one."

The next afternoon four-year old Michael was in the fields at the back of their bungalow.

Mum wanted to know what he was doing there.

Michael shouted back, “I am collecting feathers for Khan, he has lost his head gear.”

Poor Michael had mistaken me for a Red Indian. It took him a long time to understand and realise that I wasn't the same kind of Indian as in Cowboy and Indian movies.

****

Sadly, Michael’s first marriage to Steph wasn’t successful and ended up in a divorce. Michael and Steph had five children, Bernadette, Neva, Kenneth, Anthony and Katie.

After some time Michael met Trish and got married to her. They have four children between them, Naomi, Jake and the twins Porche and Michaela. This means that the total number of Michael’s children is now nine.

It is wonderful to see Michael and Trish managing to look after all their children so well. They both work hard to bring them up properly; the children are always smartly dressed and well behaved. Despite their sizeable family, they both make sure that the whole family always go on an annual holiday. For the last few years their favourite holidays have been cruises; they have been on a Mediterranean Cruise and are planning a Caribbean Cruise in the near future.

At one time we all used to wonder as to who was going to follow in mum and dad’s footsteps by having a large family of ten children. No one in the Hubberstey clan had the courage to carry on with the trend set by their parents, but at least Michael can claim that he has *almost* reached their target. However there is still time yet!

****

Many Asians are under a misconception regarding the care that British folk give to their elderly parents; in fact I have touched on this subject earlier. A lot of English people and the families I have come in contact with do care for their elders; if they can help them in any way they do so.

However my statement doesn’t mean that *all* British families are like that. Whilst I was working in the CAB I came across some heartbreaking stories as to how some young people abandoned their elderly relatives.

Also I have heard a pet sentence, “I don’t care,” uttered by so many young people, British whites as well as Asians, but when I explained properly to them just how much trouble, and how many difficulties their parents had gone through to bring them up, often they do realise and some regret having such feelings.

CHAPTER EIGHTEEN

As mentioned previously, our group of friends in Preston during the 60's included Wasim, Mahmood, Sattar, Baqui, Patwari, the Kumar Brothers, Roy, Passi and me. We were a good mixture of Indians and Pakistanis and met at least once a week. All the boys were well educated so weren't jealous of each other as we got on well together. Wasim was a Pakistani, who would recite poetry written by Faiz Ahmed or Ahmed Faraz's; whilst Roy, an Indian, would recite some of the poems by Ghalib, Allama Iqbal and Jigar Muradabadi.

Whenever we went out we were all immaculately dressed, well mannered and fluent in English. One day Wasim's cousin came to see him from Bradford. He was a Captain in the British Indian Army during the Second World War who had served and taken part on the front line in El-Alamein. At 6 ft 3 inches tall, with a 50 inch plus chest, he was an extremely imposing figure.

Wasim asked me, Mahmood and Roy to accompany him to take his cousin to Blackpool, or some other nice countryside or seaside place. On our journey we stopped at a place to have something to eat and drink. We noticed the owner of that restaurant was reluctant to serve us. Wasim's cousin asked the waiter to send the owner across.

When the landlord came over to us, Wasim's cousin used his British Regimental accent and said, "We notice that you seem to be rather reluctant to serve us. Can I introduce us all to your goodself?"

The landlord kept quiet.

Wasim's cousin continued, "My name is Captain Chaudhry, I have fought against Germans for people like you in North Africa under General Montgomery and won the Victoria Cross. By the way these gentlemen are doctors, serving in Blackburn and Preston hospitals."

The poor landlord was now apologising a lot, "I am sorry Sir if you got that impression, as we most certainly had no intention of ignoring you."

I knew that Mr Chaudhry was in the army during the Second World War, but I didn't know that he had won the Victoria Cross. Anyway, Mr Chaudhry's bluff worked well and we were given full attention. After our meal the owner came over to our table and talked to us for a long time. It just goes to show that it doesn’t take long for someone to change their perceptions from their first impressions.

Once again we were given the same wonderful reception in a cricket match held in Preston.

CHAPTER NINETEEN

It was now the middle of 1961. I was pretty sure that Kath and I would spend the rest of our lives together. Luckily Kath was of the same opinion, but I hadn't asked her mother or father yet. Before taking the big step I wanted to explain a few things about myself to her.

I explained to Kath, "Before we commit ourselves we should understand each other very clearly. First of all for a successful marriage, I believe that it is very important that both husband and wife are of the same faith.

Secondly Kath, you already know that whilst I appreciate and enjoy fish and chips, I couldn't possibly live on them for the rest of my life."

She not only agreed to learn to cook curry, but she actually became an enthusiastic cook of all things spicy and authentic curries.

Thirdly we **both** agreed that if we had children, it would be better for the children too, if they had Muslim names and were brought up in the Muslim faith.

I consulted June on this matter and being a very liberal minded girl, she completely agreed with all my views, but she just wasn't sure about her parents' reaction. So in the end I plucked up my courage, and one afternoon I went to see Mum. Luckily Dad was at work, so there was only Michael with her.

When I told Mum of our plans to get married, she was in favour, but as expected she couldn't speak for Dad.

Before leaving Mum's house I said, "I'm going to see Dad about this matter myself."

After I had approached him, he wanted some time to think about it. I believe he consulted with his family, but after a while he gladly gave us both his consent.

I had crossed this bridge quite nicely, but then came the question and crunch of seeking **my** parent's consent. It wasn't easy writing to my father on this subject. As mentioned earlier the boys in my family were very scared of our father, so first of all I approached my elder brother and sisters.

Through my sisters my predicament reached our father. As soon as this request reached him, he wasn't very pleased at all, but called an extended family (clan) meeting.

According to my sister, sparks were really flying about in that meeting; the main objector was one of our old, eccentric and traditional aunties. As she was the oldest, she had a lot of authority in family affairs. One of her reasons of objection was that she wanted to keep our family blood as pure as possible.

She declared at the meeting, "We have educated, and good looking girls over here. Why does he want to get married over there?"

She turned to our father and said, "Tell him never to come back to this family if he does that."

After a lot of discussions and arguments the meeting was adjourned. Our father promised the meeting that the matter before them was serious, therefore it had to be tackled and resolved in a proper manner.

Our father himself was an educated person who had worked under British administration for a long time. He had always liked and was used to doing things in a proper manner. He wrote me a very compromising letter, asking me to send him Kath's address.

With fear and reluctance on my part, I did so.

Then he wrote a two paged A4 sized letter in English to Kath. It was written in very official and formal English, enquiring about her family, her father and mother, her brothers and sisters then asked her to send him some photographs.

Kath was a bit nervous of writing her first letter to him, but after that she managed to write him a few letters. While he was corresponding with Kath, he wrote to me also.

In the end he called another clan meeting and told them, "If it is Mudassir's wish to marry this girl, then we should accept her into our family and wish them good luck!"

After he had sorted out the family objections, my father wrote to me asking, "By what Muslim name will Kath be known?"

I wrote back to him saying, “Actually we would both be very honoured if you would suggest a Muslim name for her.”

There was a meeting of the immediate family, including my younger sister Beeda Baji, my nieces Rafia, Saeeda and nephew Akhtar. They didn't want to give her an old fashioned or a traditional name; instead they wanted her to have a modern name.

In the end Fernaz was suggested as her Muslim name. Kath was pleased to be known by this name. I was delighted that my parents and family had taken part in one of the most important events of my life. They may know her as Fernaz, but to others she will still be the Kath we all know and love.

There were still some people in the clan who weren't sure about my father's decision, but on his word alone, they accepted it.

He wrote me a very long letter, in which he poured his heart out. Then he mentioned my mother's, sisters' and all my family's best wishes for my wedding. My sisters and nieces were happier than any one else for us.

During the time when Kath and I decided to get married, Wasim met a Scottish girl called Alma. I knew they were serious about each other and wanted to get married. It was very important for Wasim and me that Kath and Alma embraced Islam before we got married.

Sattar was quite active in the community and knew an Imam of a local mosque. He made arrangements to bring the Imam to perform our Nikah (Wedding vows) in a Muslim ceremony.

It was arranged that the Muslim ceremony would take place in the morning, whilst in the afternoon a Civil marriage ceremony would take place in the Registrar's office.

******

Mudassir and Kath signing the marriage register in 1962

Before the Nikah obligations could be undertaken, Kath and Alma formally embraced Islam by a personal declaration in accordance to the same recitation of an Islamic vow first set out one thousand four hundred years ago. The simple and brief ceremony was conducted by a local Imam and 'witnessed' by our few selected guests.

The Muslim ceremony took place in Curwen Street; guests included both Kath's and Alma's immediate families and our friends. Our civil ceremony took place at the Registrar's office located at Guildhall Street in Preston.

By the time we arrived at the Registry Office everyone was more relaxed and in a celebratory mood.

Just before the ceremony, the Registrar turned to Kath and the guests and informed them, "Being a Muslim, Mudassir Khan can have four wives."

Kath told him. "I already know all about that."

The ceremony was simple and dignified.

****

Karamat Chaudhry had bought a house in Curwen Street off Ribbleton Lane. I rented the front room of this house for £2.00 a week. A married West Indian gentleman called Conroy, and a single Pakistani young man Qamar Abbas Sheikh, rented the upstairs bedrooms. Sheikh worked in the CSP department at Courtaulds.

Qamar Sheikh was a newly arrived Pakistani young man. He came from a respectable family and was a very well educated man. We were on the same 'A' shift, and went to work together. After a few months Conroy moved out and the landlord's cousin Sadiq Chaudry moved in.

Sadiq was an old soldier who had fought the Japanese on the Burma front. He was a proper gentleman and a very good cook. He worked on 'B' shift which always followed our 'A' shift. He cooked wonderful and tasty curries. I don't know how many times Sheikh and I pinched curry from his pans. Our curries just weren't as tasty as Sadiq Chaudry's, no matter how we prepared them.

Once we the lodgers asked our landlord to put a heater in the kitchen so that we wouldn't feel so cold while we were cooking. As the landlord was reluctant to give us this facility, we resorted to Plan B. When Sheikh and I returned home after work at six o'clock each morning, we would switch on all four rings on the cooker. One way or another we managed to keep warm in a very cold kitchen, but on the other hand this generated a heavy bill for our landlord as we had a pre-agreement that he would pay for all the electricity used at the property.

****

It was June 1962 when through Courtauld's internal transfer system, the whole team of male operatives in the coning department were transferred to different departments. Some were sent back to CSP, a few went to box spinning, others were sent to the new yarn testing department, whilst those remaining were transferred to other departments.

Due to my textile educational background, I was transferred to the duracol department where the blends of different shades were prepared with different dyestuffs. These blends were used for spun dyed yarn in the box spinning machines. After the colourist's approval, the blends were taken from our department to the next floor up, to be poured into the hoppers of the box spinning machines.

As I had studied textile chemistry, colour and design at Blackburn College, this department suited me well. I could apply the theory that I had learnt at Blackburn College into practical work.

Within days I became familiar with the recipes for the different shades and preparation of blends. Ken Green, the Duracol department's manager was a wonderful person. When he found out that I had so much theoretical knowledge of dyed yarn, he explained the practical side of this process to me.

Ken treated his workers fairly. Every week he allocated different jobs to workers, such as making blends for the box spinning machines, or putting buckets in suction pots and colour checking. There were six other male workers in this room, George Zelinski the leading hand, our foreman Ken green, Bernard Cohen, Sam, Martin and a Hungarian lad called Joe.

Although there were hundreds of Jamaicans, Italians, Polish, Indians and Pakistanis in the different departments and sections, there were only one or two Asians on the other shift, but I was the only Asian on 'A' shift in Duracol.

Duracol department was directly under the supervision of the works chief chemist and colourist Mr Flanagan. I also remember Mr Parks who was the assistant chemist and general manager of the department.

As I was already familiar with dyestuffs and pigments of different manufacturers, such as ICI, CIBA, GIEGY and others, it didn't take me long to make friends with the four assistant colourists. On the night shift, whenever I was on colour checks, I spent a lot of time in the lab with the on duty shift colourist, helping him to finalise the colour-match, which taught me more skills and gave me so much more experience at the same time.

****

It was April 1962 when Dr Dowling confirmed that Kath was expecting. We were both pleased, but at that time we were only living in a rented room, which really worried me. I wanted to buy my own house, but due to lack of finances I was unable to raise the deposit required to buy a house of our own.

Kath's younger sister Neva was quite close to Kath, she sometimes stayed with us in Curwen Street. Neva was a great help to us, as she was a helping hand to Kath for housework and carried the shopping from town.

None of my friends, even my closest friends like Sattar or Wasim, knew that Kath was expecting. She always dressed sensibly, covering her whole body in such a way that nobody could guess she was expecting.

During that time Kath had learnt to cook some curries. She started with egg and potato curry like I had done, then progressed to cooking different sorts, such as chicken, meat, or vegetable curries. She was a bit scared at the beginning, but slowly mastered so much, that even Pakistani women have praised her curries. After a while she learnt how to cook Pulao, Zarda, and Halwa.

****

It was a freezing cold morning on the 23rd November 1962 when about eight o'clock in the morning, Kath told me that she was ready to go to the hospital. She had already arranged for an ambulance for this emergency and had booked a bed in Chorley hospital. We didn't have a telephone or a car at that time, so I ran to the public telephone booth in Skeffington Road. In my hurry and confusion, after ringing for an ambulance, I rang Doctor Dowling too.

Instead of our usual doctor, another doctor turned up at the house before the arrival of the ambulance.

I had never seen this doctor before, but he introduced himself as Dr. Cowling, and asked me, "Have you got some hot water, towels and soap ready?"

I had never had an emergency to deal with like this in my life. I was already nervous and confused. I was just about to go into the kitchen to put the kettle on for the hot water, when two very calm ambulance men walked in. I gave a huge sigh of relief!

Dr Cowling and the ambulance men talked for a minute or two, but to me this seemed ages. Kath was already in the final stages of labour, so they eventually made a decision to rush her to hospital in the ambulance.

Dr Cowling told me that he would follow the ambulance saying, "You accompany your wife in the ambulance."

On the way the ambulancemen assured me that they were well qualified and equipped to deal with cases and emergencies like this, and if need be they would pull up at the side of the road and help to deliver the baby.

I couldn't believe what I was hearing. For a minute I thought it would be like it happens in some African countries and parts of South Asia, where perhaps some women give birth to their child behind the bushes.

Whilst all this drama was unfolding before my eyes I really missed home at that moment. In Pakistani families these sorts of emergencies are mainly dealt with by the other women in the community. Men are hardly ever involved at all; in fact they are usually kept out of things of this kind altogether.

It was about 10:00am when we reached Chorley Hospital. Two nurses with a stretcher were already waiting at the door; they wheeled Kath in. Dr Cowling introduced himself and me to the nurses and we followed them. The nurse brought a gown and mask for the doctor and asked me to wait in the waiting room.

About fifteen minutes later, Dr Cowling and a nurse came into the waiting room and told me that I had become the father of a little girl.

I asked, "Please can I see the baby and Kath?"

I was told that as the child was born prematurely, she had been placed in an incubator, so I would need to go to see her there.

It was my first chance to see a newborn baby. I plucked up courage and entered the room in which the babies in incubators were being taken care of. I was terribly nervous, but Dr Cowling kept talking and explained everything to me.

I noticed that my daughter had lovely olive skin, jet black hair, and beautiful big brown eyes. She looked quite small to me weighing just 6lbs. I was so thrilled to see her!

When I left Kath and our new baby daughter my first errand was to go to the GPO to get a telegram form to send off to my father, confirming that not only had Kath and I got the precious gift of a baby daughter, but that they were both doing well. I was filled up with so much pride and felt so joyful.

I was supposed to be working on the afternoon shift from 2:00 until 10:00pm; instead I sent a doctor's note to Ken Green explaining the reason for my absence. He was so surprised to hear that we had a child, as I had never even told him about my family circumstances.

When I next visited the hospital I took the GPO form with me so that Kath and I could word the telegram together for my family. I also presented my wife with a large bunch of flowers that I had purchased earlier; then Kath and I gave the box of chocolates to the nurses to share amongst themselves in order to express both mine and Kath's gratitude to them for their help in delivering us such a beautiful child. I left there feeling so very happy and blessed at becoming a father especially now knowing that Kath had come through it all so very well.

At work our shift followed 'C' shift and regularly I used to see Sattar at work as he was finishing, but when on this particular day he hadn't seen me at work, he came straight round to our house in Curwen Street to find out why I hadn't appeared at work? He also asked after Kath, wondering where she was.

When I informed him that she was in hospital he became worried and said, "She looked all right yesterday, what happened?"

"She has given birth to a child," I told him.

Sattar had mixed feelings for us, worries, happiness, concern and excitement. He had a look on his face that was filled with so many questions.

"When, how, where? I mean where is she now? You never said she was expecting."

"I know; we didn't tell anybody, but we have a most perfect daughter; she is in Chorley hospital."

Sattar was genuinely pleased and excited. He immediately announced that he was going out to buy a carrycot, baby blankets and other things related to newborns. He was so happy that in the evening he accompanied me to Chorley so that we could both see my daughter, but unfortunately only the father was allowed on the ward, so Sattar came back very disappointed.

The only means of transport in those days that we had were either local or Ribble buses. I used to leave Curwen Street at 6:00pm to catch a Ribble bus at the bus station to reach Chorley at 7:00pm.

During that week it had snowed heavily and was bitterly cold. It felt as if it was going right through one's bones. Winters were generally bitterly cold in those days. If it snowed heavily, it used to stick to the roads and pavements for days, or even weeks.

The return journey from Chorley hospital was terrible. Waiting for a bus at an open bus stop near the hospital was real torture. No matter how I tried to keep myself warm, I was always freezing.

As I said before, I had no idea what to do next for either Kath or the child, so once again I went to June for advice. The very next day I went along with June and Sattar to do all the necessary shopping.

I bought a pair of shoes, a dress and a blue coat for Kath, while Sattar bought a carrycot, a little rattle and a few more baby things. By then the news had reached Wasim, Mahmood and our other friends. I couldn't say no when Sattar wished to name the child.

He suggested the name Shahnaz, which we all agreed on. In the beginning there were a few objections about the name, in that it was unusual and very difficult to pronounce, but after a while everybody got used to it except Kath's father, who had difficulty pronouncing it for a long time. He overcame this difficulty by calling Shahnaz, Cheyenne, after a popular Western series on TV in the 60's.

Because Shahnaz was a premature child, she and Kath had to stay for a full week in Chorley hospital, but as soon as they were discharged, Sattar and I brought Kath and Shahnaz from Chorley Hospital back to our house in Curwen Street in a taxi.

Sattar arranged for an Imam to come and recite the 'Adhaan' in Shahnaz's right ear. It is a Muslim obligation that all newborn Muslim children receive the holy words of the 'Adhaan' soon after birth.

Throughout this time I was kept very busy being in constant touch with my parents and other relatives. All of Kath's relatives were very thrilled with their new baby niece. However Kath's sister Neva adored Shahnaz, she asked if she could look after her if we ever wished to go out in the evenings.

We both agreed to her kind offer. On occasions when we did have an evening out, Neva lovingly took the responsibility of looking after her little niece as she had promised.

Before long we received a telegram from my father on behalf of all the family, expressing their joy and happiness on the birth of our daughter.

****

Quite often, I'm asked if I have ever experienced racism. My answer is always, "Never, ever socially, but in the forty-one years of my working life, perhaps I faced it two or three times at the most."

Though what I experienced was not racism, but discrimination. The first time was in duracol department. An advertisement appeared in Preston's *Evening Post*, for an assistant colourist to work on three shifts in the duracol department at Courtaulds.

The required qualifications for the post were five 'O' level (now GCSE) subjects, including chemistry. I didn't pay much attention to it at the time, but the next day at work Ken Green called me into his office.

"Have you seen the advertisement in the *Post* for an assistant colourist?" he asked.

"Yes," I answered. "It's in last night's *Post*."

"Why don't *you* apply for it?" Ken suggested to me. "You have all the qualifications, besides which you are already doing the job so you would be silly **not** to apply for it," he continued.

The next day I applied for the post. Ken Green was really pleased with me. He felt sure that I would definitely get the job.

After a week or so, I received a letter from Courtauld's Chief Chemist which read:-

Dear Mr Khan,

After considering your qualifications, we do not find you suitable for the post.

Sincerely yours,

(signed)

Chief Chemist.

I wasn't surprised, because I already had a feeling that the management were willing to employ coloured people only on menial jobs not on the better paid, or ones that carried any kind of responsibility. Deep down it was something that I was quite well aware of and was one of the reasons that I did not want to stay in England permanently.

When I showed this letter to Ken, he was furious and said to me, "Write another letter to that b*****d, and ask him why he didn't find you suitable?"

Reluctantly I wrote another letter to the chief chemist, asking him for the reason for turning me down for this position?

His reply was, "Your qualifications are higher than the capacity we can offer."

This time I wasn't satisfied with his answer. I wanted to see the works chemist, so I asked Ken to make an appointment for me to see him.

The following week on my day off, I went to see the works chemist. He was very sympathetic towards me, and started out by giving me all sorts of reasons for not considering me for that job.

When I insisted that I must know the **real** reason for turning me down, he uttered the same usual sentences that even today I still hear.

Feeling uncomfortable and fidgeting in his chair he starting saying, "I personally have nothing against coloured people, I like you as a person; I know you are a very good worker and thoroughly conscientious. I would have liked to appoint you to this post but my hands are tied. I'm very sorry, but it is Company policy."

I couldn't believe my ears as this did shock me, I was really annoyed and challenged him, "Mr Parks, why beat about the bush, why don't you just admit that it is *you* who doesn't want a coloured person to take up such a position?"

Mr Parks tried to give me a lot of explanations then tried to console me by saying, "There will be other chances."

However I was in no mood for listening to his pathetic excuses. I simply got up and left.

At that time there was no Race Relation Board, or any other similar public body, that I could have approached to seek advice or take the matter further. The only organisation I could approach was the General Workers' Trade Union, but they couldn't do anything.

As I didn't get any positive response from anywhere, I thought it best to leave Courtaulds. There was also another reason for me to finish there; a series of practical training had been arranged for me at Ciba, Sandoz, and Giegy, the manufacturers of dyestuffs in Basal, Switzerland. This training course was due to start in July 1964. The duration of it was for almost three months. I therefore left Preston in July 1964 leaving Kath and Shahnaz in Preston.

After completing the training in Switzerland, I should have proceeded to Pakistan where in Hyderabad a job had already been arranged for me at Amin Textiles Ltd, however I fell ill in Basal and changed my mind, so instead of going to Pakistan I returned to Preston.

At that time Kath and Shahnaz were staying with Kath's parents. I could have found a job in Preston, but instead I decided to try my luck elsewhere, so we moved to Blackburn in the middle of October 1964.

I could have gone to my old friends in Blackburn for accommodation, but as I was now a family man I needed a family house. Our search proved to be a difficult task.

Kath and I, together with Shahnaz, who was now almost two-years old, walked at least five miles looking for a flat or a house in Blackburn. It was cold, raining and windy. We called at almost all the places where I thought there might be some accommodation available. We visited Estate Agents, the Citizen's Advice Bureau (CAB) and the *Evening Telegraph* Office for help, but nobody could do anything for us.

By now it was almost 7:00 in the evening, and dark. We were soaking wet, cold and tired. In the end we decided to call on our friend Cathy, who lived in a flat in Duckworth Street, Blackburn.

Luckily she was in and welcomed us, making us cups of tea and something to eat. She was pleased to know that we were planning to move to Blackburn. It was so wonderful to sit down in a warm room, see a friendly face and be in a cheerful atmosphere. Cathy knew that the house on Park Road where she used to live was still vacant, and the landlord lived in Lambeth Street.

Feeling a little revived now by the hot tea and food, we plucked up some courage and walked all the way to Lambeth Street from Duckworth Street. Kath and I were each carrying Shahnaz in turn.

It was so tiring walking up Lower Audley, then onto Audley Range, before turning into Lambeth Street. Soon after we arrived we managed to speak to the landlord, Mr King. Thankfully he was willing to let us have this flat for £1.10 shillings a week.

The rent he quoted was very reasonable, so we accepted it immediately. At that time if the landlord had asked for even £5.00 per week, we would gladly have agreed to it. The flat was over the top of a shop that was used as a warehouse for direct supplies.

The two gentlemen who ran this business used the downstairs for their post. They came once or twice a week to collect their mail, but they never stopped for very long in the shop downstairs.

Although we were going to use the two bedrooms upstairs, we had to come downstairs to the kitchen to make a cup of tea or to cook. Unfortunately there was no bathroom, so we had to go to Freckleton Street Baths to have a proper bath, so once again I had to put up with outside toilets, as the toilets were out in the yard.

All the rooms in the flat were cold and damp. To top it all, on the ground floor the backroom window was smashed and there was a great big hole in the window.

There was only one single bed for Kath and me to share, but thankfully Cathy had left her sofa and chairs when she had moved out. Luckily we had our own bedding, pans, pots, and other utensils.

It was a very difficult time for us because we didn't have a job between us, so what little money we had was running out fast. Going to the DSS or any other agency or friends for help would have been an embarrassing act. We were determined to come out of this hard time through our own merit and efforts.

In the next two days we managed to move to Park Road Blackburn. The following week I went to the Employment Exchange in King Street. The system for finding a job in those days was totally different than it is today. In the Employment Exchange there were different sections, such as Management, Building Construction, Textiles, Engineering, and Miscellaneous.

As my interests rested in textiles, I naturally went to the textile section first and sat down in the queue. When my turn came, the clerk took down my details. I didn't tell her about my educational background, because firstly I was desperate for money, secondly I didn't want to be refused with the excuse that I had higher qualifications.

The clerk told me that there were a few jobs in Whiteley's Albion Mill, Waterfall Mill and Unity Mill, all part of the William Birtwistle Group. She gave me three cards bearing each mill's address, and the manager's name.

I had enough money for the bus fare to get to Wm. Birtwistle's Waterfall Mill in Queen Victoria Street. I went to the reception at Waterfall Mill, knocked at the window, and when a female member of staff appeared, I gave her the Waterfall Mill card.

As soon as she saw the card she said, "I am sorry, there is no job."

"Could you ask the manager please, if there is anything at all?" I asked her politely.

"I am telling you, there isn't anything." she replied.

I was furious, but I knew that I was in no position to argue with her, so I went straight back to the Employment Exchange.

It was about 2:30 in the afternoon and I was determined to find a job of some kind that day. When I told the girl at the Exchange what had happened, she also became annoyed.

Without saying anything, she picked up the phone and had a lengthy conversation with someone.

As soon as she finished the conversation, she turned to me and said, "I am sorry I have just spoken to the weaving manager; could you go back and see him?"

"Are you sure that there is a job? I have already spent money and time," I told her.

The clerk herself was annoyed and embarrassed, but she assured me that there was a job for me there. I caught the Mill Hill bus once again, and when I reached Waterfall Mill reception I didn't ask for the job.

This time I asked the girl, "Please can I see Mr Halstead the weaving manager?"

The receptionist was Ann. She worked in Waterfall Mill for a long time. In later years we became very good friends, but she never forgot my first day at Waterfall Mill.

Also working with Ann in the office were a few other teenage girls and boys. One of these was a young girl called Madeleine with long, dark, wavy hair who used to come out into the various departments carrying a metal tray, filled with little cans every Thursday, which was payday. Each can held a person's wage, and each worker was allocated a works and payroll number when they started work.

As Madeleine entered the department, she would walk along the line and each worker would state their number. She would hand over the complete contents of the corresponding tin to the worker. A few notes and a handful of coins as appropriate were counted out into each individual's hand and she waited for them to check it themselves immediately, as no one was allowed to say they were short or over except at the time they were paid. It was hoped that each worker remembered to bring their purse or wallet with them each Thursday, otherwise they would have nowhere to keep their money. Later on though, a wage packet system was introduced.

****

Over forty years later when I ventured to convert my stories into this book, I also started searching around for an Editor. I could not believe it when the editor I actually turned to was none other than the same Madeleine from Waterfall Mill office. As fate would have it, what an unbelievable coincidence this was! Naturally we had a lot to talk about once we got over the pleasant shock. Little did I think or believe that once she had formatted the first storage disk containing the draft copy of my life history, she would actually hand my disk back to me in an old wage packet, just like the ones that I used to get paid in.

This was due to the fact that many years after leaving Birtwistle's, Madeleine worked for the same printer who had originally supplied stationery to the whole William Birtwistle Group. When her boss died, he left her a room filled with stationery from years earlier, which Madeleine still finds a use for. The links that loosely bind us together are amazing aren't they?

****

After a few minutes, Mr Halstead came to reception and took me to his office. "There are a few jobs in the weaving shed," he said, "however I am impressed with your spoken English. Would you like to learn weaving?"

I intentionally didn't mention my educational background because I feared I might face the same problems that I had in Courtaulds, so I agreed to his suggestion of learning weaving.

Mr Halstead took me down to the weaving shed.

I immediately noticed that the noise in the shed was unbearable. I was then introduced to Tommy Livesey the shift manager. I was told to start work the following Monday on day shift starting at 7:30am and finishing at 4:30pm, with a one hour dinner break between 12:00 and 1:00pm.

I was so desperate for the job and some money that I didn't even ask about my weekly wage. On the last Monday of October 1964 I started work on Mr Livesey's shift. He took me to Christine, an experienced weaver, who was going to teach me practical weaving. She lent me a reed hook to draw the ends through the healds and reed. To be a proper weaver I needed other things too, a steel comb, a pair of scissors and an apron. I bought these things during my lunch hour.

Christine was about eighteen-year's old, a pretty girl and a patient and wonderful teacher. As she was on the morning shift, her shift finished at 2:00pm when the afternoon workers started.

While the shift was changing over, I went to have a smoke, (bans weren't in place in those days but being a mill with flammable material about, there were designated smoking areas). After five minutes or so I went to see the shift manager, Harold Hindle, who handed me over to another weaver called Joan Bond, who fully explained to me the working system of the weaving shed.

Besides the shift manager, there were overlookers, weavers, helper weavers, spare weavers, spoolers, unifil cleaners, oilmen, loomsweepers and other such workers in the weaving shed.

Within a week I became used to weaving. It was simple, one up, one down, weave. It was very easy for me to follow the practical side as I already knew the theory.

At that time there were only two Asian spare weavers, one on each shift. The one on Mr Livesey's shift was Rashid Chaudry. In later years we became very good friends.

Rashid asked me, “What wage have the management started you on?”

"To tell you the truth," I replied, "I don't know, because I didn't ask."

Rashid was a bit surprised but said, "It will be about £10.00 a week, because you are a trainee."

The wages were paid on Thursdays, but all the new starters had to work a week in hand, which meant that one had to work for almost two weeks before getting paid any wages.

Somehow, I don't remember exactly how, but Kath and I managed to exist that first week on barely nothing, however when the following week started we only had one pound between the three of us.

By now Shahnaz was almost two-years old, so we knew that we couldn't manage with just a pound till Thursday, so I had to ask Rashid if he could lend me a pound. I felt terribly embarrassed about asking him, but I was forced to borrow.

On Thursday I got a wonderful surprise, my wage was £13.14 shillings. This wage was for a fully trained helper or spare weaver. Mr Halstead must have found me capable enough of becoming a helper weaver very soon. I gladly repaid £1 to Rashid with a smile.

I was transferred to Mr Livesey's shift to be Christine's helper weaver. Later I made a lot of friends in the shed and started to enjoy the work. While I worked at Waterfall, Kath found a job at Hall Street Mill, which raised the question as to who was going to look after Shahnaz while we were at work?

I mentioned this problem to Rashid, he was very sympathetic and promised me that he would ask his wife if she would look after Shahnaz? Luckily she agreed. Kath and I were both on double day shift, so one week we worked 6am-2pm, and the next week 2pm till 10pm.

It used to be heartbreaking for us when Kath used to wake Shahnaz up at 4:30 in the morning to take her from Park Road to Shakeshaft Street. It was not surprising that Shahnaz hated getting up at that time, as would be the case for any child, and it made her cry a lot.

Each journey would mean the same routine. Kath would carry Shahnaz all the way up Lower Audley, then on to Audley Range, eventually reaching Shakeshaft Street at about 5:15am. Kath then had to walk back all the way to Hall Street via Audley Range, Lower Audley and Bolton Road.

At the end of work Kath had to travel and reverse her morning journey in order to collect Shahnaz at 2:30pm.

William Birtwistle Allied Mills Ltd, Waterfall Mill, Blackburn. (Known locally as Fish's)

CHAPTER TWENTY

We were desperate to save some money, so that we could put a deposit down to buy our own house. We managed to save about £50, but out of this sum we had to put £40 deposit on a house in Ingham Street. It was just a two-up and two-down property.

We were about to sign the contract for the purchase of this house, when we saw the advertisement in the *Evening Telegraph* for the sale of our landlord's house in Lambeth Street. The house in Lambeth Street was heavenly compared to the one in Park Road, where even the downstairs window was broken.

The price for the house in Lambeth Street was £700, and the deposit was £100.00. I had a word with the agent who was selling the house in Ingham Street; he didn't like me going back on our previous arrangement, so I eventually had to compromise and agreed for him to deduct £10 from my deposit, leaving us with just £30.00.

Kath and I didn't want to lose the Lambeth Street property, which left me with no choice but to ask Rashid if he could lend me £70 for approximately eight or ten weeks?

Rashid willingly lent me the money and I took the deposit to Mortimer, Gorse and Ross the local estate agents immediately. This house had originally belonged to a builder, who had installed a beautiful three-piece bathroom suite, and a modern kitchen. The house was well maintained and had modern coal fires in both the living and sitting rooms.

Without any further delay we managed to buy this house, and moved to Lambeth Street in May 1965. Besides us there was only one other Asian family on Lambeth Street; they were an Indian family called Hafizjis.

****

During the 60's the Birtwistle Group dominated Blackburn in textiles. There was another firm Mullards in Blackburn on Phillips Road, but their main works was in Simmonstone; between the two places they employed thousands of workers. The Phillips Road works worked on a three shift system, which meant they paid a higher rate than that of the textile mills.

This rate of pay attracted me greatly, so I went along to the Phillips Road site. The works were very impressive, with smartly uniformed commissionaires at the main gates. I was directed to the personnel office where a lovely girl attended to me, giving me an application form to fill in. I completed the form in no time and she took it into the office.

A smartly dressed gentleman in his late thirties came into the waiting room and took me to an interview room.

We had a pleasant and long chat then he said, "Everything seems to be fine Mr Khan. Now I want you to go to our surgery for a medical test."

"Fine, thank you very much," I replied.

The nurse in the surgery measured my height, weighed me, tested my eyesight and gave me a test for colour blindness. She was very pleasant and gave me a written report to take back to the personnel office.

Once more the smartly dressed man in the personnel office received me with a big smile and asked me to wait in the waiting room. A few minutes later a middle-aged man came out and took me into the interview room.

With all the English pleasantness and mannerisms he said, "I am sorry Mr Khan, but I can't offer you the job."

"Oh, is there no job?" I asked.

"Yes, there are jobs," he stuttered on trying to explain the situation to me.

"Is my medical report not good," I enquired.

"That is perfect, there is no problem there." His facial expression was changing every minute.

"Then please, can you give me the reason why you can't offer me a job?" I said with a little annoyance in my voice.

He was restless in his chair; changing his posture he said, "I don't know how to tell you," before uttering those well versed words and sentences that I had heard so many times before. "I have nothing against coloured people, I think they are very good workers, but at present it is Company policy not to employ them."

I was so shocked that I couldn't speak for a few seconds, but then I composed myself, and said to him, "Can I ask you something?"

"Yes of course!" He tried to use his English charm and manners to their fullest extent.

I couldn't believe my ears, I was really annoyed and said, "Your commissionaire at the gate, or your receptionist, or even you yourself could have told me the same thing, when I first arrived. Why did you waste all this time?"

Again he tried to justify himself, by saying, "You must appreciate Mr Khan, that it is the *Company's* policy and nothing to do with me."

Then a thought flashed through my mind, "Be honest, you expected me to fail the test and medical, then you would have been justified with your decision for not employing me, without bringing discrimination into it."

He was too embarrassed to answer me, so without saying anything I got up and left.

This was the second time that I had faced blatant discrimination in England, but at that time there was no race relation act, or laws to deal with cases like these.

****

As we were in need of money I thought it best to go on night shifts, as it paid 20% more in wages than double day shifts at my current position at Waterfall Mill.

I asked Mr Livesey if I could be transferred to the night shift. He wasn't very pleased initially, but when I told him about my circumstances he agreed.

The following Monday I started work on the night shift. The shift manager on nights was Bill Gardner. Besides Bill, there were five other English workers, they were overlookers. The weavers, helper weavers, spare weavers, and spoolers were all Asians.

Weaving wasn't difficult work and I mastered it in no time. There were times when Bill Gardner wanted to talk to a weaver, or someone else wanted to talk to Bill, but there was always a language problem, so they used to send for me to interpret.

After a year or so Mr Halstead left and Mr Maher took over as the weaving manager. Mr Maher was quite a nice person, with a good understanding of Asian workers.

It was in 1966 when many Asians started to come and settle in Blackburn. The main employer in Blackburn was the William Birtwistle Allied Mills Group. The group had twelve textile mills in Blackburn, one in Preston, one in Abbey Village, and one in Ribchester.

The majority of Asians who came to Blackburn, Bolton and Preston in the 60's were from the rural areas of India, Pakistan, and Bangladesh. Most of them were unskilled and ignorant of the English language. Others were educated even to degree level, but because of their lack of good English communication skills they weren't given jobs where they could use their educational qualifications.

During the 60's the merchant ships that came to Liverpool used to have an Asian crew. As soon as a ship docked at Liverpool, some of the crew would desert the ship and go to stay with their friends in Blackburn or Preston.

I believe that in the 40's, 50's and 60's, once the sailors had landed in England (legally or illegally) nobody would ask them about their passport or other documents. They could quite easily go to a National Insurance Office to get an Insurance Number so they could start work. Now fifty years on things have tightened up considerably, England is endeavouring to apply strict controls for each immigrant that enters the country as we have become very overcrowded.

****

After a year or so Mr Livesey died suddenly with stomach cancer and Bill Gardner left for another mill. Frank Maher left too and the whole structure of the Waterfall Mill management changed.

While Mr John Clements was the general manager at Waterfall Mill, George Welsby was transferred from Unity Mill to work as the weaving manager at Waterfall Mill. Tom Ward, an overlooker on the night shift, was promoted to be the night shift manager and Ron Mitchel, who had just arrived from South Africa, was appointed as one of the shift managers on double day shift.

Since I had first started at Waterfall Mill, I was always doing interpretations and translations for the management and workers. One Monday night when we started work at 10pm, Tom Ward came to me, telling me that Mr Welsby, the weaving manager wanted to see me. I thought it could be for a translation, or maybe for some instructions that he wanted me to pass on to weavers or workers.

As I entered his office with Tom Ward, Mr Welsby had a folder in front of him and was reading a paper. He offered me a seat, so I pulled up a chair and sat down in front of his desk.

He closed the folder and said to me, "I have been looking into your file. I can see that you have a good background in textiles. On top of everything else, Tom speaks highly of you. We are going to create new posts of weaving supervisors on all three shifts. On the night shift we think that you are the most suitable person for the job, and I would like to offer you this position."

As I had encountered such a bitter experience in Courtaulds and Mullards, I simply wasn't expecting any offer like this. Although I was pleased, I wanted to think about it. I asked, "Do I have to give you my answer now?"

"No, but you must let us know before this coming Friday," said Mr Welsby.

By Thursday, after discussing the wages, duties and conditions for this job, I gladly accepted their offer. I thought I might get some sort of resentment from the English overlookers on the night shift, but to my horror it was the Asians who in the beginning gave me a bit of a headache. I found out later that this particular Asian, who was supposed to be my best friend, turned out to be jealous of me. On the face of it he was still my best friend at work and socially too for family visits, exchanging presents at Eid, Christmas and birthdays. I was both disappointed and hurt when I found out that this 'friend' had tried to discredit me quite a few times; sadly I only found this out when I left the Birtwistle group in 1975.

The first problem that the Waterfall Mill management faced was when some male English workers complained that the male toilets were not being used in the usual Western way, so were being left wet through and dirty.

Through Tom Ward, I received a message that John Clements, the works manager, wanted to see me the next day. So the following afternoon I went to see Mr Clements. He was very understanding, and wanted to know the background as to how and why there might be wet toilets?

I had to explain about Asian toiletry and cleanliness, as I did the first time to my landladies in 1956. I suggested that it would be better if one toilet out of the three existing cubicles could possibly be modified to Eastern style for Asian use? The following week the maintenance department did the required alterations, which led to no further complaints. For my suggestion to help solve this problem I was rewarded financially.

My bilingual skills came in very handy, as I was always in demand to do interpretations or translations. The second problem came when one of the loomsweepers wanted to pray during working hours.

Ron Mitchell the shift managers sent for me to interpret and help solve this problem for them. The elderly loomsweeper came from a Pakistani village and was a strict practising Muslim. He wanted to offer his two of five obligatory daily prayers at work in the afternoon. One prayer took about twenty minutes, whilst the second in the late afternoon, took about ten minutes.

It was an awkward situation because the man was very keen to offer his prayers. Ron, who was a very reasonable person, didn't know how he could allow thirty plus minutes for him during the working day.

I had a long chat with the elderly man, explaining to him that I would try my best to come up with some sort of solution, but asked him "What if the manager does not agree with me; what would your reaction be?"

"I would be willing to give up the job," he said.

His answer gave me a bit of hope to bringing about some kind of compromise between the two.

I asked Ron, "How many official breaks is the loomsweeper entitled to?"

Ron said, "He is entitled to three breaks. The first one is between 9:30 and 9:45am for 10 minutes; then he has a one hour dinner break between 12:00 and 1:00pm, with the last ten minute break between 2:30 and 2:40pm."

I asked the loomsweeper, "How important are your tea breaks and dinner breaks compared to your prayers?"

"Khan saab," he said, "I don't bother about tea or dinner breaks, I just don't want to miss my prayers," he replied with confidence.

So I said to Ron, "I have a suggestion that might appeal to both of you to help sort this out."

"I would like to listen to it. If it is workable, then I would like to adopt it," Ron replied.

So first I explained my plan to the loomsweeper in Urdu; then I turned to Ron and said, "If you add up all his break times, they add up to one hour and twenty minutes. If you would allow him, he wouldn't take his tea breaks, instead he would divide his dinner time and use that time for prayers."

Ron liked this suggestion and said, "Have you asked him about this arrangement?"

"Yes, I have cleared it with him and he agrees to it," I answered.

Both parties were happy with this arrangement and nobody knew about it, or ever had any further complaints.

With petty problems like these I soon established myself as a good interpreter, translator and adviser on Asian matters, regarding culture, food, and the Asian way of life.

Since I had first started at Waterfall Mill I had got to know nearly everybody in the mill. It was not only in the weaving shed that they got to know and hear about me, but also in other departments. They too started sending for me to do interpretations.

The were many people I got on well with at Waterfall Mill, but I naturally recall some more than others due to my particular work responsibilities and social circle. Amongst them were John Clements, John Memon, Fred, Frank Maher, George Welsby, Tommy Livesey, Harold Hindle, Bill Gardner, Tom Ward and Ron Mitchell, Colin Campbell, Ron Yates, Cyril Danson, and David Redfern.

I remember David Redfern well as he started as a trainee overlooker at the time when I was a weaver. Later he became a fully fledged overlooker once he had completed his training. We used to try to wind each other up on different subjects, but never insulted or offended one another.

I can also recall some of the many Asian weavers and other workers to this day. Amongst them were Rashid Chaudry, Mohammed Sadiq, Abdul Hai, Maulana Mohsin, Mohammed Khan, Chaudry Mohammed Hussain, Mohammed Ishaq, Munshi and Babu.

There were many others who I cannot recall clearly, but from time to time when I was perhaps in Accrington, Blackburn, Bolton or Preston, someone would approach me with a huge grin on their face, and call out "Khan Sahib".

We would then chat for a good few minutes. In reality I could not remember them, but they would soon realise this and politely remind me of their identity. I suppose there must be something about my personal appearance which might have remained familiar to them. Whenever I had such an encounter, our conversation would evoke fond and pleasant memories from the past.

It is so gratifying to me to find that in later years many of my former colleagues, or some of their children went on to become very successful businessmen in their own rights.

Mr Mohsin is one such person who epitomised 'hard graft' and honest values. There was a time when he would work a full nightshift in the mill, then during the daytime would manage to run a small retail business, leaving himself barely a few hours for sleeping. Besides his desire to give a good quality of life to his family, he also took on very important and responsible roles amongst the small, but growing Asian community in Blackburn and the surrounding areas. With his vast knowledge of Islam, Mr Mohsin took on the role of a Maulana, an Islamic cleric and a spiritual leader.

From the moment he arrived in Blackburn, Maulana Mohsin showed great pride in being a Muslim living in a non-Muslim country. He was not only a religious person; he always informed and guided others about their religious values and duty to compromise with Western values. He enlightened us on the importance of Islam, Islamic teachings and Islamic values, always stressing that every member of society deserved respect.

Our lunch breaks would only last for about thirty minutes, but he made them into very interesting sessions, despite the fact that sometimes these breaks would be taking place in the early morning hours.

In late 1969 we heard that the higher management of the William Birtwistle Group at Osprey House were thinking of closing the night shift at Waterfall Mill. One Wednesday evening the Directors from Osprey House were all gathered at the mill prior to the start of the night shift. At about 10:15pm Tom Ward informed me that the Directors wished to address all the workers and instructed me to ask the workers to gather in the canteen.

Naturally everyone became very concerned at this unusual event, as normally we only got together around the start of the Christmas festivities or annual holidays. People were feeling deeply worried about the prospect of losing their jobs. Most Asians were already working to support their extended families in their own countries. Their dependents relied heavily on the regular financial support being sent by a family member from England.

Mr Harry Whittaker, Mr Bill Doidge, Mr Steedan the Financial Director and Bill Fryer, were all present in John Clements office along with George Welsby and John Memon.

Just before we went into the canteen Mr Clements briefed me, as I was to provide an instant interpretation of the developments and consequences of what was being said.

Shortly afterwards Mr Whittaker and Mr Doidge addressed the meeting and outlined the bleak situation. As rumoured the night shift at Waterfall Mill was to close down.

Fortunately the Birtwistle Group had other mills in the surrounding areas in Blackburn, Preston, Abbey Village and Ribchester. Some overlookers, weavers, spare weavers and spoolers were offered jobs in other mills within the group, but sadly there were also some redundancies.

After the main address by the Directors, Mr Welsby read out the names of each individual worker and the mills where they were being offered a job. Some were sent to Albion Mill, others to Unity or Lower Darwen Mills, whilst a few were offered jobs at Abbey Village or Florence Mills.

Finally my name was announced and I was informed that I would be transferred to Osprey House. This came as just as big a surprise to me as it was to the others; I wasn't expecting anything like that.

The next day I went to Osprey House for a formal interview with Mr Doidge, Mr Whittaker and Mr Pomfret. There I found out that Tom Ward and Mr Clements had recommended me for a newly created position and I was now included in the Osprey House staff. My duties took me to different mills in Blackburn, Preston, Ribchester and Abbey Village. To reflect on my new level of responsibility I was informed that I would receive a petrol allowance for these journeys.

Osprey House in Aqueduct Road Blackburn was the nerve centre of Wm. Birtwistle Allied Mills Ltd. At one time this group had sixteen textile mills in and around Lancashire. All the major policies for individual mills and businesses were made at Osprey House which was the Head Office

As expected Osprey House was a beautiful, purpose built, single storey building, furnished and decorated to a high quality standard. The reception area was decorated in soft, pleasant and attractive shades.

The receptionists were attractive and polite. Elaine, who had a very pleasant personality and a melodious telephone voice, always had a beautiful smile on her face. All the Directors had their own individual offices, all of which were equipped with modern furniture and up to date facilities.

Osprey House had its own fully equipped motor garage, where the servicing, repair and maintenance of the group's fleet of staff cars, vans and trucks were carried out. The trucks and vans were used for transporting bales of cotton, yarn and fabric and machinery from one mill to another.

Every two or three years the staff cars were replaced by new ones. The staff entitled to get company cars were the Directors, general managers of the mills and the heads of departments. Junior staff travelling between the mills to carry out their duties, were each allocated an appropriate mileage allowance.

There was a fully equipped testing laboratory based within Osprey House, where raw cotton, yarn and fabrics from the different mills were tested. There was also a works study department which was responsible for both the efficiency and quality of work in the mills. A team of works study staff would go to different departments of certain mills, and after their studies were completed they would make a report of their findings. Once these findings met with the approval of the work study officer, the reports were then forwarded to the various works managers.

After my transfer to Osprey House, I naturally came in regular contact with the Directors as well as Mr Pomfret the head of the personnel department.

Mr H. C. Whittaker had started work as a young boy at Bank Mill, Great Harwood. On his own merits he rose through the ranks until eventually he became the weaving and production director of the group. Besides these two responsibilities, he also held the responsibility for being the personal assistant to the chairman Mr A. H. Birtwistle. In truth, Mr Whittaker was regarded as being next to Mr Birtwistle himself.

One afternoon in my early days at Waterfall I was on my way to the weaving shed in Waterfall Mill, when a smartly dressed man stopped me at the top of yard next to the entrance and main gates. Without realising who he was I got talking to him; during the conversation we were both laughing cheerfully. People going past us glanced at me with curious looks. I thought that my conversation with the gentleman was quite normal until later, when a worker in the shed approached me.

"Hey! Do you know who you were talking to?"

"No, I really have no idea," I replied.

The worker told me, "That man is regarded as 'God' in the Birtwistle group. Whatever he says will be the final word, as nobody ever dares to go against his decisions. Then the worker told me that the man in question was the weaving director, Harry Whittaker.

Later on I too realised the importance and authority of Harry Whittaker in the group.

Both Mr Whittaker and Mr Doidge seemed to have a soft spot for me. Although I was really on Mr Pomfret's staff, quite often I would be sent for to meet Mr Whittaker and Mr Doidge over matters related to Asian culture and customs.

During the Second World War these two gentlemen had spent some time in India. They both had very pleasant memories of those days and often used to talk to me about them. Once when Mr Doidge was with Bob Forrest, the spinning manager and I were speaking to to Jimmy Shaw in the roller covering room. After our mutual greetings, Mr Doidge started talking about the time when he was in Delhi and a young Indian boy had stolen his felt hat.

We were all in a rather humorous mood so I said, "I assure you Mr Doidge, that boy was definitely *not* me."

This produced laughter all around.

During his stay in India, Mr Whittaker and a young Indian man became sincere friends. Mr Whittaker told me once, that not only did I look like his friend, but I even *sounded* like him, and as such I always reminded him of his old friend.

During my work at Osprey House I came across Mrs Violet (Vi) Birtwistle Shutt. She was the group chairman's sister and one of the members of the Board of Directors.

She used to arrange trips for the local schoolchildren and elderly people to Albion Mill (Whiteleys). She often used to ask some staff members to take the visitors on a guided tour of all the different departments in the mill. After these tours the visitors and the guides were treated to refreshments. Several times I was called upon to accompany the visitors as a guide.

Mrs Shutt married into a very wealthy family from Preston. I believe the family owned a successful corn business.

At Christmas time in the 1960's, Mrs Shutt used to pay for the office parties, every staff member throughout all the mills from the office junior up was always given a lovely gift.

Mrs Shutt was also interested in sports activities for the staff, as there were a couple of netball courts in the Birtwistle Group, inter mill matches were frequently arranged. Mrs Shutt did the teams proud by laying on coach transport to and from the courts either in Blackburn or Preston. She also ensured that complimentary refreshments were provided. Trophies for the winners and runners up were engraved with names of the two teams who had won through to play in the final.

In this way young female office staff got to meet and know one another after work. They were encouraged to take part in netball and represent their own mill at the game. Competition was fierce but friendly, and many long lasting friendships were forged in this way.

Madeleine Baylie, one of the young girls in the office in the 60's, actually met her boyfriend through netball as the Blackburn games were played at Albion Mill (Whiteleys). Stewart, (later to become a Taper at Waterfall Mill) saw her practising on the court and asked her out on a date. A few years later they married and have two children Andrea and David.

****

As the Asian community was increasing in Blackburn, one of my friends called on some people to get together and form a support organisation. Eventually the Young Men's Muslim Association was formed. A General Secretary was duly elected, while an educated gentleman newly arrived from Pakistan, was elected to serve as President.

By 1968/69 Whalley Range and the London Road area of Blackburn were getting well populated by Asians. They were mostly Muslims from India and Pakistan. Those who had lived here for some years and could afford to, sent for their families to join them in Lancashire. As the Asian population grew, the grocery shops, dress shops and other specialist shops emerged in various Lancashire towns. This was the start of a trend when corner shops run by Asians became a familiar sight.

One Conservative Councillor showed a lot of interest in the welfare of newly settled Asians in Blackburn. He suggested that we should meet to chalk out a programme in this connection. The following week we met in the old town hall.

My friend and I represented Y.M.M.A., whilst a Police Inspector, the Conservative Councillor, the Editor of a newspaper, and two other gentlemen represented their departments. In that meeting it was felt that there was a need for some organisation for liaison between the Asians and the indigenous community.

The first ever 'Race Relation Organisation' was proposed. The Counsellor, along with two other Counsellors, a Police Inspector, and the Newspaper Editor, invited my friend and me to become members of this organisation.

At that time I didn't realise that there were a few people who didn't want to do anything in supporting the launch of the proposed organisation. But soon after waiting in the wings for glory, they 'jumped on board'. Sadly, their main intention was self-glory and publicity by having their names published in local newspapers.

These individuals could not converse or write in Urdu, (the common Asian language) let alone English, but they gained prominence due to support from companions from their own villages in India and Pakistan, a trait which was to become an integral part of the Asian way of life throughout the United Kingdom. It was a terrible feeling to be let down by so-called 'educated' Asians, who placed greater importance on personal glory over a constructive venture to benefit a wider society. It was such a shame that they were more interested in interfering and criticising from the sidelines, than simply discussing and putting in place the true aims for everyone.

****

Although I was directly responsible to Mr Pomfret and Mr Doidge in the Birtwistle group, I also made myself available to other mill managers and assisted whenever there were any issues related to Asian language or cultural problems.

By 1970 a large number of Asians had settled in towns like Blackburn, Preston, Bolton and Burnley. At Waterfall Mill during the 70's on night shifts, apart from the overlookers and the managers, the majority of workers were Asians. For the double day shifts the mills were employing young Asians and training them to become spinners, winders or weavers.

The Birtwistle Group had a training school in their Lower Darwen Mill. It was under the jurisdiction of Mr Pomfret. May Dunn was a very competent training instructor, however she sometimes used to have difficulty in explaining things to Asian trainees, because the young Asians weren't used to the Lancashire accent and dialect. Time and time again I was sent for to do some interpretation for her.

After six to ten weeks training in the training school, the trainees were sent to their spinning or weaving departments. As a follow up, it was my job to keep a record of each trainee's progress in the mill.

For that I had to visit different mills in Blackburn and John Hawkins Preston, Abbey Village Mill, and Ribchester Mill.

I had a 1965 Ford Zephyr 6. I used to get my tank filled with petrol every Monday morning and travel to all the mills during the week.

****

It would perhaps be appropriate to mention here, that in the beginning I had some doubts about my acceptance by some of the English workers in the mills, as I was a visitor from head office. Right up to the 70's and 80's the overlookers and their union were very strong. The management was more or less helpless when it came to any disputes with overlookers.

To be honest I never met with any resentment apart from on two occasions. The first happened at Florence Mill. A group of young Asian boys had completed their initial training in weaving in Lower Darwen Training School, and some went to Florence Mill on Whalley New Road. My job was to help complete their follow up training and keep a record of their weekly progress.

As usual I went to the manager, Mr Welsby's office at Florence Mill, and explained the reason for my visit. Mr Welsby was really pleased to see me, as he already knew me from Waterfall Mill.

After talking to Mr Welsby, and with his permission, I went down to the weaving shed and spotted some boys in one of the alleys. I asked one of them who was in charge.

He pointed to an overlooker. I approached him, introduced myself in a proper manner asking him how these trainees were doing?

"Waste of time, they are no good at all," he replied.

"Why, what have they done?" I enquired.

"They try to be clever," the overlooker said.

I couldn't understand what he meant by, 'try to be clever'. So I asked him, "What do you mean by that?"

"They talk in their own lingo, and they are ignorant."

He then made specific remarks which were strongly racist in both vocabulary and tone. In today's present time the individual would have been prosecuted for making those offensive remarks.

At this point, I knew he hadn't had many dealings with Asians. I calmed him down and invited him to go somewhere quieter for a discussion. It was time for our tea break; we went to the canteen and sat in a quiet corner. I listened to him very patiently. His main complaint was that these young Asians didn't have manners. I assured him that I would have a word with the young people and that he would definitely find a difference in their attitude next time. He and I talked for about twenty minutes on different subjects, including Asian workers.

Later on I had a brief word with the Asian boys and told them to behave themselves. I went back to see the overlooker, before leaving the weaving shed.

He was apologetic for the things he had said in the beginning and said, "I am sorry lad, I was out of order to receive you like that. I wish more Asians had your sort of attitude, approach and patience."

"Oh don't worry about that, I am sure we can work together and get along without falling out with each other," I said.

We shook hands and I left for Osprey House. When I reached there the receptionist Elaine told me that Mr Pomfret wanted to see me right away.

I thought that it might be something serious, but her smile conveyed a good feeling.

As I entered Mr Pomfret's office I was greeted with a big smile and he said, "Ah, just the man I want to see. I have just received a phone call from the manager in Florence Mill."

"Yes, Elaine said you wanted to see me," I told him.

He offered me a seat, which I gladly accepted.

"Oh, what did he have to say?" I asked with curiosity.

Smiling, Mr Pomfret said, "You handled the overlooker very well."

He thought before continuing, "Actually, he was full of praise for you; in fact he couldn't speak highly enough about you."

Then Mr Pomfret told me in detail how the overlooker had complimented the management for appointing the right sort of person for the job.

The second time I had to deal with someone who had become a little more awkward with me, it was in regard to the manager at Abbey Village Mill. He was quite an intelligent person, who had completed a part-time textiles course at Blackburn College while working in the textile industry.

After working as an overlooker he had been promoted to the position of manager of a weaving shed. At the time of my transfer from Waterfall Mill to Osprey House, he was the general manager at Abbey Village Mill.

I had never met him, but I had heard about him. It was said that he was a conceited man who thought too much of himself. He regarded himself as being the only one fit enough for promotion. He never said so in actual words, but one could feel that he didn't like anybody from Osprey House. He was of the opinion that the people there just sat about all day long drinking cups of tea.

Whilst doing follow up reports I noticed that I needed to see some trainee weavers who had returned to Abbey Village Mill and were working in the shed. I drove to the mill, but instead of going straight to the weaving shed, I went to the general manager's office and explained the purpose of my visit.

He listened to me and said rather sarcastically, "I don't know why somebody has to come here; we have our own supervisor and instructor for this job."

I couldn't keep quiet and said, "I am sure you have, but now it is Company policy to centralise the training system."

Then I saw my chance and had to be blunt saying, "Look Sir, both Mr Whittaker and Mr Pomfret have instructed me to carry out this programme. Naturally I intend to do it to the best of my ability. If you have any objection, or complaint about me or my work, you can get in touch with either one of them."

He tried to explain things, but I was in no mood for listening to him so I said, "Do I have your permission to see these trainees?"

"I suppose so," he said reluctantly.

"Thank you," I said politely before leaving his office

Apart from those two incidents I never met with any resentment, or experienced anything like that in my eleven years with the Birtwistle Group.

Due to the nature of my role and my previous position in the company, almost everybody in all the departments at Waterfall Mill knew me, and within weeks the majority of people got to know me in the other mills also. As mentioned my base was at Osprey House where I would start my day. After checking my post, I would decide which job was most important. Priorities were always interpretation (in case of disputes), translations and visiting all the mills during the week. If there were trainees in different mills I would go to visit them; if some were doing well, I would recommend them to be sent to the weaving shed or spinning room.

From May to September I thoroughly enjoyed visiting Abbey Village, Ribchester, and Preston mills. Managers and other staff at these mills were very good, particularly so the mill canteen managers, who were very kind to me. Sometimes I used to reach these mills near to lunch time. I really enjoyed the fish and chips at John Hawkins in Preston. I also looked forward to having cheese and onion pie with chips and mushy peas at Ribchester Mill.

Around this time some illegal immigrants started coming to Blackburn. Some came as students to Blackburn College, but after attending classes for a few weeks they would disappear.

Others came as visitors, overstayed their allotted period and started work in one mill or another in the Birtwistle Group, or some other place. Quite a few came as crew on foreign merchant ships to Liverpool, as soon as the ship docked at Liverpool, their friends or relatives collected them from the ship.

During the 60's and 70's the Immigration department didn't really bother. Then all of a sudden they realised that people were abusing the system. A nationality division was set up in Blackburn Police Station, where Sgt. Phillips was always kept very active rounding up illegal immigrants.

One afternoon I was about to leave Osprey House for Unity Mill in Lower Darwen, when I got a phone call saying that I was required at Waterfall Mill urgently.

I drove to the mill concerned, and on arrival I was informed that there were some people waiting for me in Mr Clement's office. With Mr Clements were Sgt. Phillips, PC Fishwick and an Asian man.

Mr Clements introduced me to the Police Officers. Sgt Phillips explained the situation, which was that the sergeant and the other officer suspected the man in question was illegal in Britain, so the Sergeant would like to talk to him.

This man worked as a loomsweeper in the mill and didn't know any English. I therefore acted as interpreter whilst PC Fishwick recorded the interview in English.

Purely by accident this became the start of my role as a professional interpreter. My name was at the top of the list in the Blackburn courts, the police station, DSS Offices and with solicitors. I also acted as an interpreter in a few cases in Crown Courts at Manchester and Lancaster.

Once when I appeared in Manchester Crown Court, a top Asian Barrister challenged my qualifications and ability to be an interpreter. Somehow he had found out that I was a Science Graduate, and not a degree holder in languages.

With the Judge's permission he gave me a passage of about ten sentences in English, and asked me to translate it into Urdu. The court was filled with barristers, solicitors, police officers and the general public. Although I was nervous for the first few seconds, I recovered quickly and asked the Judge to excuse me for four or five minutes. The Judge was very kind.

With a big smile at me he said, "Take your time Mr Khan; there is no hurry."

"Thank you my Lord," I replied, immediately getting busy translating the passage. This took me about two or three minutes to complete.

As soon as I finished the task, I handed the paper over to the usher, who passed it over to the barrister. He asked me a few more questions regarding my academic qualifications and my reasons for coming to England. This relaxed me and I started talking freely. All of a sudden the barrister beckoned the usher and asked him to pass the piece of paper containing my Urdu translation back to me.

Then he turned to me and said, "Mr Khan, would you be kind enough to translate this piece into English?"

That surprised and shocked me, but later on I realised that this barrister wanted to check my presence of mind. Again this only took a few minutes to translate the piece back into English.

At this stage the Judge turned to the barrister and said, "Are you satisfied with Mr Khan's capabilities?"

"Yes my Lord, I am well satisfied," the barrister said with a smile.

The court was adjourned for lunch; I was just about to go out to meet the police inspector whom I had come with, when I saw this same barrister rushing towards me.

Approaching me he got hold of my right hand, shaking it he said, "Mr Khan, I am terribly sorry that I had to put you through all that."

I almost felt like swearing at him, if not hitting him, but instead I simply said, "It's quite all right Sir, I hope you were satisfied."

Walking along the corridor he put his left arm over my shoulder and explained, "I had to put those questions to you, not just to satisfy myself, but to show the court that you have a full command of both languages, oral and written."

The day trial finished in Manchester Crown Court; the barrister asked me to join him for lunch. It was my first visit to such a high profile restaurant, but I was confident enough to communicate well with the other barristers. I had a wonderful lunch, which was all the more enjoyable as I did not have to settle the bill.

This trial in Manchester established me as a qualified interpreter and translator throughout Blackburn, Bolton, Preston and Burnley. My fees were based on different daily rates, depending upon what sort of court I was appearing in. During this time some more interpreters popped up thinking it was an easy job to do and lowered their fees.

Once, one of the police inspectors said to me, that a certain Asian interpreter's fees were a lot lower than mine.

My answer to him was simple and straightforward, "I am sorry but I can't lower my fee. By all means please feel free to get the cheaper one."

Later on I found out that the interpreter in question wasn't even high school educated and struggled to gain work as an interpreter.

CHAPTER TWENTY-ONE

As Shahnaz was almost four-years old in 1966, Kath and I were concerned about her learning the holy Qu'ran. There were mosques in the Whalley Range area where children could go to learn the Qu'ran, but these were too far away for us to attend.

Luckily later on I found out there was a trainee weaver Mr Makda in Waterfall Mill, who was very knowledgeable in Islam, and qualified in religious scriptures. When I asked him if he could teach the holy Qu'ran to my daughter, he was more than willing to come to our house to teach the Qu'ran to Shahnaz.

After some time, the Muslim residents of the Audley district where we lived converted two adjoining houses in Lambeth Street into a Mosque and 'Madressah' (Religious school). Later on Shahnaz started to visit the mosque in order to continue her studies.

Mr Makda had moved away to Birmingham, but whenever he was in Blackburn he would always visit us. He still remained interested and pleased with the progress that Shahnaz was making with her Islamic education.

Shahnaz, with Mr Makda
her Islamic teacher

In 1967 Kathleen and I started to plan for the education of our daughter Shahnaz, as by now she was almost five-years old. We were living in Lambeth Street, and St.Thomas's Primary School was only a short distance away. We took it for granted that it would be very easy for Shahnaz to attend that school.

One Monday afternoon in May or June, I thought I'd better go and get things moving for Shahnaz's admission into St.Thomas's Primary School. I went to the school and made an appointment to see Mr Rothwell the Headteacher, the following Friday.

We had a long and very pleasant chat about the English weather, Indian sub-continent and the rest, but in the end Mr Rothwell shocked me when he spoke.

"I am sorry Mr Khan, but you will have to get your daughter into Scotland Road Primary School."

"But that is almost a quarter of a mile away from where we live," I told him. I felt sure that Mr Rothwell could read the expression of annoyance on my face.

With his charming attitude he said, "It isn't my decision. It is the new policy of the Education Authorities that immigrant children should be spread into different schools."

"I quite understand Mr Rothwell, that it is not **your** decision, but is there really any logic in it?" I carried on talking and explaining,

"We live just two minutes away from your school, and my daughter would have to cross only one road to get to it. She will have to cross at least *four* main roads before she reaches the other school. Please tell me where the sense is in that?"

Mr Rothwell was sympathetic, but also very reluctant to give me a straight answer, but finally said, "To tell you the truth Mr Khan, the Education Authority doesn't want too many immigrant children in one school. I am allowed to take only a certain number of these children at this school."

"That's fair enough, but I will take this matter up with the Education Authorities in this case," I told him.

The following Monday I went along to the Education Offices. I have never been an aggressive person, so when a young girl appeared behind the counter, displaying full English manners and politeness, I asked her, "Can I see the Education Officer, or someone of that calibre?"

She looked a bit surprised, but picking up a pen and some paper asked me, "What is it about?"

"It is about my daughter's admission into a school," I replied.

Putting the pen and paper back down on the counter she answered, "You should go to the school then."

"I have, but there seems to be some problem there, so can I see somebody about it please?" I asked her politely.

By this time her questions were becoming needless and very annoying, but I remained calm. She then went away for a little while, a few minutes later a young man appeared and took me into a cubicle.

"What can I do for you?" he asked.

I explained the situation and problem to him, then I asked him, "Is there any logic at all in me sending my daughter a mile away from home, when there is already a school situated much closer to us?"

He came up with the same answer that Mr Rothwell had given to me, that it was the policy of the authorities to spread the immigrant children between the different schools in Blackburn.

His answer was typical, "This way immigrant children will be able to learn the English language properly."

I had to laugh and said, "I take it then that you think my daughter *doesn't* speak English?"

A blank expression crossed his face.

"By the way, my wife is English, and we speak English in our house," I explained.

He insisted that my daughter would have to go to Scotland Road School, as nothing more could be done.

In the end I got up saying, "Oh no mister, on no account can I take the risk of sending my child to a school so far away, when there is already an adequate school in Lambeth Street. I'd rather keep her at home and teach her myself." I was determined to send Shahnaz to St.Thomas's School.

After a week I received a letter from the Education Office stating that there was a place for Shahnaz in St.Thomas's School, so would I get in touch with the headteacher there.

Shahnaz started at St.Thomas's and was a very popular child, not only amongst her friends, but with her teachers too. She fully participated in all the school activities and sports. In her final year at St.Thomas's School, Shahnaz played the main role in the Christmas drama, 'Super Star'. The play was produced and directed by one of her teachers Mr Worswick.

She was a favourite pupil of Mr Pemberton the headteacher, Miss Smith, Mr Worswick and Mr Sloan. (Mr Rothwell left after a while).

****

In 1966 we were happy at Lambeth Street; we started making friends and increased our social circle. Amongst our new friends were Mr and Mrs Rashid Chaudhry, Mr and Mrs Munir, and Mr Sadiq and his family.

At weekends we visited each other's families. I have always been on good terms with my in-laws. As mentioned before, one of my younger sisters-in-law Neva has always been close to me and Kath. Whenever Kath and I wanted to go somewhere and couldn't take Shahnaz with us, it was Neva who always looked after her.

During the summer holidays, or some warm and nice weekend, if we were going to Blackpool, Southport, or some other interesting place, we always took Neva with us.

Neva turned fifteen in 1966 and had finished her schooling at Easter of that year. Kath was already working in the winding room at Birtwistle & Oddie on Wharf Street. Kath therefore suggested to Neva to enquire at that mill if they had any vacancies? Arthur Sutcliffe the manager saw Neva and offered her a job as a trainee weaver.

At that time Kath and Neva's parents were living at Bradkirk Lane farmhouse, which was situated in an isolated place. There was no direct bus service from Bradkirk Lane to Blackburn for Neva to reach the mill on time. Also she had to walk two miles just to reach the main road to catch a bus to Blackburn. Naturally her mother and Neva were worried about the situation.

Kath and I had settled in well at our Lambeth Street house. It had two bedrooms. Initially we had set up the second bedroom for Shahnaz, but as I worked on the night shift, Shahnaz often slept in our bedroom with her mother.

Kath and I thought that as our second bedroom was lying vacant, it would help Neva and be company for Kath, if Neva stayed at our house during the week whilst I was on the night shift. We put this suggestion forward to Mum, who was really pleased with this arrangement.

Neva had grown up to be a very good looking and smart young lady. She attracted not just young people's attention, the older men too turned around to have another look at her mini-skirt or mini-dress. Young people always wanted to be near her, while the elders were rather careful, as sometimes she would talk to them in a very frank and bold manner.

Neva and I always held a mutual respect for one other. As a joke, we would say a lot of things to and about each other; but whenever it came to responsible business or serious talks we respected each other's views and priorities. I'm glad that we never offended each other.

Neva made friends with the Whitehead girls. Joan Whitehead was a teenager too. Sometimes they both went out, but Neva was always home before 10:00pm, or if she went to the pictures she always came home before 10:30 in the evening.

I somehow felt responsible for her welfare. A good sense of respect was always maintained between Neva, Kath and I. Neva lived with us as a member of our family, so naturally I used to talk to her on most topics.

On a few occasions I corrected her on her attitude towards life. It could have been contrary to British culture, but Neva took notice of what I used to tell and advise her. Somehow Neva knew and realised that I didn't approve of mini-dresses or skirts in the house, so when she came home she used to change into trousers.

After completing her training Neva worked as a weaver on days for a while, before going onto shifts. After some time I noticed a change in her. When Neva was on the morning shift she would go out for the evening. In the beginning Kath told me that Neva went to see a friend from the office. However a few weeks later Kath told me that Neva was seeing an overlooker from the weaving shed.

"Oh, is she? Who is he?" I asked.

"It's Jim Mercer," Kath informed me.

My concern was only for Neva's future. I didn't want anybody taking advantage of her. After talking to Kath in detail I said, "Why don't you ask Neva to bring him to our house sometimes?"

So one evening Jim came with Neva to our house. I found him to be a mature and responsible sort of person. As we were both working in textiles we had a lot in common to talk about; Jim was a successful overlooker at Birtwistle & Oddie.

Neva and Jim got married in June 1968, and went to live in Great Harwood. The following year they had a daughter Jackie, followed later by their son Darren and a second daughter Sandra. We were regular visitors to each other's houses, Jim and I usually talked about the textile industry, which sadly was now on the decline in Lancashire.

Once Jim showed interest in going abroad, I knew for sure that some Lancashire textile firms had set up factories in African countries such as South Africa, Nigeria, Ghana, and Sudan. At that time Whitehead and Sons of Burnley were in the process of starting a weaving shed in Kaduna, Nigeria. They were looking for overlookers from Lancashire.

Jim applied for a job to go to Nigeria. He was successful in getting the position and went to Kaduna in 1972. Neva and the children followed a little later on.

****

In Birtwistle & Oddie Neva was quite popular amongst the weaving shed's male workers. In fact she left a lot of pleasant memories with quite a few people. One of them was Jack Cameron. Jack was an overlooker in Birtwistle & Oddie and knew Neva. Later on he came to Waterfall, so I got to know him well.

After almost thirty-five years I met Jack in Asda in Blackburn. Within minutes we recognised each other, though we had both grown a lot older since we had first started working in Waterfall Mill.

After our initial greetings Jack said, "By the way, how is your sister-in-law Neva?"

He was really pleased for her when I told him, "She is happily married now and has a family."

Thinking back to his old days, he said, "They were good old days, weren't they? Neva was a lively girl and the talk of the shed. In fact every single person in the shed liked her."

CHAPTER TWENTY-TWO

By 1967 we had purchased our first car, a 1960 Triumph Herald 1200. We went all over Lancashire in that little car. Although I drove the car, I didn't know anything about looking after or maintaining it. On the other hand, Kath's younger brother Ken was quite expert in mending cars, so every time something went wrong with our car, Ken would always manage to put it right.

Ken had just started courting a girl called Cathy from Accrington. He hadn't yet passed his driving test, but already he'd got a Standard 8. Cathy's father, Mr Charlesworth, didn't approve of anybody driving a car without first passing their test. At that time Ken lived with his parents in Bradkirk Lane. Ken used to come to our house in his car in the evening, leave his car at our house then I would take him to Accrington in my car to see Cathy.

Cathy Charlesworth was a beautiful girl of about eighteen; she and Ken made a wonderful couple. After getting married they settled in a house in Stanley Street, Oswaldtwisle. They had a daughter called Sharon who was educated in Oswaldtwistle. After completing a catering course she moved to Scotland, some time later she got married there.

Cathy has always been a family orientated lady. She made sure that she kept in touch with all family members, including our family. She would visit our house with Ken and Sharon at least once a week. In return we would visit their house. I used to look forward to tasting her freshly baked sponge cakes.

All her life Cathy has been an energetic girl. She managed to hold down a full-time job, and always kept her house very neat and tidy. With such regular family visits, Shahnaz and Sharon were obviously quite close to each other.

One Saturday afternoon Kath and I were in Blackburn town centre, when we met Mr and Mrs Charlesworth with Sharon. At that time Sharon was only about three or four-years old. As soon as

Sharon saw us she ran to us and I lifted her up into my arms. Mrs Charlesworth was a bit surprised at Sharon's reaction.

While Kath talked to Mr and Mrs Charlesworth, I asked Sharon, "Would you like to come and see Shahnaz?"

Sharon said, "Oh yes I want to see Shahnaz."

We assured Mr and Mrs Charlesworth that Sharon would be fine with us. We went home and Shahnaz and Sharon played together until it was their bedtime. They went to bed quite late at about 10:00pm.

At about 10:30pm Shahnaz came down saying, "Sharon is crying in bed."

"Why? Is there something wrong?" Kath asked rather worriedly.

"Oh no, everything is alright, but she wants to go home," Shahnaz explained to us.

Kath went upstairs and brought Sharon down. We tried all sorts to keep her at our house, but when she started sobbing I couldn't resist any longer. We got ready and took Sharon back to Oswaldtwistle. It turned out that Sharon had never been away from home before and just wished for familiar surroundings. As time went by though, Sharon and Shahnaz stayed over at each other's homes.

****

Once again I faced racism or discrimination, whichever you prefer to call it, when I wanted to insure my Triumph car. I called in at an insurance office in Richmond Terrace to get a fully comprehensive insurance quote for my vehicle. The girl behind the counter took down the particulars of the car and myself then gave me a figure. I was a bit suspicious about this quote, because it was so much higher than I had expected.

Kath was waiting for me outside the insurance office. After discussing the quote given to me, I asked her to go and ask for insurance using the same particulars of car. Kath went in, but came out with a very different figure, which was an awful lot lower than the one I'd been given.

Within minutes I went back to the same insurance office with Kath. The girl behind the counter got really nervous; she didn't know what to say, or how to justify herself.

She came up with the same classical answer, "I'm sorry, but it is Company policy."

However we insisted that they honoured the lower quote given to Kath.

****

It was around 1968 when I felt that my parents had done such a lot for me. They had spent a lot of money educating me. Not many parents, unless they were millionaires, would send their sons or daughters to England for their higher education. I therefore decided that it was time I did something for them in return.

Before I committed myself, I put my thoughts and ideas to my wife. I explained to her the background of these thoughts, and Asian cultural values. Luckily she agreed with me that they most certainly deserved something in return.

I wrote to my father and mentioned our intentions. He was overwhelmed and clearly overjoyed with the idea.

In Eastern countries including India, Pakistan and Bangladesh, it is widely thought that English people are like birds. The young ones stay with their parents while they are young, but as soon as they are grown up, they fly away and lead their own lives, particularly so when they are married.

The other misconception in the Asian community is that in Western culture, as soon as a young man gets married, his wife becomes his number one priority, and unless his wife agrees they rarely do anything for their parents, even when visiting their ageing parents they always have to consult their partner first.

Very rarely did I find elderly parents living with their children or grandchildren. If they are too old to be looked after by their children, they are put into old peoples' homes.

Whenever I speak to English people on this subject, they come up with the explanation, "My Mum (or Dad) is too fussy and independent."

However when I personally spoke to some elderly parents who were either living on their own, or in an old folk's home, their first reaction and answers were always the same. "I like to live independently," or "I was in their way."

After a while when it came to serious talks, I found out that most of them missed their families terribly, they often felt so depressed and lonely. They just wished there was somebody there for them to talk to when they got up in the morning or when they turned into bed at night.

It is a fact of life, that when one is healthy, fit and active, one doesn't need anybody to help them. People can be independent, sarcastic, arrogant or even pompous, but when they are ill, or are unable to do their usual things, then they really do need someone to be with them.

On this topic I could wholeheartedly say that Kath's parents were either extremely lucky, or they'd brought up their children in such a proper way, that their children always gave them priority over everything, even over their husband or wife.

Kath's brothers and sisters always took care of their parents, to the point that sometimes they even fell out with their 'number ones'. Jimmy, Ronnie, Ken, and Alan visited their parents regularly, while Michael stayed with his parents all the time. Likewise the daughters visited their parents every week. Michael being the youngest of the ten children, stayed with his mother right to her dying day.

****

When my mother, father and family heard about the suggestion that Kath and I wanted to get a house built for them in Hyderabad Sind, they couldn't believe it.

It is well known in Pakistan and India that not all Asian daughters-in-law would willingly help their parents-in-law. In fact some hardly get on with their mother-in law at all. I had to reassure my father that it wasn't just a suggestion; we really did mean to get a house built for them.

My father wrote to me saying, "You have a wife and a daughter, I wouldn't like to deprive any of you of anything. You should look after their interests first. It is so nice of both of you to think so much of us."

Before we committed ourselves fully to my father, Kath and I decided to put a squeeze on our expenses, so that we could start saving up as much money as we could. To do that, first of all we sold our car. We used to get three daily newspapers and three weekly magazines. We cancelled all of these except *for The Lancashire Evening Telegraph,* our local newspaper. We decided not to buy anything for us or Shahnaz for a certain period of time.

In this way we managed to save enough money to send to my father. In order to transfer this money to Hyderabad we had to go to Manchester to the National Bank of Pakistan, as there wasn't any Pakistani Bank in Blackburn.

Before remitting any money to my father, I wrote to him suggesting, "Perhaps the old house should be erased, so that a new house could be built in its place."

At the same time I requested my elder brother Muzammil to help me, by going to Hyderabad. I assured him that he wouldn't need to worry about the finance involved at all, as I would be sending him enough money to cover all of the expenses involved.

Before Muzammil Bhai reached Hyderabad, father tried to get the necessary planning permission for his new house approved by the local council authorities; however the clerks in the offices were giving him the run round.

It is the usual practice in countries like India, Pakistan, and Bangladesh that if one wants to get something done by an office; one first has to please the clerk. It is usually in the form of money that a client offers to the clerk or the officer concerned. Then there is another way to get things done. If you are in some Government employment, you ring and speak to the office concerned, send a message, or go yourself, then all of a sudden you get priority treatment.

I call this bribery in every sense, but the people in these offices simply name it 'speeding up the process'. Our father was experiencing the same problem. The clerks were sending him from one office to another with lame excuses. Their main purpose was to harass him, which they thought might result in them getting some money from him. Our father was distressed by their behaviour, and he wrote to Muzammil about it.

The following week, Muzammil Bhai reached Hyderabad, and without wasting any time at all, he went along with our father to the Council offices.

Later on father wrote to me saying, "As soon as Muzammil introduced himself as being from the police, the same clerk and officer, who previously wouldn't even talk to me properly, were busily running around after me."

At every office they went to, father was offered a seat straightaway, then was asked if he and my brother would like to have tea or coffee? This sudden change in their behaviour and attitude helped to speed up the process, which enabled the house to be completed in the middle of 1971.

With our financial help and active physical help from my brothers and nephews, the house was built without any further trouble or problem.

During the time the house was being built, the family temporarily moved to my younger sister's house. Luckily the house was completed just before the monsoon season began.

Our father was very happy and full of joy at moving into the newly-built house. He wrote a lengthy letter to me praising our help, and particularly that from Fernaz. In my family at least this went a long way to dispel misconceptions about English girls. As soon as the house was built and completed, we received the following wonderful letter from my father.

My dear Mudassir and Family,

I hope that by the grace of God you, Fernaz and Shahnaz are all in good health and spirits.

I am so happy and delighted to say that I am in one of the upstairs rooms of our newly-built and completed house, busy writing this letter to you.

As you know, during the months of May, June and July it is very hot, and just before the middle of July people look forward to having some rain. As soon as the monsoon season starts, we hope and pray that the rain will come down, as this will then bring the temperature down and allow us to get rid of the prickly heat.

Whilst the rain during this season does come down, sometimes it rains so heavily and lasts for so many hours, that it brings some of the houses down.

I am sure you remember that our drainage system is not of a very high standard, so whenever it rains too hard the drains overflow and all the streets are so flooded that our daily life is greatly disrupted.

Every year I used to really worry during the monsoon season, as the old house was in need of so many repairs.

But today as I write this letter, the monsoon season has already started, since this morning the dark clouds are coming over. It has been so very hot for the past few weeks. I am sure it is going to rain, because the cool breeze has just started blowing, which is always a sign of rainfull. Thankfully it will serve to bring the temperature down.

Since this morning both your young and old nephews and nieces, have all been very excited, as they have been making plans to go to the Rani-Bagh (gardens) for the seasonal party.

After a long time, I too am going to enjoy the downpour without any worry. As soon as it starts raining I am going to put my deck chair on the verandah and listen to the sound of the raindrops.

At this moment my thoughts are with you and Fernaz, as all of this has become possible through the love, affection and loyalty of both of you to us. Our dreams, happiness and enjoyment, have all come true, thanks to you both.

However I must also give some credit to your brother Muzammil that his contacts in the town hall and other Local Government Offices, made it possible to get this house built without further delay. As you know before Muzammil arrived on the scene I went to almost all the offices, but I received the cold shoulder by all the officers and their clerks. When Muzammil came with me to those very same office, and introduced himself as the Lahore Police official, the same clerks and officers who couldn't be bothered to talk to me properly, stood up to shake hands with him and were very attentive. They even provided tea and cold drinks for us. They couldn't do enough for us. Mubashir, Tafazzul and Akhtar too worked very hard during the construction of the house.

You, Fernaz and Shahnaz are always in our thoughts and prayers. God bless you all, our best wishes are always with you. Your mother and sisters send their love and best wishes to you, Fernaz and Shahnaz.

Your loving Father,

Shabbir Hussain

****

Father's letter pleased us all so much; we were very happy that we had been able to do our little bit to help make life easier for my parents. They were such wonderful parents who deserved only the very best. The house made such a difference to their lives, especially so during the monsoon season.

CHAPTER TWENTY-THREE

I visited Albion and Waterfall Mills regularly and also got to know a few people in Albion Mill. They were Jim Shaw, Margaret Hill, Eileen Crane, Bob Forrest, Len Whalley and Jimmy Crawley.

Jim Shaw was a true Lancastrian and proud Englishman. He was in charge of the roller covering department. He never spoke ill of anybody; as a matter of fact he hated gossips. Jim was popular and liked by everybody in the Birtwistle group. Whenever the Directors came to visit Albion Mill, they would call on Jim first and have a cup of tea with him before going to different departments.

Jim would never offend anyone; he was always ready and willing to give a helping hand to friends. Jim's wife Ellen and sons David and Jeffery were all good decent people.

****

Margaret and Eileen were spinning and cardroom instructors; both were expert in their jobs. Sometimes they used to call me to interpret for them as they had a few young Asian doffers and spinners. During lunch times the shift managers and foremen from the spinning department used to come to Jim's room.

Bob Forrest the spinning manager was an intelligent young man. He was also a very down to earth and approachable manager, which made the workers feel at ease with him. They could discuss their problems and grievances freely.

During summer the temperature in the spinning and winding rooms rose quite high and became unbearable. To look after and please his workers, Bob used to arrange for cold drinks to be available to them.

Bob had three shift managers, Len Whalley, Jimmy Crawley and Andy. I met Andy only a few times because he was on permanent night shifts, but I used to see Len and Jimmy quite often. They were mature and sensible shift managers; their shifts ran efficiently with hardly any problems. Len, the handsome young man, got married to a beautiful girl called Marilyn.

I met her years later when she was working in Blackburn Town Hall, and I had translated a few documents for her without realising at that time just who she was. It was a total surprise for both of us to meet when I took those documents to the town hall. It was lovely to meet Len too after almost thirty years; obviously we both had aged a bit, but Len hadn't really changed much at all.

While I was working at Whiteley's I met two students, Michael Clements and Baba Thundi. Baba was from Nigeria and was a full-time textile student at Blackburn College. Michael was in his final year of the textiles course. Michael and Baba were both working in Whiteley's in order to gain some practical experience.

Michael was one of the few Englishmen I met who loved spicy food, especially curries. At his request we had a curry session during lunch time in Jim Shaw's roller covering room.

Everybody, including Bob, Margaret, and Eileen enjoyed the curry and rice lunch. Unfortunately Jim Shaw couldn't enjoy it because I forgot to tell him that he should take out the black pepper seeds. On his very first bite he chewed the black pepper, which was a really hot experience; after that the poor fellow couldn't take any more curry and rice.

****

By the end of 1971 I longed to visit Pakistan with my family; I wrote to my father about our plans. This news caused lots of excitement for the whole family. In Hyderabad they immediately started making plans for our reception, as to who would be at Karachi Airport to receive us, then who would accompany us on a tour of the whole of Pakistan? Then there was another question as to who would be with Kath and Shahnaz all the time? All this commotion occurred long before we had even set a date or booked our tickets.

Saeeda my niece, Akhtar and Guddu my nephews, were all young in those days and our father valued their suggestions and opinions. Father had worked for, and had a long service with the Pakistan Railways. He had lots of friends and contacts in head offices, and he also maintained good relationships with station staff between Karachi and Hyderabad.

In 1955 Mr Matlub Hussain was our father's assistant station master at Nawab Shah Station. By 1971 he had been promoted to the position of senior station master at Karachi City Station.

Once our travel plans were finalised our father went to Karachi to see Matlub to plan our tour of Pakistan. Matlub Hussain had a high regard and a lot of respect for my father; he promised him that everything would be sorted out ready for our tour.

He said, "They are going to get VIP treatment on the train from Karachi to Peshawar."

He also told my father that an air-conditioned compartment would be reserved for us from Karachi to Lahore, then from Lahore to Peshawar. On behalf of Pakistan Railways he was going to arrange our stay in both Lahore and Peshawar.

CHAPTER TWENTY-FOUR

Kath and I had now managed to save enough money to make the trip to Pakistan. We were busy getting things together to take with us and felt really excited about our forthcoming trip to see my family.

After consulting with father we agreed to travel during September or October, because the weather in Pakistan would start cooling down during these months.

In the last week of May 1972 I received a letter from my niece Saeeda informing me that quite suddenly my father had been taken ill. Everybody, even our father himself, thought that it was a little temporary illness and that he would be all right in no time. He insisted that I shouldn't change our plans to go to Pakistan. I was getting letters from Saeeda almost every third or fourth day. In every letter she was trying to comfort me by saying that Abba (our father) wasn't seriously ill and that he would recover very soon.

In the middle of June I received a letter from my brother saying that Abba had been admitted into Liaquat Medical College Hospital. This news worried me greatly. Up until this time we hadn't even had our vaccinations for travelling, though we had got our passports sorted out. I quickly made appointments with Dr Sayner our GP for our vaccinations. At the same time I also got in touch with the travel agent specialising in trips to Pakistan. I was rushing about and trying to put things together just in case I had to leave suddenly.

****

From a very young age Shahnaz used to have a lot of problems with her tonsils. Dr Duncan had recommended her for an operation in Blackburn Infirmary. During the first week of July 1972 we received a letter from the infirmary stating that a bed was available for Shahnaz and that her operation would take place the following week.

I was still getting letters from Saeeda almost every third day. The news about our father wasn't very good. His condition was deteriorating, but he had instructed Muzammil Bhai to write to me saying that he would be all right soon, so I shouldn't change my planned programme for the trip to Pakistan in September '72.

Some kind of instinct told me that I was heading for a worrying and difficult time. Shahnaz was in hospital for a week and Kath and I visited her every day. We were both worrying simultaneously about Shahnaz in Blackburn and Abba in Hyderabad.

On 16th July 1972 I received a telegram from my brother Muzammil saying that our father had passed away. This news shattered me and set me rushing about for an air ticket. I managed to get the ticket through Syrian Airways.

The next problem I faced was that in those days no aeroplanes flew directly from Manchester to Karachi. I had to travel to London Heathrow to get to Karachi. The Syrian Airways flight from Heathrow was on a Sunday, but due to the lack of train services there was no connection for my flight. The only option left open to me was to travel by air from Manchester to Heathrow. It was also July holiday time in Blackburn, which meant that the whole of the Birtwistle group of mills were on their annual holidays except for a skeleton staff arranged to work at Osprey House.

As I had to leave for Hyderabad as soon as possible, I desperately needed to see either Mr Pomfret or Mr Doidge, as I didn't want to go off to Hyderabad without first obtaining a leave of absence. I therefore made my way to Osprey House. As both Mr Pomfret and Mr Doidge were away on holiday during that week, I was a little concerned as to who I could speak to.

I asked Elaine the receptionist if there was somebody who I could see?

She said, "Mr Whittaker is in; would you like to see him?"

"Oh yes please, that would be fine." I answered her feeling rather relieved.

Elaine rang Mr Whittaker to ask him if he would see me.

Mr Whittaker always spoke with a loud and crispy voice, even on the phone.

I could hear him clearly saying, "Send him in Elaine."

Whenever and wherever I met Mr Whittaker he always greeted me with a handshake. This time was no exception.

Shaking hands and offering me a seat, Mr Whittaker said, "Now then, what can I do for you?"

I explained to him about my father's death and how much I now needed to get over there as soon as possible.

He was genuinely sorry to hear about my father dying.

I explained to him in more detail, "I had been planning to go over to Pakistan in September with my family, but due to my father's untimely death, I will now have to go there alone."

"When do you want to go?" Mr Whittaker enquired.

I was reluctant to speak, but I plucked up courage and said, "My seat is booked for next Sunday."

"In that case you must go ahead," he told me.

Then he picked up his phone and asked his secretary to come into his office.

As she entered he said to her, "Will you leave a note for Mr Doidge saying that I have allowed Mr Khan to have a leave of absence as from today."

There was another thing I wanted to clarify with Mr Whittaker, "I'm sorry Mr Whittaker; I don't know as to when I will be able to return to Blackburn."

He turned to me and said, "You need not worry about that, you just come back when you are ready."

Thanking him, I got up to go, but as I reached the door he said, "Have you got enough money for this trip?"

"Yes thank you, I have been saving for a while," I replied.

Still he wasn't satisfied and said, "I'll write a Company cheque for you; use it if you want."

I was grateful for his offer but said, "No, thank you Mr Whittaker, I really have more than enough, but thank you once again."

Although I had sorted out the air ticket, vaccinations and leave from work, I was still worried about reaching London for my onward journey to Pakistan. The only option left to me was to fly from Manchester to London.

The question of getting to Manchester Airport was also a concern as Kath didn't know how to drive then and I didn't really want to ask any of my friends. Ken and Cathy were on their annual holidays in the Isle of Man. I took the liberty of ringing them there and luckily they were in their hotel at the time. When they heard about the situation that I was in they returned home a day early.

The next day Ken, Cathy, Sharon, Kath and Shahnaz came to Manchester Airport to see me off. I reached Karachi via Zurich, Athens, Damascus, Bahrain, and Tehran.

It took almost sixteen hours for me to reach Karachi, arriving on the 22nd July 1972. I missed my father terribly. He had mellowed a lot in his old age and had been looking forward to meeting the three of us so much. It was very clear to me that he had changed such a lot over the years.

Although it was terribly hot during the day in Hyderabad during July, the evenings were as pleasant as ever. On the evening of my arrival, I immediately went to the cemetery to visit my father's grave with my brothers and nephews.

****

After a week or so I got used to the heat and started meeting relatives. I had been away for so many years and my first visit back was due to such very sad circumstances. So many people had different questions for me. They had a lot to ask me regarding British culture and the way of life in England. They were under the impression that in England as soon as a boy or girl reaches the age of sixteen or eighteen years of age, they become independent and don't bother to listen to their parents. The other thing that bothered my younger sister was that she had heard that in England a wife goes with any man and no one bothers about it. I had to do an awful lot of explaining in order to convince her that in England the ladies are not at all like that.

The first few weeks in Hyderabad were very difficult for me. I had a lot of explaining to do about me staying far too long in England. It wasn't easy to satisfy them. I met my old friends there too, and some from Blackburn College. Saeed, Sabir, Inayat, Palli, Halim, Qureshi, Hassan, Ashraf, Salim and a few others were amongst those who I managed to meet up with again.

I had taken enough money with me to cover all the religious and customary obligations for our late father. One such event was to mark the fortieth day after his death, when we planned to invite family and friends to remember our late father and offer up prayers for him. Once the list of guests was finalised the number reached over a thousand.

Whilst discussing the guests with the immediate family, I made the mistake of saying, "Do we have to invite so many people?"

Everybody looked at me with disgust.

All of a sudden Amma (our mother) said, "We know you now live in England. Things may be done differently there, but we live here. Your late father made a big name for this family and we aim to maintain that. Whether you like or not we are going to invite the same number of guests, or possibly even more!"

It is traditional in our family that we hold a remembrance service on the 40th day following the death of a loved one. Relatives and guests came from Lahore, Rawalpindi, Larkana, and Karachi. We had to accommodate and pay for the upkeep of out of town guests for almost a week. The event went off smoothly without any problems.

Once the commemoration was concluded, my stay in Hyderabad became slightly 'normal'. A few people couldn't wait to ask me to stay in Pakistan and send for my family. I was even offered jobs in textiles, which included many perks associated with qualifications and experience. I didn't find the circumstances favourable for my family in England to settle in Pakistan.

By the end of October I decided to return to England. My mother, my siblings and the rest of the extended family were all upset by this news; thankfully though everyone was very understanding and accepted my decision.

One evening when all the visitors had gone, and Amma and I were left on our own, she asked me to sit next to her. She started talking about Shahnaz and after a while asked me, "Is Fernaz all right?"

At first, I didn't understand Mum's question properly, so I said, "Yes, she is fine."

"Have you taken Fernaz to any doctor for a check up?" Mother enquired.

"But there is nothing wrong with her, Mother," I assured her.

Still she wasn't satisfied with my answers. A little bit concerned she blurted out in a forthright manner, "Then why is there no brother for Shahnaz?"

At this point I finally understood what she meant. I laughed and said, "Amma, it was intentional, we wanted to keep to a small family."

She was a bit annoyed and said, "That's not right, a family isn't complete without two or three children, and it is most important to have a son in the family."

Although I was taking it all light-heartedly, Amma was very serious about it.

She said, "We know and accept that you are going to stay in England for good, so your next generation will be brought up in England. However to carry on with both your own and your father's name, you should have a son."

Just to keep the peace, I promised her that we'd definitely think about it.

The next day news of this conversation reached my sister Beeda and nieces Saeeda and Rafia. They kept teasing me all day about it. In the end my sisters Aapi and Beeda convinced me that it was our late father's wish also that Fernaz and I should have a son, and a brother for Shahnaz. So my mother made me promise that I would discuss this with Fernaz as soon as I returned to Blackburn.

I left Hyderabad on 15th November 1972. It was heartbreaking for me to leave all my relatives and close friends. I couldn't hold my tears back at the time when my mother and sisters embraced me. We were all emotional, but I had to leave. At Karachi Airport some of my college friends came to see me off.

I reached London the next day via Doha, Qatar and Damascus. I had to wait at Heathrow for four hours to catch a flight to Manchester. At Manchester Airport Fernaz, Shahnaz, Ken, Cathy, Sharon and Kath's parents had all come to meet me.

After a few days rest I called at Osprey House to see Mr Pomfret, Mr Doidge and Mr Whittaker. Fortunately they were all pleased to see me. Mr Doidge was even kind enough to allow me a few more days rest before I returned to work. I resumed my duties on 22nd November 1972. The following day Shahnaz was ten-years old, and she celebrated her birthday with her school friends.

****

It was just before Christmas 1972 when it was confirmed that Kath was pregnant again. As expected, Amma was really pleased with this news. My niece Saeeda used to write to me regularly. She started writing messages from Amma to Fernaz, as to what precautions to take during the pregnancy. They were all hoping and praying for a boy, because I had told them categorically that if the next child was a girl, we were going to be content with two girls, as we would not try again for a boy as happens in most Asian families.

However they were all sure that the next child would be a boy. In June 1973 Saeeda sent me a list of ten boy's names, with a note saying that they liked all these names, but we could choose for ourselves the one that we liked best.

It is customary and traditional in our family that the honour of naming the newborn child goes to the elder of the family. So honouring this custom, Kath and I left this task to Amma.

Although there were ten very good names, we wanted to select one that was more easily pronounceable. Out of the ten names we finally chose to name our son Suhail. To be perfectly honest this name has been my favourite since I was a teenager. I also added Rana to this name and hoped for the best.

****

Through their new policy, the higher management at Birtwistles, decided to rearrange the shift systems of their mills. In doing so, Waterfall Mill was put on three shifts of morning, afternoon and permanent night shift.

To manage Waterfall Mill, Mr Bill Bickerton was transferred from Unity Mill. Along with him the three shift managers Roy Lund, Colin Pearson and Ronnie Dickinson came from the same Unity Mill.

I had met Bill Bickerton, Roy Lund and Colin Pearson when I used to visit Unity Mill to see the trainees. I met Ronnie Dickinson for the first time when they were setting up the night shift at Waterfall Mill. I got on very well with these people and helped them to interview new Asian workers for the night shift.

Bill Bickerton was quite young to be a works manager, but he had a wide experience of managing a mill, plus he always handled all issues sensibly. Later on after Mr Whittaker's retirement, Mr Bickerton became the weaving Director of the group.

As the shifts in Waterfall Mill were in the process of being established a considerable number of Asian workers were on double day shifts, I had to be at Waterfall Mill most of the time for interpretations. Roy Lund was a quiet sort of person, while Colin Pearson was talkative, but both were successful shift managers.

In March 1973 Kath had to finish work due to her pregnancy. One afternoon I was with Bill Bickerton in his office when he asked me how things were with my family. Almost everybody in the group knew that we were expecting our second child.

I told him that all was well, but since my wife had finished work, we were feeling a bit of a pinch financially.

After listening to me he said, "We already have supervisors on the day shifts, but we are considering appointing a supervisor on the night shift. I think that you are a suitable person for this post. I would therefore like to offer this position to you. Would you take it?"

I was really pleased with this offer and said, "Thank you very much, but it would really be better if I consulted my wife about it first."

Then Bill Bickerton mentioned what the increment in my salary for going onto the night shift would be. He also told me that my status in the staff and pension scheme would not be affected.

I talked to Kath about it, explaining carefully to her that by accepting this offer at least we wouldn't feel any financial hardship. I decided to accept the offer from Mr Bickerton and the following week I informed him of my decicion.

I was a bit concerned about both Mr Doidge and Mr Pomfret as to what their reaction would be regarding my new position. I needn't have worried at all, as Mr Bickerton had already talked to them both and neither had any objection concerning my transfer to the night shift.

Ronnie Dickinson the shift manager was very fair and friendly to everyone. We had a very good understanding and I was on good terms with him. I thoroughly enjoyed working on this night shift. Every month Ronnie and I attended a monthly management meeting with Mr Bickerton and the other shift managers.

All the overlookers on night shift were English. Except for one or two, they were all quite young, between the ages of twenty-five and thirty. A couple of them had small families.

One particular night, one of the workers called Jay came over to me at about 10:30pm. He told me that he had left his wallet at home and as it contained quite a substantial amount of money, he wanted to go home and collect it.

Jay didn't have any transport, so he asked me if I would give him a lift.

I was quite willing to do this, but I had to see Ronnie about it first. Ronnie didn't have any objection so I drove Jay to his house in Blackburn.

As we reached his house he said, "Come into the house."

"No thank you," I replied, "I'll just wait for you in the car."

But he wouldn't hear of this and kept insisting, "Oh come on in, we'll have a cup of tea. I'd like you to meet my wife."

I had always had this fear in my mind that things might not be as harmonious as some people might think. On his insistence, but with great reluctance, I agreed only to meet his wife for a moment.

We got out of the car and I followed him to his house. He went in through the front door, but as he opened the vestibule door, I could see that the room was dimly lit. What we saw shocked us. I really couldn't believe my eyes.

His wife was sitting on the sofa with a young man in an intimate and very compromising position. As well as the embarrassment of having me as a visitor, this truly infuriated Jay.

He leaped towards the young man, grabbed him by his collar and shouted, "Who the ……hell are you?"

The wife started screaming, and struggled to adjust her clothes, "Leave him alone; leave him alone."

"I'll deal with you later, you ……. bitch," Jay screamed back.

At this point I thought, "To heck with a cup of tea or meeting the wife; I shouldn't be here." I turned around and flew to my car. I sat in the car just thinking about my dreaded suspicious feeling before going into the house with him.

I didn't want to be a witness to this sordid incident. I could hear the arguments and screams for about ten minutes. In the end Jay came to the car still panting with temper. Without uttering a single word he sat in the car. I drove off and we travelled the whole journey in complete silence.

Once we reached the mill he finally uttered, "You can't trust anybody these days, can you?"

I didn't know how to answer him, so I kept quiet. As far as I was concerned the incident was firmly in the past. I got busy with my work during the shift. As usual we had our dinner break at 2:00am, when all the overlookers came to Ronnie's office.

As I entered the office one of the overlookers said with a big grin, "Hey, come on tell us what went on at Jay's house?"

"Nothing, nothing went on," I said.

Laughing the other overlookers said, "Come on now; don't play the innocent. Tell us what you saw."

I tried to dodge and avoid their questions but they wouldn't leave me alone.

In the end one of them said, "Look, Jay has already told us all, but we want to hear what *you* saw?"

"It is a shame for him, that's all I have to say," I said.

Jay didn't come in with any of us for his dinner break, so the others were enjoying gossiping. One of the young ones, who had a young wife and a child, was laughing the most.

He smiled saying, "All right then, just tell us the juicy bits."

This really annoyed me. I turned to him and said, "Hey listen, how old are you all?"

One by one they told me their ages.

Then I said, "Please, don't be offended, but with all due respect to your wives, can I ask their ages too?"

They were a bit reluctant, but they finally gave me their answers to my question. I continued to question them further, "And if you don't mind, could you tell me what time you left home to come to work tonight?"

They all agreed that they left at about 9:30pm, but queried as to why I had asked that question.

I explained, "We live in a free society, so anything could happen between 9:00pm and midnight, especially if one is on their own."

This must have worked well, because after that nobody mentioned any more about that incident at Jay's house.

CHAPTER TWENTY-FIVE

I had a small Hillman Imp car in 1972; it was a good little runner but I wanted to have a change. It was August 1973 when I decided to buy a bigger car. The following Sunday, we spotted a green Ford Escort at the Empire garage on Aqueduct Road. Shahnaz, Kath and I really liked it. I spoke to the owner of the garage and we agreed on a price for the Ford Escort and arranged to collect it the next day. The garage owner agreed to do the MOT on the Escort and on Monday I went to the garage and drove this new car home.

I was really excited about my new vehicle and went to work in it that evening at 9:30pm. About midnight I was in the shed when Ronnie Dickinson came running to me.

"Hey, hurry up, you must go home quickly," he told me.

"Why, what's the matter?" I asked curiously.

"Your wife has just rung, and she is ready to go to hospital."

Ronnie seemed far more excited and nervous than I was about this news. By now everyone was aware that Kath was expecting our second child.

Before I could put my jacket on, Ronnie ran across the shed's yard to look for Jack the night watchman, to ask him to open the gate for me. He really rushed Jack until the gates were fully open.

I reached home in Lambeth Street within fifteen minutes, to find Kath and Shahnaz had just finished watching the late night film *King Kong* on BBC2. They were both as calm as anything.

As I had gone through a panicky time at the birth of Shahnaz eleven years earlier, I was nervous this time too. Hurriedly I put Kath's suitcase and other things into the boot, while Shahnaz and Kath got into the car.

I tried to start it, but the car wouldn't start for at least seven minutes. By this time it was almost one o'clock in the morning. The noise was terrible, especially so this early in the morning. There was no telephone in our house, so in the end I thought of going to the end of Lambeth Street on Audley Range to the telephone booth to ring for a taxi. I was just about to set off to the phonebox, when our two doors away neighbour Victor, came out of his house in his dressing gown.

"Having problems, Khan?" he asked.

"Yes, the blasted thing won't start." I said in annoyance.

Without hesitation Victor said, "No problem, I'll get my car out of the garage."

Before I could say anything, he started walking towards Pringle Street, as his car was in a garage there. Victor was walking down Lambeth Street in his gown.

I said to him, "Hey, at least get changed, you are in your pyjamas."

"It doesn't matter, it's after 1:00 in the morning; nobody will see us."

Kathy and Victor knew that Kath was expecting. Kathy was about to drop off to sleep when she heard all the commotion. Kathy woke Victor up asking him to find out what was going on. They had both been our friends for at least twelve years. We knew Kathy before our Shahnaz was born, as she used to come to see us in Curwen Street, Preston.

Kathy had always been a very caring girl, and possessed a very soft nature. She would always go out of her way to help others, and often spent her last penny making people happy.

In company Kathy always stood out as a smartly dressed woman. She had very good taste in selecting clothes and colour matching. She was also well known for her jewellery.

In the early 60's when Shahnaz was only two or three-years old, Kathy bought her lots of things. If the truth be known, Kathy used to spoil Shahnaz by buying toys and expensive clothes for her.

****

In 1963, whilst living in Preston, I was going through practical training with British Northrop, the loom manufacturers in Blackburn. There were trainees there from India, Pakistan, Nigeria and Lancashire in the same class.

Amongst the other boys there was a young man from Jordan. He was Victor Dada. Victor was actually a Palestinian. His family had moved to Jordan during the 50's. He was fluent in English and quite familiar with the English way of life.

One evening Kathy came to see us in Preston and asked me, "Do you know anyone called Victor in Northrop?"

It turned out to be same Victor who was in my class at British Northrop. Kathy married him and moved to Jordan, but both returned to England after five years.

****

Victor and I came back with Victor's car and set off to Bull Hill Maternity Hospital in Darwen with Kath and Shahnaz. When we eventually left Kath it was after 2:00am. Shahnaz and I went to bed at about 3:00am.

The next morning I woke up at about 6:45. After a quick wash and change I rushed to the telephone kiosk in Audley Range. It was just 7:00am when I rang Bull Hill Maternity Home. "Hello, this is Mr Khan, can you tell me about my wife Kath; she was admitted after midnight."

"Yes, she has given birth to a child," the voice on the phone declared.

I was so excited I didn't know what I was saying, "What is it, what is the weight and how is it?"

"Hey Mr, hold your horses, the child is just born, give us a chance. By the way it's a boy," the nurse told me.

I couldn't believe my ears, I wanted to ring again to make sure, but I didn't have enough money on me to phone back. I hurried along Lambeth Street. As I was approaching our house I saw Kathy coming out of her house. She was surprised to see me up so early.

"I have just rung the hospital. It's a boy," I said joyfully.

"That's wonderful, congratulations, please give my best wishes and love to Kath when you go to visit her," Kathy said.

I wanted to tell this good news to the whole world. I rushed home and shouted for Shahnaz.

She jumped up at the sound of my voice. It had been after 3:00am when she went to bed, but she too was waiting to hear the news.

I said, "It is Suhail. He was born at 6.50am today.

Shahnaz didn't know what to say to me, but I am sure she was as happy with this news as I was. Although she had had only four hours sleep she was very cheerful.

While Shahnaz was in the bathroom, I went out to see if the car would start. Would you believe it the blasted thing started straight away on the very first turn of the ignition key!

After a very light breakfast Shahnaz and I shot off to see Kath's mother and father. They lived at Woodfold Farmhouse, next to the famous Henry Sudell's Woodfold Mansion.

Mum and Dad had just got up and were still in their pyjamas and gowns. They were as thrilled as us with this wonderful news.

After the congratulations and good wishes Mum asked us, "Have you two had any breakfast?"

"Yes thank you, we have had some toast," I said.

Without saying anything she went into the kitchen and came back with two bowls, a packet of cornflakes, a jug of milk, and ordered us, "Sit down, you are not going anywhere without a proper breakfast."

I tried to explain to her that we didn't need any more breakfast, but she wouldn't hear of it. In the end we both had to sit down and have something to eat. We left soon afterwards as I wanted to send telegrams to Hyderabad and Karachi.

Before going home we called at Ghiwala's, an Indian grocery shop in Furthergate. I parked the car at the lower end of Lambeth Street. The Ghiwala brothers were Ghulam and Yusuf, both came from India. They ran the grocery shop and also worked in Birtwistle's Albion Mill on the night shift.

I bought some groceries and went out to start the car. Again I had the same problem, for it didn't matter how I tried the car just wouldn't start.

In the end I had to ring Empire Garage. They were very quick to respond and sent out a mechanic. He spotted the problem immediately and managed to start the car. He asked me to follow him and take the car to the garage, so that the fault could be rectified.

By now it was almost 11:00am. Facing the Empire garage there was a mobile café on some spare land. It was actually a long caravan that had been turned into a café. It had tables and chairs and served proper hot meals. The café had a jukebox, a pinball machine and slot machines. As Shahnaz and I needed to spend time somewhere while the mechanics worked on our car, we went to this mobile café, spent some money on the slot and pinball machines, and at about midday we thought we'd have our dinner there. It was tasty fish and chips with mushy peas for lunch.

When the car was repaired our next job was to go to the General Post Office in Blackburn town centre, so that we could send some telegrams to Pakistan. We sent one to Hyderabad and another to Karachi. It's customary in our family that all the messages of happiness or condolence are sent from the eldest in the family.

The telegrams read,

"Suhail arrived safely today at 6.50am.
Khan and Shahnaz."

The next day we received a telegram from Aapi, my eldest sister in Hyderabad which read:

"Congratulations from all of us on Suhail's arrival.
Aapi."

After this we went to Waterfall Mill to see Roy Lund the weaving manager. Roy, Colin and the other people in the shed were very pleased and happy for us.

After listening to my story about running around all day, Roy said, "Why don't you have a night or two off?"

I thanked him but said, "I'll come into work at the start of my shift, and after settling everyone down, I'll go home if that is all right?"

Roy agreed.

I was quite capable of looking after myself, but I had never before had to look after anyone else. I was a bit worried as to what Shahnaz was going to have for her evening meal? Luckily we had enough curry for that evening, so Shahnaz and I managed quite well.

The visiting times at Bull Hill were 8:00 until 9:00pm. As children weren't allowed to visit, I had to leave Shahnaz playing out with her friends whilst I went to visit Kath that evening.

In the maternity ward all the other newborn babies were next to their mother's bedside. The ward was quiet when the nurse brought Suhail to us.

I looked down at my baby son nestled in my wife's arms. I felt so proud of them both; my family now seemed to be complete. Our son had paler skin than Shahnaz had when she was born, and his eyes were very dark brown almost black. He was also a little bigger than his sister had been, weighing in at 7lbs 3ozs. He was quiet for few minutes, but that didn't last too long as he started screaming. His cries started all the other babies in the ward off causing the poor nurses to come rushing in.

One nurse picked Suhail up and said, "Now then young man, look what you have done, you've got everybody going." She took him back to the nursery; I left after cuddling Kath, just after 9:00pm.

My sister-in-law June who lived in Leyland with her family, very kindly agreed to have Shahnaz for a week while Kath was in Bull Hill. So the next day, which was Wednesday, Shahnaz and I went to Leyland. As usual June was cheerful, full of life and really pleased for us. Shahnaz always felt at home with June and her children. June and her husband Brian treated all children with love and affection.

During Shahnaz's stay at June's, Brian would keep the children busy by taking them to Leyland baths to swim, and in the evenings they'd go out for a walk, so shahnaz was never bored there.

June later informed me, "As Saturday approached, Shahnaz didn't want to go out to play with the children, instead she kept looking along the road to see if her mummy and daddy were coming to take her home."

Especially so that Shahnaz would not be disappointed, June and I had arranged that I would visit them in Leyland at about 2.30pm on the Saturday to collect my daughter and take her home. June and Brian had been especially wonderful towards us during that time.

During the week while Kath was in Bull Hill, I didn't have much time to do anything at home due to me being on the night shift, except go to work, come home, sleep till at least 3:00pm, then I had to get ready to visit Bull Hill. 'I was such a lucky man,' I thought, 'for I now have my wonderful wife and *two* beautiful children.'

I neither felt like cooking any curry, nor had I really enough time, but I found an alternative. On Higher Eanam an Asian had just opened a little café and takeaway.

At about 5:00pm I would take one of our small pans with me in the car, then buy three chapatties and curry for the pan, as takeaway trays weren't yet introduced. In the café while serving me, the café owner's wife used to look at me as if she was going to ask me something. I can only assume that she thought that my wife had left me.

Thankfully we never talked much. I would collect my curry and chapatties and rush home. After getting ready at about 7:30pm, I would go to Bull Hill then get off to work at Waterfall Mill at 9:30pm.

****

On Sunday the 26th August 1973, Shahnaz and I got up early. We were both ready by 8:30am and left for Bull Hill Hospital. Kath was waiting for us with Suhail. He was well wrapped up in a little white shawl and blanket.

A nurse carried him outside to the car. We thanked her and a photo of us all with her was taken before we left. During that week we received lots of greeting cards for Suhail. Many people from Albion Mill, Waterfall Mill, Greenbank Mill Preston, and Ribchester Mill sent different items for our new baby.

Margaret Hill, one of the instructors in Albion Mill, had knitted him a lovely shawl. Sister Brocklebank bought little mittens, and Ronnie Dickinson and his wife bought socks and a hat. Ann Robinson and her partner Bert got our new baby a sleeping suit and other people in different mills very kindly bought different items.

That same evening Ken and Cathy, Ronnie and Maude Dickinson, Gwen and Norman, and Wasim and Alma all came to our house.

Later, I also arranged for an Imam (a Muslim cleric) to come to our house to recite an Islamic prayer known as an Adh'aan in accordance with Islamic practice, it was gently recited into Suhail's right ear.

The next day, Kath and I visited her parents with Shahnaz and Suhail. Again Kath's father had to compromise with the name Suhail, as it was rather a strange name to him. As dad liked his drink, he could relate the baby's name with 'sup-ale', but later on he never had any difficulty in pronouncing the names Suhail or Shahnaz.

CHAPTER TWENTY-SIX

Life was going on as usual. I was happy working on the night shift at Waterfall Mill and was constantly in touch with the higher management within the Birtwistle group; I was also regularly contacting my close relatives in Hyderabad and Karachi. I was taking Suhail and Shahnaz's photos almost every week and sending copies of them to my niece Saeeda.

In 1974 due to lack of trade the management had to re-organise the shift system, and because of that the night shift had to be closed. Once again I was transferred to Osprey House and Whiteley's Albion Mill.

Whilst helping out in the spinning and winding rooms I was continuing visiting different mills, such as Waterfall, Florence, Abbey Village, Ribchester and Jack Hawkins Greenbank Mill.

We were well settled in at Lambeth Street. Shahnaz was now almost twelve and Suhail had celebrated his first birthday. Soon after his birthday we received a letter from the town hall informing us that our house was in a compulsory purchase scheme for the redevelopment of the area. The letter specifically stated that either we would have to move into a house on a council estate, or buy our own house elsewhere.

Kath and I had always been reluctant to move to a council estate due to the poor state of the houses at that time. We started looking for a house in other parts of Blackburn where the general condition of houses was better. We didn't want to move too far away because of my work and Shahnaz's school. We viewed a lot of different houses; some of which we liked but financially we weren't able to afford; in the end we found a house with two bedrooms within our budget.

This house in Pringle Street had been modernised by a builder. The inside walls were newly plastered, so there wasn't even any wallpaper covering the walls, or paint on the woodwork. I signed for the purchase of this house in November 1974; however I was allowed to have the keys earlier in order to decorate the house before we moved in.

I started painting the doors and windows in the evenings before work. Although there was central heating in the house, the gas supply wasn't connected. To keep myself warm I needed a heater. Cathy and Ken were kind enough to lend me their oil heater, which kept me going throughout the winter months.

I was spending most of my time decorating the house. I was busy painting and wallpapering even on Christmas Day, Boxing Day and New Year's Day. By February 1975 the house was ready and we moved into Pringle Street.

We have always been lucky in having good neighbours. Until 1990 Pringle Street was a wonderful street to live in. The residents in that area had a neighbourly sense of looking after each other. It was like a community, all based on goodwill.

In 1975 there were only two or three Asian families in Pringle Street. On one side of us lived an Indian family, whilst next door to us on the other side lived Connie and Dick. Besides their son Russell, who was about fourteen at the time, they had two married daughters, Elizabeth and Lorraine. Lorraine lived with her husband Alan in the same block, while Elizabeth lived in Blackpool. The residents on our block were always very friendly.

These were Jessie, Edith, Kath, Julie and her parents, Mrs Brown, Gloria and Barry. Connie and Dick turned out to be wonderful neighbours; they were always willing to help. Connie had all the information about Pringle Street and its residents. If I needed, or wanted to know about somebody in Pringle Street, I would just ask Connie and she would give me the full details.

She had a soft spot for Shahnaz. During the summer while Shahnaz was taking her 'O' Level exams, Connie would bring a plate full of food for her. Her instructions used to be that this was just for Shahnaz.

In September 1980 Shahnaz, Suhail and Kath went to Spain on holiday. Because of work I stayed at home. During that week I was on the afternoon shift. One evening I finished work at 10:00pm and reached home at about 10:15pm. As I was getting changed I heard a knock at the door.

I was surprised to see Connie standing at the door with a plate of fish, chips and peas. "What is it, Connie?" I asked.

"It's your supper lad," she said, offering me the plate.

"But I have cooked curry for myself Connie," I pleaded

But she wouldn't hear of it, so I had to accept the supper. I thanked her, and tried to explain that I could look after myself quite well.

During the warm summer evenings, almost all the neighbours in Pringle Street would come out of their houses after tea, then stand around and chat away with each other till ten or eleven o'clock.

Connie and Dick were two of the best security guards around that area. I am convinced that the Neighbourhood Watch Scheme was based on this very helpful couple. I remember once Kath's elder brother Ronnie called at our house while we were out. As soon as Ronnie knocked at our door, Connie came out of her house like a shot.

She asked, "What do you want? Who are you?"

"Are they in?" Ronnie asked.

Connie wasn't satisfied with Ronnie's question, she said, "Who? Who do you want?"

Ronnie had to explain to Connie, "I'm Kath's brother and I've just called to see her."

Connie asked his name and noted almost everything about Ronnie, what sort of car he had, even what he was wearing.

Connie's younger daughter Lorraine lived at the other end of our terrace with her husband Alan. Their son Graham was about the same age as our Suhail. Lorraine used to work part-time at Les's newspaper shop at the corner of Pringle Street and Queens Park Road.

Because Les had other business interests, he hired part-time workers for the shop. At one time Lorraine, Shahnaz and Gwen ran this shop between them.

Quite a few people in Pringle Street knew us, but because of her pleasant nature and working at the shop, 90% of the residents in Pringle Street knew Shahnaz by name, far better than they knew us.

One winter evening Kath's sister June and her husband Brian came to Pringle Street for the first time to see us. They didn't remember our house number. They asked some passers-by if they knew where we lived, describing the Asian husband and his English wife.

"We know they live here, but we don't know which one is their house," was the common reply.

June and Brian asked a few more people in the street, but nobody could tell them. In fact not many people in the street knew us by our names.

Then June said to a passer-by, "They have a daughter called Shahnaz."

"Ah, I know where Shahnaz lives. She lives at that house," the passer-by told them, pointing directly to our door.

****

Being at Osprey House, I sometimes used to be at a loose end, so I would help the managers out, by acting as a temporary foreman for their different departments. Bob Forrest the spinning manager at Albion Mill asked me to take charge of the winding room for a few weeks on shifts. I agreed to do this for him.

In that winding room the majority of workers were young women between the ages of nineteen and twenty-five. There were three young men also.

The following Monday, before starting the shift, I gathered all the workers into the office and told them about myself and my family. I'm glad to say that my action worked beautifully. When I finished there the girls bought me a tie and a cigarette lighter.

I was quite content working for the William Birtwistle Group, but between April and May 1975 rumours started circulating stating that the group was going to close altogether. In the beginning the management didn't admit this, but in the first week of June it became official that the group was going to close which meant that the whole workforce would be made redundant.

I had no choice but to look for a fresh job somewhere in Blackburn. I obtained a job in the carpet manufacturing firm Donaghadi, which worked on a three shift system.

I met a few Asian workers at Donaghadi, namely Shaheer Ahmed, Hafeez Khan, Rafique Ahmed, and Ali. I got on well with Shaheer, Hafeez and Ali. Shaheer and I became close friends and a few times we visited each other with our families.

In October 1975 Shaheer Ahmed left Donaghadi to take up employment with a textile firm. I later visited Shaheer in London Road; he told me he was working for Blackburn Cord Company, the manufacturers of stitch-bonded fabric.

Shaheer told me, "The firm is wonderful, but it has a very limited number of Asian workers."

I was a bit surprised to hear such a statement in 1975. Then he explained in detail the working conditions and the facilities the firm offered to its workers. These good things, together with the decent wages, attracted me a lot, I wished to take up employment with Blackburn Cord Company.

The following week I rang Blackburn Cord's knitting department manager, Mr Anthony Finnigan. He told me that there was no vacancy in his department

A few weeks later Shaheer told me that an Asian from the 'A' shift had left to go to India, which meant there was a vacancy. I rang Mr Finnigan again.

Before he could say anything I said, "Mr Finnigan, I know there is now a vacancy in your department."

He still sounded a bit reluctant to give me a positive answer.

"At this stage I am only asking you to see me, at least it would give you an idea as to what sort of a person I am," I suggested to him.

He paused for a moment before answering, "All right then, when can you come to see me?"

"I am free tomorrow till 2:00pm." I said.

Mr Finnigan must have looked in his diary. He said, "Could you come tomorrow at about 10:30 in the morning?"

I was doubly quick to accept his proposed time for a meeting.

The next morning I got ready to go to see Mr Finnigan. I always carried a briefcase with me whenever I went for an interview. This morning was no different. I reached Blackburn Cord on Highfield Road at about 10:20.

I opened the door and approached the reception. Without me uttering a single word, the lady behind the counter looked straight at me.

In an arrogant tone she said, "There is no vacancy - no job."

I wasn't ready for that, I was a bit shocked at first, but I composed myself and said, "I beg your pardon?"

"No job; there is no job," she said with some annoyance in her voice.

By this time I too was annoyed, so I asked, "Who has come for the job? I have come to see Mr Finnigan on a personal matter. Would you be kind enough to tell him that I am here?"

She didn't even ask me my name, or any other thing, but rang Mr Finnigan.

After a few minutes he came down, shook hands with me and took me into the interview room. He asked me a lot of questions about my experience in textiles. I am sure I satisfied him with my answers.

Mr Finnigan gave me the general background of Blackburn Cord, explaining to me that the firm was newly established, but its products were already very popular on the market. He went on to tell me that the firm has a bright future, so people who started work for the firm would have a good chance of promotion.

Mr Finnigan was willing to give me the job but said, "As far as I am concerned you are a suitable person, but I would like you to meet our general manager."

I agreed to meet him; it was Mr David Warsop.

This time Mr Warsop asked me a few more questions, then turning to Mr Finnigan he announced, "Yes, he is suitable."

Mr Warsop left us while Mr Finnigan took me to the knitting department.

While walking to the knitting room Mr Finningan asked me, "How did you find out about this vacancy?"

"I hope no action would be taken against him if I tell you," I answered.

Mr Finnigan smiled and said, "Yes, I can assure you of that."

"It was Mr Ahmed, Shaheer Ahmed," I replied.

The knitting room was a very brightly lit large room, which was spotlessly clean. Even the floor of the whole knitting room was painted with grey gloss paint. The temperature in the knitting room was quite high; I felt myself sweating within minutes of entering.

Mr Finnigan explained the shift system. It was based on a continental shift system of twelve hour shifts. There were four shifts, ‘A’, ‘B’, ‘C’, and ‘D’. If two shifts ‘A’ & ‘B’ were on their twelve hour shifts, both ‘C’ & ‘D’ shifts would be off. The two shifts worked for three days or nights then they would be off for three days.

Mr Finnigan told me that for my first week I would work on day shift from 7:30am to 4:30pm, then I would join the ‘A’ shift. It was the first or second week of November 1975 when I started at Blackburn Cord.

I started work on ‘B’ shift at 7.30am. The shift manager on that shift was Alan Baines. He left me with an experienced person who was to train me.

I was surprised by the facilities the firm provided for all its workers, regardless of their status. Iced cold water was free, while out of the vending machine one could buy cold orange, lemon, lime, or coke for just a penny. From the same vending machine, there was a choice of hot drinks, tea, coffee, chocolate, or soup for only a penny.

During lunchtime the workers were given free food with the choice of a meat pie, potato pie, steak pie, chicken breast, eclairs, doughnuts or ice-cream. On Wednesday and Friday nights all the workers on the night shift were treated to hot fish and chips from the local chippy.

Because of the high temperature in the knitting room I felt very uncomfortable, but managed to learn the basic things about the knitting machines and the knitting process.

After one week’s training I was transferred to the ‘A’ shift, which was on night shift from 6:00pm to 6:00am. At that time Malcolm Drever was the shift manager. I reported to him and he put me on the Mali knitting machines in partnership with Kingsley Owen.

On this shift, the other notable personnel were Jack Miller the carder, Vic Lucas the mechanic, Bernard Gagan the threader,

Kingsley Owen, Tony Inglis, Peter, and old Albert with a team of cleaners.

I didn't come into contact with David Warsop so often, but when I was promoted to be in charge of the Batcher's section I was directly responsible to Mr Warsop. At the end of each shift I had to give a full report regarding the production, quality and problems on the batchers.

David Warsop was a quiet person. He hardly spoke to anybody on the shop floor, but he was a very good manager who always had time for his workers. He would give an impression of being a quiet person, but he was a man of great knowledge. He helped me whenever I needed his assistance.

Tony Finnegan was just as helpful to me as David Warsop. One of my nephews was in America; he wanted to apply for a visa to visit me in Blackburn, but was having difficulty in obtaining it. I asked Tony Finnigan if he could give me a letter of employment and a reference in order to confirm my sponsorship for my nephew.

The employment letter and reference that Tony Finnigan gave were so wonderfully worded, that the British Embassy officials in America didn't hesitate to grant a visa for my nephew.

The other occasion was in 1987, when as a result of my heart attack I had to go to Blackpool Victoria Hospital for a bypass operation. Tony Finnigan gave a lot of support to my wife and daughter, telling them not to worry about anything. He also offered them financial help if they needed any.

Malcolm Drever was the shift manager of 'A' shift. When I started on his shift he had his right foot in bandages, as he had hurt his big toe. Malcolm was always a cool minded person; I never saw him losing his temper or worrying about anything. He was a qualified engineer and had a vast knowledge of both textile technology and textile machinery. He always helped his shift workers in every way. He didn't act just as a shift manager; when needed, he would help a Mali-mechanic, knitter or a threader.

Vic Lucas was a shift Mali-mechanic on the 'A' shift. He was a quiet sort of person, but had a good sense of humour. When he wasn't too busy he would help the knitters to run the machines.

Bernard (Barny) Gagan was a threader on our shift. He was a true comedian. Actually he was a heart patient who took life very lightly. He knew he wasn't going to live too long, and for that reason he didn't fall out with anybody. Sadly, he died in the late 1970's.

The carder on the 'A' shift was Jack Miller. During official breaks at work Jack Miller read books. When I got to know him he turned out to be a very friendly and sociable person. He knew a lot of jokes, if he didn't bring a book to read he would make us all laugh with his humour. Sometimes he spoke with a broad Lancashire accent, particularly in a Chorley dialect. He would tell us about the coal mines and some really funny stories related to this industry.

Jack was very interested in his two daughters' education. Both his daughters, Christine and Geraldine, were at Larkhill High School, a fee paying private school in Preston. He always held Larkhill School in high esteem. This school was a girls' only Convent school originally run by nuns who were particularly strict about the education and behaviour of their pupils.

One afternoon Jack and I were in the works canteen talking about different things. "Which school does your daughter go to?" Jack asked me.

"She is at Shadsworth High School," I told him.

As usual Jack talked about the importance of education and showed a lot of interest in Shahnaz's progress at school. In the end he said, "How does she do in her class and exams?"

I didn't pay much attention to what Jack was saying, but said, "Oh, she seems to be doing all right. At least her reports show that to be the case," I replied.

Jack continued the conversation about Shahnaz asking, "What are your plans for her educationally?"

"I hope she goes to university and finishes off with a degree," I answered him.

Closing our conversation Jack stated, "I would like to see her progress reports from school."

The next day I took Shahnaz's school reports to show Jack. In my mind at least her school reports, even her primary school reports, were always brilliant. In all her subjects the teachers at Shadsworth

High School had given her high grades, and made very good remarks about her conduct and behaviour.

Jack read these reports with interest, then folded them back up, saying, "Your daughter seems to be an intelligent and clever girl. Why don't you get her into a private school?"

I did try to get Shahnaz into a private school in Blackburn, but was unsuccessful, I said to Jack, "I tried to get her into Westholme Girls High School, but their fees were so high that I couldn't afford them. That's why she had to go to Shadsworth High School."

Jack thought for a few seconds before saying, "Why don't you ring Larkhill High School and get your daughter into that school?"

The next day Jack gave me Larkhill School's phone number. At the same time he explained to me that if the school agreed to consider Shahnaz's acceptance, she might need to take a test, as usually without passing this test, the school wouldn't accept any pupil.

On my day off I rang Larkhill High School. They asked me to send two of Shahnaz's progress reports.

The next day I told Jack about the response from Larkhill High School.

His reaction was wonderful, "Now they will ask your daughter to take a test."

The following week while I was at work Kath received a phone call from Sister Gabriel, the principal of Larkhill High School.

"We have looked at your daughter's reports. She can start here next term."

"Thank you very much, so she can start next year?" Kath questioned.

"No, no. Next term starts on Tuesday of next week," Sister Gabriel explained.

Kath was excited, nervous and confused, she asked, "Would you like to see us and Shahnaz before she starts next Tuesday?"

Although Sister Gabriel was busy with other matters, she said, "Of course I would like to see you. Would it be possible for you to come tomorrow?"

The next day all four of us made our way to Larkhill High School in Preston. Sister Gabriel was wearing a nun's black dress. She was small in height, dainty and softly spoken, but she had enough qualities to impress anyone who spoke to her.

As we entered her office she offered us seats, but there were only three chairs. Suhail was first to grab a chair and sat on it. We took the other two chairs, which meant that poor Shahnaz was left standing.

Looking at the situation Sister Gabriel turned to Suhail and said, "Are you not going to let your sister sit down?"

"No," the stern and firm answer came from Suhail.

Automatically Kath guided Suhail onto her knee allowing Shahnaz to sit down.

We had a pleasant chat with Sister Gabriel. As we were about to leave I asked, "What about Shahnaz's school uniform?"

"Oh, if you go to Linguards in Fishergate, they will be able to fix you up with everything she requires."

Shahnaz, Kath and I were a bit careful how we answered Sister Gabriel. The only person who was neither impressed, nor frightened of Sister Gabriel was Suhail. At that time he was just about three-years old.

Over the next few years Shahnaz did her 'O' levels, and 'A' levels at Larkhill High School. Later she studied at Preston Poly, where she gained her B.Sc. (Hons) before studying at Strathclyde University where she completed her PhD.

after gaining her PhD degree in Glasgow

In my family in Pakistan we have doctors, surgeons, girls who are schoolteachers, college lecturers, university lecturers, solicitors, lady dentists and fashion designers. There was however previously no one with a PhD degree throughout our whole family.

I was so very proud when Shahnaz's thesis was approved; she fulfilled my very old wish. I phoned my elder brother Muzammil in Karachi with the good news. He was so thrilled to hear how well Shahnaz had done, that he arranged a family party for the next day to announce the wonderful news to everyone.

I couldn't let this happy occasion go by without a celebration. After consulting with Kath and Shahnaz we hired Hoghton Village Hall. There was the question of caterers and drinks for those invited, as we had to cater for both English and Asian guests.

Shahnaz's friend Mary McDonald took charge of catering for the English food. For the Asian food I got in touch with Mr Aslam Khan of Manchester Sweet Centre in Whalley Range, Blackburn.

Mary arranged the seating in the hall, prepared the salad and sandwiches, as well as ordering all the pies and soft drinks. Kathy and Victor Dada took on the responsibility for getting the cakes. An order was put with Mr Aslam's samosa centre to supply two types of samosas and pakoras.

Amongst the guests were all the members of the Hubberstey clan, including the children, all our long time family friends in Pringle Street, Lambeth Street, Leamington Road, and naturally our work colleagues. Most of Shahnaz's friends from Glasgow came up the day before especially for the party. The total number of guests was approximately two-hundred and fifty.

It turned out to be a very successful party and almost everyone invited turned up. It started at 7:00pm and lasted till after midnight. There was no shortage of food or drinks. The spicy food was very popular. Everybody said that they had thoroughly enjoyed the evening, and Shahnaz was absolutely loaded down with greeting cards, presents and best wishes.

****

When Shahnaz started working it was for Umist, followed by working for the Water Board. From there she went down to Poole to design some machinery for Siemen. She impressed the firm so much that she was offered a position as a technical director working for Siemen, which she accepted. She still works for them in Surrey and is very much a career lady.

Some years later our son Suhail went to Witton Park School, taking and passing his 'O' levels there. Then he went on to further studies at Blackburn College, firstly passing his 'A' levels then obtaining a BA in Administration. He then took a job in Burnley at Duerdens before becoming an advisor to schools. Now he works for British Telecom as a telephone operator working on emergency calls and still lives with us at home.

Suhail with his sister Shahnaz after he had received his B.A. Degree.

CHAPTER TWENTY-SEVEN

After a week's training I started work on the 'A' shift; I was put with Kingsley Owen an experienced worker on that shift. Kingsley was an international sort of person. He loved hitchhiking and had travelled all through Europe, the Middle East, through South Asian countries, Australia and New Zealand. He had a wonderful attitude towards life. He loved and appreciated all life, not just for human beings, but all animals and insects too.

On his way to Australia and New Zealand he had hitchhiked and worked through the middle-eastern and Far eastern countries. These experiences had given him a good chance to familiarise himself with different religions and cultures. He had such a great respect for all religions and cultures.

Mostly Kingsley was cheerful, but one particular morning when we came onto the morning shift before six o'clock, Kingsley looked very depressed at the start of the shift. I tried to talk to him but his answers were very short.

I was a bit concerned and worried, so I said, "Come on Kings, what's wrong?"

"Nothing much, but this morning on my way to work I passed the slaughter house at the end of Harrison Street," Kingsley replied.

I was still confused by his sad face, so I said, "You do that every day."

"Yes, but this morning while I was passing there I heard the noise of the cows; I think they are going to be slaughtered today. It depressed me to think that for our food we have to take some innocent lives."

I had no answer to this, but fortunately soon afterwards Kingsley came round to being his old self. Some time later Kingsley left for Australia with his wife Debbie and son Aaron.

****

On the other section of the mali machines was Toni Inglis. In the beginning, the impression I had of Toni was that he didn't pay any attention to anyone. But later on I realised that he was the reserved type. To me he was a very knowledgeable person who had travelled intensively. He was married to the equally knowledgeable Evelyn, who was a full-time teacher in a Blackburn school. Toni and Evelyn have a son called Graham. Quite often Toni and I would discuss our childrens' education and future.

During one such discussion Toni asked me if I had made a covenant while Shahnaz was going to Larkhill School and I paid her tuition fees. I was quite ignorant about this, so Toni gave me further information regarding the covenant, which resulted in me obtaining the full tax relief to which I was entitled.

****

I was transferred from the mali section to the batching section to take charge of the production and quality of the fleece produced. I had Ian Hunter and Fardella as machine operators in my team. Besides quality and quantity of the fleece produced, my responsibilities included having to liase with the shift manager and production director. Ian and Fardella were very good workers; in fact we always worked as a proper team.

I met Ian for the first time when I had just started on the 'A' shift and Ian had come on overtime. He gave me the impression of being a teacher, but unfortunately he wasn't successful as a teacher. Actually he was known as an eccentric man. People at work didn't take him seriously because he used a much posher accent than most people. They used to get fed up with Ian's slow speaking speed and difficult English words. However personally I got on well with him, but quite a few people at work thought I wound Ian up; actually I thoroughly enjoyed talking to him.

Fardella was a very strong Italian man who had been in England for a long time and spoke good English.

After Ian Hunter and Fardella I got Alan and Ian Lewis as batcher operatives. Both were very cooperative and good workers; I never had any complaint against either one of them. Alan and Ian were father and son; they went with the family to New Zealand, but came back after a few years. Ian was a fast and efficient worker, while Alan was a very conscientious and reliable person.

Ricky Grieves and Alan Grundell worked on the batchers for a while with me, before they moved on to different jobs. Ricky was a friendly sort of person. Socially we became very good friends and visited each other's houses with our families. He carried out his job efficiently, and at the same time he learnt the job of batching charge hand. Later on he was promoted to be a charge hand on the 'B' shift.

Alan Grundle was always a pleasant and playful person. Not only at work, but he was cheerful and full of life socially at home too. He opted to come off the three-shift work and took the job as a forklift driver.

Brian Johnson initially started as a stitch bonder, but later was promoted to be a carder. Brian was a good all rounder. There wasn't any job that Brian couldn't handle from painting and decorating the house, to gardening, even the car's body repairs were an easy task for him to carry out.

In the engineering department I got to know almost all the engineers, fitters, and electricians. They were Terry, Barry Riley, Dominic, Les Campbell, Ashley, Stan, Ken and a few more. Barry Riley was a very sociable and friendly person. Barry was also very interested in Indian history, so we talked a lot on this subject.

****

Way back when I was at Osprey Dyers we had a big boiler for steam there. We needed an engineer to look after and maintain the boiler and the eight dyeing machines.

I spoke to Barry Riley about this job and he readily agreed to come to our dye-house once a week. He would come to the dye-house in his own time where he was free to go round the machines, the boiler house and the dye room. If some part needed replacing on any machine, or a repair of any kind, he would do it. He was a really great help to us.

With the reorganising of the shift system, Malcolm Drever was transferred to the engineering department and Wilf Westwell took charge of the 'A' shift as shift manager.

Wilf Westwell also came from Chorley. He was a conscientious and caring shift manager. He always had time for his shift personnel.

Wilf had started his working life in the mining industry. He had a wide knowledge of mining and told us a lot of interesting stories about miners and their way of life. Some of the accidents he told us about in the mines were horrific.

As there were a few Asian workers in the factory Wilf showed a lot of interest in Asian religions, cultures and the Asian way of life. During our night shift he sometimes used to join us during our meal breaks and discuss these subjects in detail. We always respected each other's views on a lot of topics.

As I mentioned, Wilf had a good understanding with his shift workers. He used to invite certain people socially to his residence in Chorley. Once Wilf invited my wife and I to spend an evening with his friends, where we met his wife Marian and his two daughters, Pauline and Carole. Besides Wilf's family we met his lifelong friend Eddie and his wife. For the first time I met Tony Finnigan's wife too. Wilf and Marian had arranged some vegetarian food for us and we all had a very enjoyable evening.

I loved working for Blackburn Cord Company. As mentioned before it produced stitch-bonded fabric mainly for curtains. It was the brainchild, (I was told) of Sammy Wildman a Polish gentleman. I never met him but I noticed he was very fair to his workers, as in so many ways he tried to share his wealth with his staff by providing free life insurance for instance.

Up to the late1980's during Christmas time, every member of the staff, regardless of their status, would get a party and presents for their children. A night out, with dinner and dance was always arranged in a first class local restaurant for the adults. Transport was laid on to and from the restaurant for the staff and their partners. On each dinner table there would be a box of chocolates for the ladies and a packet of five cigars for the gentlemen.

To help reduce the burden of expenses at Christmas time, the company gave vouchers for Christmas shopping and a good sized turkey to every staff member.

Before the July holidays the workers got an annual bonus of between £450.00 and £500.00 each. For two years the company paid for fully comprehensive car insurance for its workers, but sadly some people abused this scheme so the Company was forced to end it.

In 1989 at my request, I was transferred from Ledatec to LedaCare, but by the end of 1990 the parent company went through reorganising its small companies. During this process the company offered redundancy to some staff members. I was waiting for a chance like that, so I readily accepted my redundancy.

Other people I came to know during my time with Ledatec (Blackburn Cord) were Ian Powell, Brian Henry, Ray Cooper, Jimmy Pitts, David Rimmer, Brian Johnson, Kevin Wignal, Frank Arrowsmith, Alan Lewis, Ian Lewis, Trever Priestley, John Gill, Ricky Grieves, Alan Grundell, Mohammed Amin, Waheed Malik, Mohammed Khan, Ismail Sange, Ashraf Sange and Suleman Rawoot.

Brian Henry was a carder on the day shift. He was promoted to the position of assistant shift manager and came onto my shift for a considerable time before he opted to collect his redundancy. I got on well with him.

On the night shift Brian used to sit with us in the canteen during our meal breaks. We used to have lots of discussions and debates on different topics. Jimmy Pitts was a wonderful artist. Sometimes I thought he was wasting his talents in Ledatec as he could have easily found good work with a publisher.

CHAPTER TWENTY-EIGHT

In December 1982 I got a phone call from one of my nephews Akhtar, who was a radio officer on a Greek ship. He was going to sign off the ship in Abu Dhabi and fly to Karachi. He asked me if I had any plans to go to Karachi with the family as Kath, Shahnaz and Suhail had never been to Pakistan and the family in Pakistan were very eager to meet them? I had saved enough for our fares, but didn't have enough to stay in Karachi and Hyderabad, so Akhtar and I agreed that he would lend me enough money for our stay.

"Don't worry about expenses while you are over there; just manage to reach Karachi, and I'll see to everything," he instructed me.

When I first mentioned to Kath about us visiting Pakistan in the middle of December she had rather mixed feelings, but said that she would talk it over with the children.

She explained to me, "I have previously had two weeks holiday in Spain, but I just wouldn't know what to expect in Pakistan. Suhail is a little too young to discuss this with, but I have talked to Shahnaz about the possible holiday."

Shahnaz did not have one single hesitation from the moment she was first told. Quite simply, she readily agreed to take this trip and was looking forward to it, wanting to see the sub-continent of her father's birth and to meet her family there. She was so thrilled and excited about it.

Together we were all convinced that a visit to Pakistan would be the chance of a lifetime, one not to be missed. So the planning began in earnest. It all happened so very fast; in fact it took us only a few days to gather everything together to go to Pakistan. It was as if none of us could really get there fast enough.

As this was the family's first big, important, and most expensive journey to date, I wanted to make it as pleasant and comfortable for everyone as I could. We decided to go by the best airline, so we chose British Airways. After some running around I finally managed to book four seats on a flight from London to Karachi. We had to reach Heathrow Airport at 11:00 in the morning, to do that this meant that we had to travel overnight.

Once again my thoughts took me back to when I was a child even up to my teens, when I used to watch Englishmen with their families travelling on Indian railways. They always travelled in either air-conditioned or first class carriages. If their journeys were overnight, they would travel in sleepers.

Air conditioned sleepers and first class carriages on Indian railways were always so luxurious and comfortable that they are rather difficult to describe. Apart from their own personal servants, they were always appointed with a railway attendant who looked after them during their entire journey. I used to wonder if I would ever be able to travel that way with my family.

For travelling to London I thought, 'In for a penny, in for a pound, why not fulfil my old wish and travel in style?' So we went to Preston railway station and booked two different sleeper compartments on a night train from Preston to Euston.

We boarded the train at about 10:30pm. In one compartment were Kath and Shahnaz, whilst in the other, Suhail and I settled down for the night. The compartments were spotless, with generous bunk beds ready made with soft pillows and spotlessly white pillowcases and exceptionally comfortable mattresses. The blankets were beautifully light but warm and cosy. The mirror shone brightly, the washbasin and other facilities were perfectly clean and all the woodwork was well polished to a brilliant shine. A great deal of care and attention had been given to the whole compartment to make us all feel very well cared for and thoroughly spoilt. The attendant was very polite and courteous. He brought Kath and I a nightcap at 11pm just before the train set off. Nothing was too much trouble for him and we all felt very special. It was a wonderfully comfortable journey from Preston to Euston in the sleeper compartments of that night train.

The next morning Kath said to me, "I couldn't sleep properly, so I just snoozed on and off."

This huge adventure for all the family kept running through my mind. I couldn't quite believe that this was actually real, as it had all come about so quickly.

"Shahnaz has slept very well indeed, so she will be thoroughly rested now," Kath told me.

The train left at 11:00pm from Preston, and must have reached Euston in the early morning hours. I too couldn't sleep properly, but dozed now and then. However Suhail was very well rested. Children are often better travellers than adults I think. We were told that we could stay in the sleeper compartment till 7:00am.

At Euston station the attendant woke us up with a gentle knock at the door. He had brought breakfast in for us on a tray. After getting ready for the long flight we got off the train. The attendant had already put our luggage onto the trolley for us.

For a moment my thoughts took me back to my childhood, when I used to watch the poor Indian porter or attendant waiting for the 'Sahib' or 'Mem Sahib' to give him some money as a tip.

I turned to Shahnaz and whispered to her, "Give £5.00 to the attendant." This really fulfilled my old wish.

It was lovely to see the smiling faces of the immigration officers at Heathrow Airport. Security was nowhere near as strict in those days as it is now.

Travelling on British Airways from Heathrow Airport turned out to be just as we had expected. We were welcomed on board by a smiling air hostess who directed us all to our seats. Suhail and I occupied the two seats in front of Shahnaz and Kath. As we settled down the hostess thoughtfully collected my jacket to hang up in her cabin, so that I could sit more comfortably in my seat.

Just as the aircraft started to taxi to reach the runway ready for takeoff, the air hostess brought some comics for Suhail to read during the flight.

Suhail and I spoke whilst on the plane. I asked him if he was feeling all right, as I knew he was very nervous on a plane.

"I am feeling a mixture of both nerves and excitement Daddy," he told me. "I am nervous because I have never made such a long journey before. I have only ever been on two short flights to and from Spain previously. Then I am excited, because it is an opportunity for me to meet all the family members that you have told me about, my aunts, uncles, cousins, and of course my grandmother. I have seen pictures of them before, you have told me all about what they are like, but it is going to be a big experience for me to finally meet them. I also feel a little nervous about all of this. Will I like them? Will they like me?"

I ruffled my young son's black hair gently, "You have nothing at all to worry about Suhail, everyone will not only like you, but they will all love you just as your mother and I do. They won't be able to help themselves as you are such a wonderful boy."

Suhail settled down to read his comics feeling a little less worried after our little chat.

The flight was wonderful and our first stop was Dubai. The landing was perfect; we were allowed to leave the aircraft in order to stretch our legs, we were also given a little time to visit the duty free shop there. It was approximately 1:30am local time when we touched down, but as soon as the door of the plane was opened the heat hit us. We had time to spend and look around before it was time to board the plane once more.

Kath was a little worried when we took off from Dubai; she had started to think about my family and wondered whether or not they would really be happy to see us all. She mentioned to Shahnaz her concerns on this matter.

In her perfectly down-to-earth way Shahnaz put her mother at ease with her good reasoning, "Look, it is only for four weeks that we are going to stay in Pakistan; if we like it, then perhaps we can visit them again; if we do not get on well there, then this can be our last trip."

The seats, crew, take off, landing, food, their service and almost everything from British Airways was just perfect. It was 3:00am when we landed at Karachi International Airport. After ten minutes or so we came down the steps.

As I stepped onto the ground a tall Pakistani airport official approached me and said in Urdu, "Excuse me Sir, are you Mr Mudassir Khan?"

"Yes I am," I replied in Urdu.

Then he turned to Kath and Shahnaz and greeted them in English, "Welcome to Pakistan."

They both smiled and thanked him. He led us to the waiting bus, which took us to the airport buildings. From the bus I spotted Muzammil Bhai and Nasim waiting in the building. They came over and met us all. Muzammil Bhai collected our passports then gave them to one of the airport officials. There was a long queue of people with passports in their hands at the immigration desk, but our passports were stamped very quickly.

We went through customs in exactly the same way; in fact our suitcases weren't even checked. As we came out of the airport building we spotted a crowd on one side.

All of a sudden I heard a shout and saw waving hands, "Mamoon!" It was my niece Saeeda's voice.

"Who are they Daddy?" Suhail asked.

"They are from your tribe," I said jokingly.

My mother wasn't there, as travelling one hundred miles from Hyderabad to Karachi would have been too much for her. However my sisters, brothers, brothers-in-law, sister-in-law, nephews, nieces and cousins were all waiting to to greet us at the airport, even though it was 3:20am.

I embraced each relative in turn and introduced my new family to the rest of my family. After formal introductions and much shedding of tears of joy, we travelled to Muzammil Bhai's flat. He had arranged a police escort for us with blue lights for Kath, Shahnaz and Suhail and a large police bus for the rest of the family members.

The children had watched in amazement as everyone shook hands and embraced us. Some of them draped red roses around our necks. We all felt like we were VIP's or the Royal Family or something like that. We then left the airport to go to my brother's flat where we initially stayed and met even more family members.

Later on I found out that Muzammil Bhai had really wanted to give an extra special reception to his sister-in-law, niece and nephew. He had spoken to his bosses and arranged in great detail all that splendid and greatly enjoyable pomp especially for us.

The four weeks in Karachi and Hyderabad were so wonderful and pleasant for veryone. My brother's flat was one of the apartments built for Government officials. Most of my sister-in-law's friends in the flats came to see us.

The next day Shahnaz and Fernaz went to Karachi's posh shopping centre with my older nephew and nieces. They bought Pakistani dresses, Shalwar, Qameez and Dupuuta. They had a very pleasant experience talking to the shopkeepers who were more than willing to sell their wares. As usual my nephews had to haggle for the items. The shopkeepers didn't really appreciate my nephews being with my wife and daughter; however Fernaz and Shahnaz loved the experience.

While Fernaz and Shahnaz went out shopping, Suhail went out with my younger nephews and their friends to play cricket on the open ground. His newly-made friends talked to him in English, whilst Suhail responded half in English and half in Urdu.

Sometimes when Suhail's new friends called for him in the morning to play out in the open ground, he would run out in his pyjamas. Once or twice Fernaz tried to stop him, but he would run out too quickly.

He would say, "Oh, it doesn't matter, it is a free country."

This made us all smile.

After a few days of staying with my elder brother and his family in Karachi we headed for Hyderabad, which was a hundred mile journey by coach. Together with my nephews and nieces we were about ten passengers. Fernaz being English and Suhail and Shahnaz being more English looking, got priority for their seats in the coach. They got front seats next to the driver while we got seats behind them.

There were so many beautiful views and sights to see as the coach sped through the countryside. I enjoyed seeing this journey and everywhere else in my country, through the eyes of my new family. It was almost a three hour journey to Hyderabad, so the coach stopped halfway.

Where the coach came to a halt, the countryside there reminded us of the scenery in many American cowboy films. We were right in the middle of barren land with bushes growing here and there, but running off this area was a straight tarmac road. In the middle of absolutely nowhere the famous North Western Pathans had set up their tea stalls.

Naturally as soon the boy in the tea stall spotted white faces he knew they were foreigners; he quickly brought a china tea service for all those requiring refreshment. These scenes were delightful for my new family, as everything was being seen by them for the very first time.

By now it was the third week of December and winter in Pakistan. Everyone, except the four of us, was feeling cold, whilst to us it was lovely and warm. It was already dark when we reached Hyderabad.

After getting off the coach we had to walk to the house where my mother lived. While my nephews took care of our suitcases we proceeded further on to meet my mother.

She was sitting in her room. As soon as I entered, I was so filled up with emotion that I just couldn't manage to control myself. With tears in my eyes I knelt down in front of her, put my head into her lap and started crying. I felt both of her hands caressing my head and neck and gently moving up and down.

She was crying also. She lifted my head, kissed my forehead then wiped away my tears. She then beckoned Kath, Shahnaz and Suhail to come and join us.

She kissed each one of them in turn gently on their foreheads, inviting Kath and Shahnaz to sit beside her, whilst Suhail sat at her feet. I felt very sure that she was very pleased to meet her daughter-in-law and grandchildren.

"If only your father could have been here to see you all today," Mother cried out.

We all felt extremely moved at that moment in time, and for a short while at least, it almost felt as though my father was with us all in that room. Perhaps we all just really wished it to be so. We huddled closer together and comforted one another.

Later on mother showed us all round her new house. She was so thrilled with it, as it was so much larger than it had originally been. She no longer had to go through the courtyard to reach the upstairs. Now there were two doors leading into the house from the street, one going straight to the upstairs apartment and one to the courtyard leading into the downstairs apartment.

Each one of the two apartments was completely self-contained, and had its own bathroom and toilet, as well as kitchen and bedroom facilities. This enabled mother to be independent downstairs, but left plenty of room upstairs to accommodate the four of us, or any other guests who might visit her.

Shahnaz and Fernaz standing one on either side of my mother (Head of the family) with other relatives in Hyderabad.

A few days later I heard that one of my relatives in a gossiping mood, had said to my mother, "How do you like a white woman in the family?"

My mother got really cross with her and told her off saying directly to her, "If someone is going to talk about my daughter-in-law, they will have to refer to her by her name."

My large extended family and our neighbours in Hyderabad, without one single exception accepted my wife and children. Once we visited one of my cousins and his family who lived about five miles from our house. We hired three rickshaws (a modified three-wheeler to carry two or three passengers) to go there. I don't know how it started but the three rickshaw drivers suddenly started racing each other.

Shahnaz, Suhail and my nieces were in different rickshaws, they were shouting with excitement and delight, but to be perfectly honest I got terribly frightened, because in Hyderabad nobody cares about, or even obeys the traffic rules and regulations. When we reached our destination I was still shaking with fear and anger, as I was cross with the drivers.

At the end of this journey my nephew and I were talking to the drivers about them travelling too fast, but these drivers told us that they would come in the evening and take us all on a tour of Hyderabad city, for which they wouldn't even charge us because we were guests in their country.

How could I possibly remain angry with them after that?

In Hyderabad we visited two Textile Mills because the general managers in those mills were my old class fellows in Blackburn College. One day was allocated to visiting a Pakistan Army Cadet College ten miles out of Hyderabad city. There we met the Commanding Officer of the college and the cadets.

We were invited out almost every evening either by a relative or some family friend. Most family members and friends spoke English, so that we didn't have that much of a language problem. This was so wonderfully thoughtful, as it enabled the whole family to converse without any problems. It also allowed my new family to practise their Urdu and those in Pakistan who wished to do so, to converse in English.

Muzammil Bhai was in the Karachi Police, so he wanted us to meet his colleagues and his boss the superintendent of police. Here, we also met the female Pakistani police officers.

At that time my nephew Dr. Tafazzul was in Karachi General Hospital. One morning he took us to visit his hospital. There too we met doctors, surgeons and nurses. Some of the doctors we met were British qualified.

Mudassir, with his late elder brother Muzammil.

Everywhere we went we were given VIP treatment. Fernaz noticed that the ordinary people in Karachi and Hyderabad have a very high regard for English people. In crowded areas they would make way for them; on the train they'd give them priority to have the best seats, and everyone treated Fernaz and Shahnaz with the greatest of respect.

My mother especially loved the times, when every morning Fernaz would go to her room taking two cups of tea, one for each of them and greet her with *Salam Alaikum.*

At home all my relatives were kind to us. One of my favourite nieces Saeeda was with us most of time and took care of almost everything for us. We had the most wonderful four weeks in Pakistan. I wish we could have stayed longer, but because of Shahnaz and Suhail's education and our jobs, sadly and very reluctantly, we had to return to England.

We all shed tears when it was finally time for us to leave, and thanked everyone for making our stay so wonderful. We promised that we would all return one day, as we had most certainly been treated so well. My family had even exceeded all *my* expectations, and made my new family so very welcome. I felt that now we were all one great family and I was so happy with that thought.

The four weeks we spent there were the happiest of times for us all. Even to this present day we still talk about the glorious times we all spent and thoroughly enjoyed during that month in Hyderabad and Karachi.

I asked my son Suhail, "How did you like your visit to Pakistan then?"

Suhail thought very hard before answering, "Well Daddy it was so very hot there, much hotter than it is in England. However the family over there did not seem to be dressed for the heat at all."

I laughed on hearing this and explained to him. "Suhail, December is their winter time, so they all feel the cold and therefore dress accordingly. In their summer time it would be far too hot for us to visit them. As they are used to it being so hot at other times, when their winter comes along, they wrap up more, just like we do back home in the English winters."

"I understand now Daddy; but we must have looked so funny to them then mustn't we?"

"I don't understand you Suhail. Tell me why you think that?"

"Daddy, I must have looked very silly to everyone else, walking around wearing a tee shirt and cap, whilst they were all wearing big pullovers and jackets."

"I know what you mean son, but they would understand that, as they are well aware of the differences in temperatures between England and Pakistan, so they would not think that you were silly at all. In fact your mother, Shahnaz and I were *all* wearing summer clothing, not just you, so they would all realise that Pakistan's temperatures in December are probably much better and warmer than all the usual summer months in England."

Suhail and I laughed heartily together; then I explained the reason for our hilarity to Kath and Shahnaz who both agreed and laughed with us.

Shahnaz spoke to me saying, "Karachi was very busy and cosmopolitan, with plenty of things to see and do, like there always is in any big city. After spending a few days there we would always travel to Hyderabad where you were raised and spent your childhood. I liked doing this, as it is also the place where most of our family live. I met my grandmother there and also aunts and uncles. I was thrilled to see them all; it was very emotional."

"Yes everyone cried there," said Suhail."

"Yes it was emotional Shahnaz and Suhail, but it was also so enjoyable too. Remember though that the tears we shed were **happy tears,** not sad ones. This was because we were so pleased to see everyone weren't we?"

"Yes Daddy and thank you for taking us all to see your family. They are all such great people. I love every one of them, but especially my grandmother," said Suhail.

"It was an excellent experience for us all to have. Thank you both so much," Shahnaz told her parents.

Tears welled up in my eyes on hearing this. Children have such a knack for speaking the truth. I felt so very proud of my son, and cuddled him close to me. I stood up and went to kiss my daughter for her words of wisdom.

"My cousins were very good to me too Daddy. They would always involve me in whatever they did, whether it was going to visit people or different places in the town. They knew that I really liked cricket in the same way that they did, so we always got together to go out and have a game whenever we had the chance. We would often go out all day playing cricket, and would indeed stay out for most of the day whenever we went out anywhere together. It was always such good fun," Suhail said sleepily.

I smiled as I listened to my son, and watched silently as I caught sight of my daughter and wife listening to him too. I knew that all my new family had enjoyed the time they had spent with the rest of my family. I felt so very proud that it had all gone so very well.

I was contented and far happier now that I finally knew that my whole family were well and truly united. I wanted to treasure this moment forever in my heart and in my mind. I was so very proud that we had been able to achieve this together - my new family and my family in Pakistan were now fully blended into one *complete* family. Letters were fine, photos were great, but actually seeing them all in person, speaking to them, shaking hands with them, hugging and kissing my mother went so much further than words alone can ever say.

I felt very humble and blessed. I knew that my father would have been very proud of me. Once more I felt his presence very close to me and tears welled up in my eyes. Suhail noticed them!

"Are you sad Daddy?" he asked me.

"Oh no son," I said leaning towards Kath and my daughter also, "I think that I am truly the luckiest and happiest man alive today in the whole world."

Tears fell down my cheeks, but I did not wipe them away; instead I proudly wore each one as a priceless pearl of pure emotion. We all held hands and captured that precious moment in time forever.

On the plane going back home to England, Kath recalled the doubts and conversation that she had with her daughter on the plane flying over to Pakistan, and said to Shahnaz, "I was so very foolish to worry about meeting your father's family and visiting this great country wasn't I? My suspicions were really unfounded and without any foundation. I feel sad that I could ever have thought that way. I was completely and utterly wrong!"

Shahnaz gave her mother a quick hug, "You were simply being the wonderful mother and wife that you truly are, protecting us from the unknown and any possible disappointments. After all with my father being the great man he is, how could his family have ever been anything different than the wonderful folk that they are? Suhail and I are both so very lucky, as we have such wonderful families on both sides. Thanks for giving us the opportunity of letting us all know that Mum." She hugged Kath close, and they both smiled together happily.

Kath and Shahnaz recalled the events of the past four weeks together, "Khan's family gave us all a wonderful reception and treated each one of us like honoured family members. We have been particularly well treated by my new brothers-in-law Muzammil and Mubashir, my new sisters-in-law Beeda Baji and Aapi were so very kind to us all, everyone was so good and caring with both you and Suhail. What did **you** think of Pakistan Shahnaz?"

"Mother, I thought that from the minute we left home, until the moment we returned to the airport has been the very best time of my whole life. Everyone was so kind and helpful to us all. I loved the shopping and seeing where father had lived. Grandma is such a wonderful and very special lady; but then she is my father's mother, so how could she possibly be anything otherwise? All of Father's family are such caring and friendly people. Even their friends and neighbours all went out of their way to ensure that everything went perfectly for us all. Nothing was too much trouble for any of them. We are all very lucky to have such a wonderful family."

Kath agreed with her daughter wholeheartedly. She just could not have worded it better herself.

****

In fact my new family liked Pakistan and its people so much, that we went back again two years later in 1984 to attend the wedding of our nephew Akhtar.

It was a wonderful and enjoyable event. Everybody in the family was surprised when they heard that Amma (my mother) was ready to go to Karachi with us from Hyderabad to attend the wedding. She travelled with us on the coach all the way to Karachi without there being one single problem.

It was very interesting for my new family to see how a wedding reception was conducted over in Pakistan, as previously they had only been to wedding receptions in the UK. Suhail and his cousins spent most of the time playing and running around, as children usually do at that age.

As in most countries, weddings are always very big events in Pakistan, with seemingly the whole town and city turning out to wish the newly married couple all the very best.

There was an overwhelming sadness on the horizon, as once again my father was greatly missed by everyone. This was naturally because my father was not there to see us or us him. He would have dearly loved to have met my new family. He would have fussed over his grandchildren, and welcomed Kath wholeheartedly.

Mother told us on the way to Karachi about the way that he had been so looking forward to receiving us, and had planned to take his English daughter-in-law and grandchildren for a tour of the whole of Pakistan. It would indeed have been a wonderful thing, but alas it was not to be, but at least for every single one of us there was not one moment that we spent there, without us all holding him dearly in our hearts and minds.

****

Sadly the following year 1985, my mother passed away very suddenly, leaving all the family completely devastated, as she was such a wonderful person. She was a softly spoken lady, who was always very considerate and extremely family orientated, who missed me so much, but still allowed me to stay in England without pressuring me to change my mind. My mother took to Fernaz, Shahnaz and Suhail immediately, she was so proud of our achievements.

In the same way that she missed each one of us, all four of us missed her also. She was so kind to each one of us. For thirteen years since my father had died, she had lived without the love of her life, but she still thought about him every single day.

Despite her small stature, mother ruled the roost, and whatever she said we did, not only out of love and respect for her, but also because she was the head of the family, so was indeed a very wise lady.

Zubeda, Aapi, Rafia, Majma,
Kath (Fernaz), Shahnaz holding Majid,
Beeda Baji and a shy girl.

Kath (Fernaz), Suhail and relatives
at Hyderabad Railway Station

CHAPTER TWENTY-NINE

In 1989 I was transferred to LedaCare, which is part of Ledatec. Most of the workers at this company were women. I worked there for almost a year. Unfortunately due to the decline in orders the firm had to reduce its staff. As a matter of fact I realised that I had made a mistake and wanted to change my employment altogether.

While reducing the staff, management offered the choice of collecting redundancy. I was offered reasonable redundancy pay, which I accepted and finished at LedaCare in October1990.

Fortunately I had taken out an insurance policy on my house mortgage against long-term illness and unemployment, so I wasn't too worried financially. The first two weeks at home with nothing to do were wonderful. I would go to town, the museum, library and some general stores, but then I started missing going to work.

A few weeks passed by and I started to get bored with staying at home doing nothing. I thought to myself, 'Instead of sitting around doing nothing all day at home, or going to the town and the library, why don't I make arrangements for a third family trip to Pakistan?'

I put this idea to Kath and Shahnaz and they both readily agreed with me; we started to discuss things and made some serious plans.

The first thing on the agenda was to sort out our passports, visas and tickets to Pakistan. As the weather is usually a lot cooler in Pakistan during the months of December and January, we decided to reach there in the middle of December.

Our passports were valid for a few more years, so we only required visas for Pakistan, which were sorted out without any problem. Once again I started running around for our air tickets. Whichever travel agent I tried, the answer always came back saying that all the airlines were fully booked.

We finally managed to get four seats on one of the Middle East airlines, directly from Manchester to Karachi, at very suitable flight times.

We reached Manchester Airport in good time and boarded the aircraft in the evening. Our journey from Manchester to Dubai was comfortable and enjoyable. Although we travelled all night without any sleep, when family members are together, nobody cares about a little discomfort.

After landing in Dubai we had to wait for about two hours before changing planes for Karachi. A bright morning greeted us on landing, as the sun was shining in full bloom.

We disembarked the plane. As we entered the airport building we were greeted by my elder brother Muzammil. One of my nephews Nasim Khan, who held a senior post at Karachi Airport, was there too. Nasim collected our passports for immigration formalities; our passports were stamped and our luggage cleared without any problem, and the four of us accompanied Muzammil Bhai to the waiting cars.

As before our stay was very enjoyable. Wherever we went to in Hyderabad and Karachi, people received us with courtesy and affection. I took Fernaz and Shahnaz to my old college in Hyderabad and showed them around. We also visited Hyderabad Railway Station, as due to my late father we still had connections with the Pakistan Railways. The Hyderabad station master was very pleased to give Fernaz and Shahnaz a guided tour of the station.

For security reasons photography at the station was not permitted, but the station master made an exception in our case, possibly because of 'The English Visitors' he allowed us to take some photos.

In Hyderabad my old college friends invited us to their homes. My sisters and nieces took Kath, Shahnaz and Suhail to their friends, everyone showed us the same wonderful hospitality as in the past.

We had planned to stay in Karachi and Hyderabad for at least five to six weeks, but because of Gulf war we had to shorten our stay; we returned to Lancashire after just four weeks.

All three of our visits to Pakistan have been very enjoyable and interesting. We all have wonderful memories of the times we visited my family and saw so many truly beautiful places. It has been very special to meet up with our family. During the time spent with them we formed a very close bond, but all too soon it always came to an end as the time arrives for us to leave and say our farewells. We have always left with true promises to keep in touch with each other, hoping that one day there would come another time when we would be visiting Pakistan to see everyone once more.

****

After our return from Pakistan it did not take me long to get bored at home.

Shahnaz noticed my uneasiness, "Why don't you do some voluntary work to keep yourself occupied, perhaps join the Citizen's Advice Bureau in Richmond Terrace," she suggested.

Initially I was reluctant to join the bureau, but eventually one morning after much insistence from Shahnaz, I made an appointment to see Peta Singer the CAB manager.

I didn't know that there would be so many steps before one could become a member of the Bureau's advisory team. I was told that I would have to fill in a form with two reliable referees vouching for me, then I would have to go in front of a panel for an interview. If the panel found me suitable to be an advisor, then I would have to go through training sessions in Preston organised by the National Citizen's Advice Bureau. After going through the initial formalities a date and time were fixed for my interview.

The panel included members of the CAB's committee, Peta Singer, Peter Turner, May Chadwick, Barry and one more member. Peter Turner, a local solicitor was the chairman of the panel.

They were all very friendly and sociable towards me, putting me at ease very quickly. They asked me all sorts of questions which I think I answered to their satisfaction.

May Chadwick a proper Lancashire lass asked, "Mr Khan, have you ever come across racism?"

I wasn't ready for this kind of question, so I said, "No, I'm sorry I haven't experienced it myself."

But May Chadwick wasn't going to let me off with that, she said, "So how would you tackle things if a client made a remark about the colour of your skin?"

I took it very light-heartedly and replied, "Well, I haven't experienced it myself, but I remember once when I was passing through New Bank Road, some young English boys were laughing at an elderly Asian man. I heard somebody saying WOG to him. I couldn't let it go without talking to these young people. I approached them and asked them if they knew what the letters W. O. G. stood for?"

When I saw the blank expressions on their faces I said, "I'll tell you then, W stands for Westernised, O is for Oriental, and G is for Gentleman. So you see W.O.G. is actually a very complimentary statement."

Would you believe it, as I left them, they had all become friendly towards me. From this one episode, it was clear that there are different ways of tackling such problems.

This sort of explanation pleased everybody on the panel; we all had a good laugh. In the end I was appointed.

I loved going to the CAB Preston for the eight weeks of training. It was a very happy experience for me. I met some wonderful people from other towns who all came for similar training.

After completing my training I started as one of the bureau's advisors. In the beginning the experienced advisors helped me a lot. Amongst them were Peta the manager, Ann Minoprio the deputy manager, Barbara, Jim, Dorothy, Malcolm, Susan and some other wonderful co-workers.

People came to us with different problems. I always did my best to advise them, or tried to help solve their difficulties. Sometimes I would either phone or write to different agencies on behalf of these clients.

Amongst our clients were young, old, men, women, Indians, Pakistanis, English, Irish, Scottish people. I must have helped them in some little way, as quite often Peta Singer the bureau manager would receive cards or notes from satisfied clients.

The card would read, "Please would you thank the Indian gentleman who consoled me and sorted out my problems. He was a great help to me; I'm ever so grateful to him."

This sort of compliment was very gratifying and encouraged me to do more for the clients. The staff and colleagues at the bureau were also very helpful and we worked in wonderful harmony.

As I enjoyed meeting, talking and advising people, Peta and Ann asked me if I would help out the bureau by going to Mill Hill to open a new office. I readily agreed to go there.

On my first day in Mill Hill Community Centre a lady client walked in, before taking a seat she said, "I know you, I remember who you are!"

I had recognised her at first glance, before she could finish her sentence I laughed and said, "You should know me, we worked together for a long time."

Actually we had first met almost twenty years earlier when she had been a weaver at Waterfall Mill. For a while we talked about the 'Good old days in the shed'.

Then I asked, "What can I do for you?"

As soon as I said this she poured her heart out. She had tears in her eyes and sounded very distressed and worried.

I put her at ease by saying, "Don't you worry, love; we'll sort it out for you."

Straightaway I picked up the phone, then took the two necessary steps and action to solve her problem. She went out smiling. I could hear her talking to the waiting clients.

"It's well worth waiting for. He is a grand lad, he'll sort out your problems. You've no need to worry."

As I used to be on my own in the Mill Hill office, if a client came with a problem that I couldn't handle, without hesitation I would ring Ann or Peta for advice. One of them would always come to my rescue with helpful and excellent suggestions.

During 1990 and 1992 I spent time with the bureau and quite a few Asian advisors came and went. Some joined the bureau till they got full-time employment, or moved to a different town. Amongst the other Pakistanis were Tariq Latif, Zubeda Chaudhry, and Ayyaz Mehmood and the Indians were Mala and Ali.

After a year or so, Peta and Ann found me suitable enough to send for more advanced training to become a Guidance Tutor. I thoroughly enjoyed my time doing that too.

Whilst I was busy with the CAB and attending college, my children were growing up fast, and throughout my unemployment, my wife Kath was always there for me.

CHAPTER THIRTY

Whilst I was a volunteer at the CAB I befriended a wonderful young man called Shakeel Salam. He was the head of the Asian News Agency and reporter for the *Daily Jang*, a national Urdu newspaper. Around that time I was very fond of listening to Urdu programmes on BBC Radio Lancashire. This programme was presented every Friday evening by Shamim Rehman, an excellent Urdu speaker, who was also fluent in Punjabi and English.

One Friday evening I heard her interviewing Dr Nasir-Ud-Din Ahmed, an Urdu lecturer at Blackburn College. The interview was conducted entirely in Urdu.

I was very impressed by Dr Ahmed's knowledge, his accent, and his total fluency and command of the Urdu language. The next evening I mentioned this to Shakeel. He had already met Dr Ahmed and he couldn't speak highly enough of him. After some discussion we both agreed that I should meet Dr Ahmed.

It was September 1991 when I went to see Dr Ahmed at Blackburn College. I was more than pleased to meet him. I learnt that he hailed from Lucknow in India and his 'pure' Urdu accent and cultured mannerisms of a 'Lucknavi' gentleman impressed me greatly.

As a matter of fact I went to see him with the intention of joining his 'A' level Urdu classes. After this meeting with Dr Ahmed I didn't hesitate to enrol on his course.

It was due to Dr Ahmed's dedication and hard-working nature that the Urdu language finally got recognised as one of the modern languages at Blackburn College and throughout Lancashire. Besides teaching at Blackburn College he was also a member of the GCSE examination board, and promoted spoken Urdu amongst the English community. He arranged different types of weekend Urdu courses for qualified Asian teachers, and encouraged many of them who were working in different industries, to join these weekend courses. He also invited Urdu scholars from many other parts of the UK to address the teachers.

Dr Ahmed is well-known as an Urdu lecturer, examiner and critic throughout the Urdu world; he is regarded as one of the top Urdu poets. Mushaira festivals (Urdu poetry reciting meetings) are incomplete without him.

I consider myself to be extremely fortunate that our teacher-pupil relationship turned into a mutual and sincere friendship. To this day I have a lot of pleasant memories of accompanying him to Urdu poetry reciting sessions in Blackburn, Accrington, Oldham, Haslingden, Bradford, Manchester and various other towns. He is a devout Muslim, following Islam in the truest sense, always being humble about his status and achievements.

One day I had the opportunity to meet Dr Ahmed's wife when I took some notes for an Urdu course to their house. Mrs Ahmed later informed me that she was pleasantly surprised to hear a good Urdu accent, when she heard me speak. I too was impressed by her, for besides looking after their house and bringing up her two girls, Mrs Ahmed also taught GCSE Urdu at Blackburn and Accrington Colleges.

Dr and Mrs Ahmed's two daughters Uzma and Naghma are a credit to their parents. Naghma was one of the very few Asian people from Lancashire who attended Oxford University. She successfully completed her degree and attained a B.Sc. and Chartered Accountancy. Uzma followed her elder sister into higher education by studying at Dundee University; she successfully completed her degree in Optics. For some time Uzma worked in the very exotic island of St. Lucia, where she became very popular with her patients. Both young ladies are like any other modern girls in England, but they have both retained a high regard for the family's Eastern values also.

In Dr Ahmed's Urdu classes I met quite a few Asians, but I was more than pleased and shocked to meet Mr Sagheer Adeeb. After all he is one of the top class Urdu writers and is well-known throughout the Indian sub-continent, the UK, Europe and America and has a huge following. His original and legendary stories are regularly published in some of the most popular Urdu magazines throughout the Urdu-world, including such publications as Bisween Sadi, Shama and Ravi.

****

In 1992, during my visit to my home town Hyderabad in Pakistan, I met some old school and college friends who had all become dignitaries in their own rights. Some of these friends invited me to Hyderabad Press Club to join them for a social evening.

While talking about Urdu as a language in the UK, one of my friends Dr Saeed commented that he had read a story in Bisween Sadi and said, "By the way Mudassir, is it true that Sagheer Adeeb lives in your literary circle in Blackburn?"

I felt really proud and was delighted to inform them, "I see Sagheer at least two or three times a week."

They all wanted to know more about him, as they were regular readers of Sagheer Adeeb's work and wished to meet him.

After the Division of India, Sagheer Adeeb came from Cownpu (India), to Rahim Yar Khan with his family. He came to Blackburn in the 1960's. He is in the truest sense an Urdu writer. He is completely carefree and hates people making a fuss of him, or making him the centre of attention. Some may even consider him to be an eccentric, but he is approachable, although he rarely goes to any large event. I was delighted and privileged to mention that Sagheer and I are on very close terms. Whenever we meet at each other's homes or in town, we always treat each other with the utmost respect and talk very frankly and honestly. He is a very unassuming gentleman and would never give an impression of being a famous writer.

****

At the time of collecting my redundancy from LedaCare I was worried how I was going to use my time, but with Shahnaz's insistences and Shakeel's suggestions, I got so busy that I hardly had enough time for myself.

I was quite happy going to the CAB and attending my 'A' level Urdu classes, but one evening Shakeel rang and told me that the Media Centre at Blackburn College was starting an access course in Journalism; he suggested that I should join this course. He told me that he was going to see Carol Duerden the head of the Media Centre.

I went along with Shakeel to speak to Carol. She was very supportive and encouraging towards us both, informing us that if there were enough students she would definitely start an access course for us.

Some of Shakeel's friends wanted to join this course. To make up the numbers, I persuaded Sagheer and two other young people to join. Carol told us about our tutor Shaheen Akhtar. She was a young Pakistani girl with a degree in journalism who worked for the *Evening Telegraph*, which at that time was our local evening newspaper, but now comes out early in the day. Because of her bad back she could not carry on with her full-time job, so had taken up part-time work teaching journalism.

Shaheen was a lot younger than Sagheer or I; in fact she was similar to our daughters' in age. But as she was our teacher we respected her, and in return she treated us courteously. Besides teaching us in class, in order to give us practical experience in journalism on a few occasions Shaheen took the whole class to Blackburn Town Hall to attend council meetings, or to Magistrate's courts to take notes on petty cases, or occasionally we attended a few news conferences. We were treated well in all these places.

The media centre at Blackburn College had both radio and television studios, where full-time students studied and learnt the skills of producing, directing, editing and presenting their own programmes.

Besides Carole Duerden, other staff at the Media Centre included John Coops, Jon Williams, Gordon Huxley and Brian. All members of staff were very helpful and popular with the students, but Gordon Huxley was a particular favourite as he would organise outdoor film shootings at many locations.

****

One evening, in the main room of the media centre while Shaheen Akhtar was teaching our class, we noticed a new face amongst us; another Asian man was sitting alone at the other end of the room. During our break we invited him to join us in the class. This was my first introduction to Salim Sameja.

Initially he was interested in photography and agreed to join our journalism group. At that time many of the Asian students in that class were unemployed, they all wanted to learn extra skills to improve their chances of gaining employment. The media staff were friendly and helpful, so we spent a lot of time there learning and working on different projects.

Salim was an all rounder in journalism. He was as good at producing a programme on the radio, as he was in producing one for television, and he did equally well producing a newspaper.

During the time when we (Salim, Sagheer and I) were Shaheen Akhtar's students, Blackburn Town Council had awarded £25,000.00 to the EMDA (Ethnic Minority Development Association) to produce a bilingual newspaper called *'AAWAZ'* (The Voice). At the same time a computer was bought with both English and Urdu packages, and eventually English and Urdu editorial teams were set up.

Salim was involved with the English section, combining his love of photography with writing, while Sagheer, Shakeel and I concentrated on the Urdu section. Shaheen took overall charge of the English section with Salim and the others.

Salim worked hard in researching and collecting stories. His main interest still remained in taking photographs at different events for the paper. A few months after the launch of *The Aawaz*, a young university student wished to start his own monthly local English newspaper, aimed not only at the Asian readership, but also at the wider community. He hoped to highlight not only the Asian community's achievements, but also its problems. He aimed to distribute the paper free of charge to the Blackburn community, financed by advertising revenue.

That university student was Zafar Khan studying at Hull University. He invited Salim Sameja, Suhail Khan, Shonti Mukherji, Fariha Qureshi and me to join him. After a long discussion it was decided that the monthly paper would be called *The Blackburn Independent*, and it would be a working project to help the students on the journalism course. Mr John Bolton, the Principal of Blackburn College, was delighted to support this joint venture.

The MP for Blackburn Jack Straw accepted the invitation to help launch the paper. The local civic leaders and dignitaries were present at its launch.

Whilst Zafar remained the Editor-in-Chief, he continued with his studies at Hull University, thus being away from Lancashire for long periods. In the meantime Salim was asked to take charge of the editorial role; the team also included Shonti, Suhail, Fariha and myself.

Salim contributed a lot into making a success of this paper. He developed contacts with local firms to generate income from advertisements, going to other Lancashire towns such as Bolton, Oldham, Rochdale and Preston. At the same time he would pursue news items, and once the content and layout were agreed by the team, he would then go to the printers to make sure that the new edition was out on time. He would work tirelessly from morning till night.

We were all volunteers, nobody, including Salim was paid a single penny. If I remember correctly, he was not even paid for any photographical material or film development.

Fariha took charge of the women's section, while Suhail looked after the sports section. Shonti and I helped Salim wherever needed. Shonti's help was mainly in editing the paper. Within a matter of months the paper was covering news around the county, it was soon re-named as *The Lancashire Independent.*

This also brought about a change in content, as the readership had exceeded anyone's expectations. New ideas were incorporated and different features became more popular. One column in particular became extremely favoured amongst a very wide readership, which also included Asian and non-Asian readership. At the same time it also became controversial amongst a small minority, particularly those who may have recognised themselves within a certain feature.

The column was known as *Sher-dil* (Lion-Heart) and it addressed topical subjects. The main reason for its popularity was because it was hard-hitting towards 'self-appointed community leaders' and corrupt individuals who were considered responsible for promoting racial divide.

The column pointed out those amongst the Asian community who had been misusing their positions for their own gains, and that of their family friends. *Sher-dil* challenged and exposed nepotism by the very people who had assumed power and control without an elected mandate. Individuals were appointed in highly paid jobs without any formal selection process, without academic qualifications, or in many cases, without suitable experience. The most common-thread for appointments was because the candidates for the posts were close relatives and friends. Young Asian men and women who had worked hard to gain qualifications were ignored because their faces did not fit the tribal DNA.

As the popularity of this column grew, the majority of the Lancashire community, including the elected politicians, other civic leaders and professional individuals took a great interest in finding out about who was going to be exposed in the next issue. The readers often wondered as to who wrote *Sher-dil;* in fact it was a closely guarded secret that has still not been revealed to me.

The column finally received an acknowledgement of the highest order when a publicly funded organisation, with assets of millions of pounds, issued a writ to sue the paper. Support for the paper and its team was overwhelming, particularly from the general readership and the politicians. At one point questions about that organisation were even asked in the House of Commons, challenging the morality of a multi-million pound company suing a group of college students. The team resisted all the threats and demands to make an apology, because they believed that what *The Independent* wrote was always true and accurate.

It is worth mentioning here that during this episode, which lasted several months, Zafar the owner of the paper, stayed away from Blackburn, leaving Salim and the rest of the team 'holding the baby' despite some challenging times in dealing with legal matters. Mr John Haworth of Haworth & Nuttall represented the case expertly.

At that time I still had some time to spare, so I accompanied Salim to several meetings. At one point, the organisation attempted to bully Salim into printing 'a two line apology' in *The Independent* and *The Evening Telegraph,* but on no account whatsoever was

Salim prepared to give in. Through the work of Mr Haworth the legal challenge fizzled out.

In the end the organisation withdrew all legal actions.

****

It was way back in the middle of the 60's when BBC Radio felt the need to cater for the needs of the Asian communities in England. First they started a half hour a week Urdu magazine programme on the BBC Home Service. Then locally, we had half an hour a week on BBC Radio Blackburn.

At Radio Blackburn, Nasim Bajwa became the first to present a half hour Urdu programme on Friday evenings. It mainly consisted of Indian and Pakistani songs. After some time Mr Bajwa left and Shamim Rehman became the sole presenter.

Shamim Rehman had the perfect radio voice. Her fluency, accent and vocabulary in Urdu and Punjabi were wonderfully precise; no one could ever find fault with her presentations.

By the end of 1980 the Asian population in Blackburn and Lancashire had increased considerably. Radio Blackburn became Radio Lancashire and the BBC increased the broadcasting slots for Asian listeners by introducing two more part-time presenters Siraj Patel and Ahmed Halim.

Although these two gentlemen presented their programmes in the Urdu language, the majority of listeners favoured Shamim Rehman because of her natural Urdu accent, fluency and extensive vocabulary. This was finally confirmed by the results of an independent public survey.

****

In the early 90's, the editorial team of *The Lancashire Independent* was approached by Mr Chris van Schaike the station manager of BBC Radio Lancashire, to conduct a survey amongst the readership. A questionnaire was prepared and circulated; public response was overwhelming. This was the first ever research of programmes that had been broadcasting for over twenty years.

The public voted for Shamim Rehman as the most popular presenter, while the survey revealed the need for changes from the outdated programme format and its presenters. The public wished to see Siraj Patel and Ahmed Halim removed. The results of the survey were passed on to the station manager, and a meeting was arranged later between Chris and the team from *The Lancashire Independent.*

The meeting was fruitful; in the end we put forward the needs of the Asian community, and some suggestions regarding the programmes to the station manager. He promised to look into these matters and take the necessary measures and steps, including the promise of increased hours.

One afternoon some weeks later, Salim came to my house and asked if I had anyone in mind who could be a good presenter in the Urdu language? He had been approached by the station manager earlier for assistance in finding a temporary presenter as Shamim was due to visit abroad. The station manager had decided that it would be an appropriate time to break from the previous format and introduce a 'new face' to refresh Shamim's temporary absence.

In those days I had mostly confined myself to my family and limited friends, I couldn't suggest any name in particular. When Salim mentioned the name Nisar Patel, I remembered him well, as I recalled that Nisar had previously assisted Ahmed Halim in presenting some items in *Mehfil.*

Nisar has a happy-go-lucky and bubbly personality. He has a unique style of addressing an audience. He possesses the art of combining Urdu, Gujerati and English and using all three languages to appeal to a wider audience and a new generation. Salim was asked to assist in making the programme, mainly with researching new stories for inclusion in the new programme. In line with BBC policy this was to be a mix of talk and music, but would also include curent affairs.

I had the pleasure of making a contribution in training and guiding Nisar, and helping to launch his new programme *Bazm-e-Nisar.* This format became very popular throughout Lancashire and Greater Manchester, in recognition of this popularity, Bazm-e-Nisar became a regular slot, as part of an overall increase in output for Asian listeners. It may have taken over twenty-five years and a survey by *The Lancashire Independent,* but the weekly output had been increased from one half hour slot to seven hours per week.

This included *Asian Talk Back,* hosted by Salim on Thursdays and Sundays, and *Bazm-e-Nisar* presented by Nisar on Saturdays.

Later the same evening *Pataka* for the Asian youth was presented by a young Indian girl called Maya. Many of the programmes included news slots, which were presented by Suhail Khan. I was asked to be a programme consultant for the Urdu output, offering training and guidance, and occasionally reading the Urdu news.

On 25th December 1993 Radio Lancashire's Asian Unit presented a two-hour special, an entire programme to celebrate the birthday of Quaid-e-Azam Mohammed Ali Jinnah, the creator of Pakistan. This was a historic moment in BBC radio broadcasting, as never before had there ever been a programme featuring moments of history, politics, and education affecting the Indian sub-continent.

Despite having no connection with Pakistan, Salim and Nisar showed great respect and admiration for Quaid-e-Azam. Salim conducted extensive research into Mr Jinnah's political and social profile, and to give this tribute its full authenticity, the programme included his original speeches from BBC Archives in London, as well as an interview with the Pakistani High Commissioner in London, which included a memorable message to the Pakistani community living in the north-west.

Mr Ishtiaq Andrabi, the Pakistani Consul General in Manchester, also very kindly accepted the invitation to join us in the studios of Radio Lancashire to celebrate the occasion, and take part in making the programme.

The programme was well received by the Pakistani community, and other communities enjoyed it too, though having said that, this programme also embarrassed the local self-appointed Pakistani leaders. These individuals had always claimed to be the loyal and true admirers of their great leaders, but to this day they have never held a single social meeting as a tribute and celebration. Sadly, hardly any one of the younger generation born in the UK has any understanding of the creation of Pakistan as a nation, or its history.

****

My roles in helping at the CAB and Radio Lancashire, and enrolling at the media centre at Blackburn College were all entirely carried out on a voluntary basis; I thoroughly enjoyed my experiences, so I attended these establishments for a long period.

For almost eighteen months I was unemployed, but financially my family and I managed to survive on the welfare benefits that I was receiving for the first time in my long employment history.

One afternoon in 1992 at the CAB, when we had finished attending to our clients and were getting ready to go home, Ann Minoprio the Deputy Manager invited me to accompany her into her office.

As we sat down she said, "I have been asked by one of our committee members Andrea Baker JP, to recommend and nominate an Asian person to become a JP. She explained that the Magistrates' service was under represented by members of the minority community."

Ann leant back in her chair and said, "You are a very good advisor at the CAB, and you have turned into a good guidance tutor; would *you* consider becoming a JP? I don't see any reason why you shouldn't make a good magistrate, you would get a thorough training."

I was delighted and felt privileged with what I heard. For a few moments I remained quietly thinking before replying, "I don't know yet; could I give you my answer tomorrow?"

"By the way Mudassir, have you ever thought of taking up teaching as a profession? You would make a very good teacher."

Later that evening I discussed this conversation with my family, and with their encouragement I agreed to be nominated as a magistrate. I didn't know at that time just who was going to propose my name, or who was going to second it, but later on I found out that Andrea Baker proposed and Mrs Elaine Holden seconded my name.

****

During the time that I was working at the CAB and attending the media centre at Blackburn College, I met Salim Sameja on many occasions. We used to meet for coffee in the town centre, or at the college café, and I used to tell him all about my first experiences in England. He showed a lot of interest and encouraged me to write down all I remembered; it was therefore partly due to him that I finally got around to writing my thoughts into this book, ***Still Here.***

****

One evening Shakeel Salam came round with his cousin Javaid to our house, Shakeel told me that an Urdu drama was going to be staged at Blackburn College. He asked me if I would like to go with them. Although I had no intention of going anywhere the next evening I felt Shakeel's sincerity in asking me, so I agreed to go with him.

The next evening we set off together, Shakeel paid for my ticket. During the interval I spotted Dr Nasir in the foyer. I went over to talk to him. During our conversation he too asked me if I had ever thought of taking up teaching.

Laughing I replied, "Dr Sahib, apart from teaching some young students on tuition, and teaching basic spoken Urdu to some English people in the industry, I have never taught anything at all."

Dr Nasir insisted saying, "A short training could be arranged for you if you are interested."

At that time I thought of it as nothing important, so with a smile I thanked Dr Nasir for his kind and sincere thoughts for me.

****

One evening when I reached home, Kath told me that Dr Nasir had left me some application forms for teaching at Blackburn College. Eventually I completed these and I thought I had returned them to the College.

Even at this stage I didn't think much of going into the teaching profession, but then one day Dr Nasir phoned to tell me that an Urdu teacher was unwell, he asked me if I would kindly go and take his Urdu class to fill in?

At first I was hesitant and nervous, but Dr Nasir gave me a lot of helpful support and encouragement. He very kindly gave me some notes and teaching materials for the class. Because of Dr Nasir's affection and insistence, I couldn't say no to him; in the end I agreed to take that evening class.

There were about twenty male and female Pakistani students in the class. Only three or four could speak proper Urdu, the rest preferred to speak in English. I must admit though, they were all very keen to learn Urdu properly.

Thank God I managed well in both languages, and the class was very impressed. I was complimented at the end of the lesson that I had a good method of passing my knowledge on to my students. That was the start of my mini teaching profession.

Following this first class I took a few more Urdu classes. Unfortunately my formal interview never took place for the post in Blackburn College, firstly because I didn't return the forms to college for registration, and secondly the college also forgot about my interview.

However this oversight was later addressed when Samina Nawaz, Head of the Urdu Section, asked me to attend a formal interview. Following this interview I was then registered as a part-time Urdu teacher at Blackburn College.

While doing all these activities I was still required to claim dole, I had to sign on once a week at the Benefit Agency declaring the paid or unpaid work I had done in the previous week. Every ten or twelve weeks I had to go before an agency's officer to explain as to how I was trying to obtain a permanent job. In fact I didn't mind it at all, as I rather enjoyed talking to these young officers.

At one of these visits, a young Asian girl clerk was interviewing me, whilst I was showing her all the copies of my letters and applications that I had sent to different firms looking for jobs.

During the conversation I said to her, "By the way, to increase my chances of getting a job, I have worked an hour extra."

She looked straight at me and said, "You can't do that. If you got paid for it, the same amount would be deducted from your benefits and you would lose all your allowances."

I couldn't believe what I heard.

She carried on, "You'll have to pay council tax, pay for your prescriptions, eye tests, dental treatments and the rest."

I kept calm for a while, then I don't know what made me lose my temper, but I threw all my papers up in the air. People in the room looked on in amazement at these flying pages.

The poor girl was shocked too but I said, "What is the point of me trying this hard to get a job, if you are going to victimise me like that?"

She started to apologise saying, "I'm sorry if it sounded harsh. Let me explain everything in detail." She bent down to pick my papers up from the floor.

I felt sorry for her at this point, so I helped her to gather them all up.

She explained to me in detail the rules and regulations of being on benefits. In the end I apologised to her for my outburst.

****

At the media centre Salim suggested to Carole Duerden that an Anglo-Asian fashion show, mixed marriages and some British/Asian musical group show should be staged, produced and filmed by media students He said that the programme would give the students an opportunity to apply some of their production skills whilst giving cultural awareness to both the English and Asian communities about each other.

Carole agreed with the idea, and gave us permission to use the studio equipment. Salim talked to Gordon, Brian, Shaheen, Sagheer, Zafar, Habiba, Linden and some other English students in the media centre, to help out in organising these events.

To stage the fashion show Salim had to work hard, and Gordon agreed to direct the show. Brian, Linden and other students were cameramen; Shaheen readily agreed to be the compere. Habiba took on the responsibility to train and manage both male and female models, while Sagheer and Zafar acted as in charge of the dresses and other costumes loaned locally by Poshak and other fashion stores. The show was staged in the college hall in front of a mixed crowd of about three-hundred. By all acoounts it was a huge success.

Later the students also got the opportunity to produce and record a pop concert involving a Midlands band called *Carpe Diem*, who was known to Shaheen Akhtar, as well as holding a debate on mixed marriages.

The quality of each one of these three shows was very good, so at a later date, all three were screened on Sky television.

I took part in all three events. In the fashion show I was the Asian bride's father. In the debate I was one of the participants talking about my personal experiences, in the pop concert I was a cameraman.

It was at the Anglo-Asian fashion show that I first met Sameja's parents, Kassam and Fatima, as well as Anwar and Shaheen, his brother and sister respecitively, who have always been kind and very sincere to me. Since our introduction we have developed family terms and a good relationship with each other.

I learnt that the Sameja family came from Zanzibar and Kenya. What surprised me about the family was that Kassam and Fatima's grandparents had left India approximately one-hundred and thirty years earlier, with no immediate relatives being left behind in the Indian sub-continent. Despite this none of their children have forgotten their religion, culture, or language. They are all fluent in English, Urdu, Swahili, Gujerati, and Cutchi languages.

It was a dull, wet and miserable afternoon when I first met Shaheen Sameja. Salim and I were on our way to the media centre when a voice calling for Salim stopped us. I saw a young girl wearing a long raincoat right down to her ankles, with a fisherman's hat protecting her hair from the rain. She was talking non-stop. As she paused for a second Salim got his chance to speak.

He introduced her to me as his younger sister Shaheen. Again she resumed talking non-stop. Shaheen is very deceiving for her age. In fact she is just like our Shahnaz who also looks a lot younger than her age. Both 'girls' look twenty years younger than their actual ages.

As mentioned earlier Salim, Nisar and I decided to dedicate two hours on Radio Lancashire as a tribute to the great leader and creator of Pakistan. We invited Mr Ishtiaq Hussain Andrabi and his assistant from the Pakistan High Commission Office in Manchester.

On this occasion we were short of helpers, so we asked Shahnaz and Shaheen to help us out with the VIP guests. They both readily agreed to this.

On our guests' arrival we all received them. After a while Salim and Nisar went to the studios to prepare for the programme which was due to be broadcasted within the following thirty minutes. I stayed in the room with the visitors, while Shaheen and Shahnaz both went off to make cups of tea.

Settling down with a freshly made cup of tea and some snacks, Mr Andrabi turned to Shaheen and Shahnaz and asked, "Which school do you young ladies attend?"

Shaheen and Shahnaz looked at each other wondering who was going to speak first. None of us knew what to say at that moment, bearing in mind that Mr Andrabi was also a VIP guest.

However Shahnaz managed to say, "Actually Sir, I have completed my doctorate and Shaheen has finished her degree. We are both working."

I am sure Mr Andrabi was surprised at this answer, but being an experienced diplomat he quickly changed the subject, and started talking to them about current affairs. It was no wonder that Mr Andrabi couldn't guess the girls' ages; they were both casually dressed in ordinary jeans and tee-shirts. Nobody could have possibly guessed their academic background or intelligence. That evening they just looked like two teenagers.

Shaheen is a girl with all good manners and charm. If she is in a happy mood she is full of fun and laughter, but if she is cross with somebody, she gives them a really hard time. I have mostly seen her as a bubbly and cheerful girl; only once have I ever seen her arguing with someone, and she gave him a very hard time.

****

During the last week of July 1992 a post for an Urdu Lecturer was advertised in the *Evening Telegraph*. It was to teach GCSE and 'A' level Urdu classes at Accrington & Rossendale College, Accrington. I sought advice from Dr Ahmed about this post; he encouraged me to apply for it. On August 3rd, I sent in my application and promptly received an acknowledgement for my application three days later.

I was invited by the college to attend two days of informal and formal interviews on 18th and 19th August 1992. The letter included a list of the other candidates, M. Ramzan Khan, Tahira Shouib, Riffat Shah, and Ijaz Ahmed. I was the first one on the list for interviews.

On August 18th 1992 the informal interview began with a 'welcome to the college' speech by the Principal Mr Austin. After watching a college video, we heard Mr D. Tyas the head of division speaking about his division. Dr Ahmed gave us a passage to translate from Urdu into English. In the afternoon the informal interview commenced with Mr Tyas and Dr Nasir-ud-Din Ahmed.

I thoroughly enjoyed the informal interview with Dr Ahmed and Mr Tyas. During our conversation we discussed and exchanged views on educational affairs.

The next day, three candidates were short listed; they were Ramzan Khan, Ijaz Ahmed and me. Ramzan Khan was the first to go in for his formal interview. After a while he came back into the room and told us that he was going home as he hadn't been successful in his formal interview. Ijaz Ahmed was next for his interview, whilst I was the last to go in front of the panel for mine.

The five people on the panel included Mr Austin, Mr Atkinson, Mr Tyas, Ms Clark and Dr Ahmed. Their seating arrangement was in a semi-circle; however I was placed in the middle in front of them all.

As I took my seat I was quite nervous but I thought, 'I have attended other interviews, this one will most likely be just like the others. The worst that could happen would be that I will be turned down; so why not enjoy it!'

As I felt confident enough to answer in both English and Urdu, I settled down in my chair. The interview was very interesting. There were all sorts of questions coming from all sides. I remember I only stumbled once, when somebody asked about the difference between the standard of GCSE and 'A' level Urdu. However I think I handled all the questions quite satisfactorily.

In the end Ijaz Ahmed and I were in the room again waiting for the results. A few minutes later somebody came for Ijaz Ahmed and Mr Tyas came for me. Again I had to take the same 'hot seat'.

After asking me a few more questions, Mr Austin got up from his seat. Coming forward towards me he said, "We are satisfied with your suitability for the post, so I would like to offer you the position, and would like your answer now as to whether or not you will accept it?"

I was delighted to hear this, so without any hesitation I said, "Yes, I would like to accept it; thank you."

Mr Austin shook hands with me saying, "Welcome to the team of Accrington & Rossendale College."

One by one I shook hands with all the panel members, and thanked everyone personally. Mr Tyas took me to the personnel office and introduced me to different people there.

To be honest, I was very pleased at this outcome; I couldn't wait to give the good news to Kath.

As soon as Mr Tyas left me I walked down Sandy Lane in Accrington. On that particular day Kath had taken the car so I had to catch the bus home from Accrington town centre. The only area I knew in Accrington was Blackburn Road, so coming down to the town centre from Sandy Lane I got lost and had to ask somebody to direct me to the town centre.

The following week at college I was introduced to Lynn Surgeon the team leader of modern languages. During the staff induction week I got to know Lyndsey Harford, Janet Royston, Katie Lee, Munawwar Jan and others. We were given a guided tour of the college and the newly-built science block.

For the first twelve months I was based at the 'fishpond' staff room where I met Sheeraz Sheerazi, Steve Hailstone, Pat Walsh, Maggie Moon and other lecturers.

The classes started on 1st September 1992, I went off to my GCSE Urdu class, where there were about twenty students. They were all British born young Asians. Because of their parental backgrounds, they all wished to have some knowledge of their heritage. Learning the Urdu language was the best way to achieve this.

In that class there were twelve or thirteen boys and seven or eight girls. The first lesson was to introduce myself to the students and get to know them. I had some difficulty communicating with them because most of them felt at ease in speaking English, whilst I was speaking to them in Urdu.

The majority of the Asians in Accrington are from Azad Kashmir, and their mother tongue is Mirpuri dialect. Most Pakistani families speak in Punjabi with their children at home. Young people hardly have a chance to speak or hear Urdu, because they had learnt the English language at school, and speak English with their English or Asian friends, so they felt at ease speaking only in English.

I made it clear to my students that because it was an Urdu class, and their main purpose in joining my class was to learn and improve their Urdu, they should try to use only Urdu in my class.

In the afternoon of the same day, I took an 'A' level class. There were only five students in that class. Within two weeks some more Asian students approached me and asked if I could start an extra class for them?

I consulted with Dave Tyas the head of modern languages over this matter. He left it entirely up to me whether or not I wished to start an extra class. The problem was that all those students were fully occupied with their day timetable, but because they were very keen to study 'A' level Urdu, I had to start a class in the evening. It was held at the college's Blackburn Road site once a week from 6:00 until 9:00pm.

In the beginning Dr Nasir Ahmed helped me a lot to prepare my teaching materials for both GCSE and 'A' levels. He gave me a lot of 'A' level teaching items that he himself had used in the past in other colleges. My teaching and subsequent exam results wouldn't have been as successful if it wasn't for Dr Ahmed's guidance and help.

During my induction week the facilities the college offered to lecturers regarding the preparation and delivery of their lessons, photocopying, printed matters, and use of the OHP had all been fully explained. In due course besides the staff room colleagues, I noticed other personnel in different meetings. By the half-term of 1992 I got to know quite a few people across the college.

In the modern languages team I met Lynn Surgeon, Charles Pearce, Jim Dickinson, Jeff Moxam, David Haworth, Cathy Wright and Linda Bell. Some time later the team leader Lynn Surgeon left, and a beautiful, active and energetic, young Mel Chadwick was appointed as the team leader.

Across the college there were a number of people who made a big impression on me. I was always on good terms with them. Due to the reorganisation and allocation of the staff rooms, I had to change my staff room from fishpond to the other wing.

In the new staff room I got to know some wonderful people, Robin Sharp, Keith, John Mckhale, David Haworth and Katie Lee. David Haworth and I were in the modern languages team. We had a lot in common to talk about, so we discussed a lot of topics in our spare time. Robin Sharp was quite a lively person. David and Robin were very fond of cricket, so he talked to me about Indian and Pakistani cricket and the players. Robin helped me a lot to polish up my Lancashire accent. A few times Robin invited me to address his classes about Asian culture and the Asian family life.

I always got a friendly reception at administration, personnel, students' services, canteen, reprographics and other departments at Sandy Lane, as well as other college sites.

One afternoon, while I was on my way to the canteen, I heard a firm but polite voice say, "Excuse me."

"Yes," I slowed down and turned my head back to see who had addressed me?

I saw a lady approaching. To me she looked more like the headmistress of a high school.

She extended her hand out to me saying, "I take it that you are Mudassir Khan the Urdu lecturer?"

Shaking her hand and smiling I said, "Yes I am."

We kept walking towards the canteen.

She then introduced herself, "I am Mary Parsons."

"I know, and I'm pleased to meet you," I said in all innocence.

She looked at me with a mixed expression of shock, surprise and pleasure. I'm sure she was wondering how I knew? A few people had already told me about her and described her appearance.

"Come on, I'll buy you a coffee," she said with a smile. She bought two coffees asking me, "Would you like to have something to eat?"

I thanked her politely, saying that a drink would be quite sufficient. We sat down with our coffees in a corner of the canteen.

Talking to Mary I felt she wasn't as stern and strict as people made her out to be.

With a cheeky smile she asked, "How did you know it was me?"

"Ah, I have ways of finding out about people," I said, with a big laugh. "I know that you teach basic Urdu to non-Urdu speakers and different skills to Asian women."

She gave me a brief account of her background, and without making it too obvious she wanted to know a lot about me. She had a good knowledge of basic Urdu, I could tell that she had the ability to pass her knowledge on to others.

In later years I found out that in fact Mary was basically a very soft person. If she liked or took to somebody, she would go out of her way to help them.

I also owe my brilliant successes in conducting the GCSE examinations to Mary Parsons. Without her instructions and help, I couldn't have conducted the Listening & Speaking test half as efficiently and effectively as I did.

Some time in March 1993 she introduced me to Ken Holmes, the examination officer and asked me, "Have you booked the hall, P. A. system loud speakers and tape recorders for the listening test, and the three different rooms required for the speaking test?"

At that time I hadn't done anything, but I promised Mary that I would do so the next day. When I tried to book the rooms and equipment the day after, I faced a lot of difficulties. I was given a lot of excuses as to why I couldn't have those items on the required dates. I felt I was being given the run around, in fact I was getting quite worried, so in desperation I rang Mary at the Blackburn Road site.

In response to my phone call she said, "Mudassir, you stay in your staff room I'm coming over."

Within half an hour she was with me. I explained my difficulties to her. She listened to me carefully before enquiring just who I had seen about the rooms.

"Right, we'll sort this all out today," she said in a firm voice. Then she took me to different people. The things I couldn't do in a whole day, Mary got done within an hour. She always had ways of getting things sorted out quickly.

For the listening test in May 1993 Mary and I agreed to meet in the morning at the Sandy Lane site. I thought I would reach Sandy Lane site earlier than Mary at about 8:00am, but to my surprise she was already sitting on the steps of the main entrance waiting for me.

Mary had a firm and powerful voice to control the young students. Nobody dared answer her back. She helped me to organise the seating arrangement for the candidates taking their GCSE exams.

I was grateful for her help during those exams; the only way I could return her favour was to help her in her basic Urdu classes for English people. Sometimes she invited me into her Urdu classes to address them in very simple Urdu. According to Mary I had a perfect Urdu accent. It helped her class in their listening practise. I enjoyed going to Mary's classes as I met some wonderful mature English people learning Urdu.

Mr Austin the principal of the college was always pleasant to me. We mostly greeted each other when passing in the corridors or car park. During my time in the college I met him only a few times, but whenever I met him he was always helpful to me.

Kath Walmsley Mr Austin's secretary was a wonderful girl. She wasn't just a very good secretary; she always had a smile on her face. Whenever I needed her help, she gave it without any hesitation. I don't ever remember her being in a bad mood.

Besides being the vice principal of the college, Tim Atkinson was also the head of the school liaison team. As a member of this team I came in contact with him quite often.

The college received a request from Rhyddings High School for a qualified Urdu tutor to teach Urdu classes to pupils in years 10 and 11. Tim asked me if I would like to teach Urdu to the pupils at the school, but he was mindful of the extra classes I had already set up at the college. I had heard that the children in English schools could be unruly at times. I accepted the chance and took it on as a challenge, and taught GCSE Urdu without encountering any problems there at all.

CHAPTER THIRTY-ONE

Later in the year some pupils in Rhyddings High School told me that two Urdu teachers before me had tried to teach them, but due to the bad behaviour of many of the children, one teacher lasted for a week and the other for only a day.

When I took up that job the children in years 10 and 11 said, "Give him a week. We'll get rid of him soon."

Not only could they not get rid of me from that school, but they also came to my 'A' level classes in Accrington College after passing their GCSE's for further education. I was very pleased indeed to see these children continuing with their education and felt I must have done *something* right!

Now some of my ex-pupils are married with children. They tell me that besides learning the Urdu language in my classes, they also learnt a lot about both Asian and British cultures.

****

Diane Waterhouse was our school liaison team leader at college. I was responsible for attracting students to our college from local high schools. Quite often Diane accompanied me to these schools as guest speaker. I thoroughly enjoyed four or five years in the liaison team.

Dave Tyas the head of languages was always supportive to the Urdu section. Dave and our new team leader Mel Chadwick never objected to my attending Urdu conferences, or staying away over the weekend in London or Cardiff. With their help and approval I managed to obtain a very good stock of Urdu literature for the Urdu section.

As mentioned above, during my first six months in the college I used to notice certain people. Quite a few of them made lasting impressions on me.

One evening I was at the Blackburn Road site ready to teach 'A' levels. I was a bit early, and was making my way to the classroom; at the same time I saw Lindsey Harford coming down the corridor.

"Ah, just the man I wanted to see," she said.

I was a bit surprised to be greeted like that, so I said, "Oh hello, what can I do for you?"

Walking towards her office she said, "Let's go to my office, I want to talk to you."

She made us both a cup of coffee. This was the first time I had spoken to Lindsey socially. I found her very agreeable, interesting and full of knowledge. After talking for a while she asked me a few more things about my background.

"Do you know our senior tutor Mr Finch?" she enquired.

"Yes, I have seen him around," I answered.

She paused for a few seconds before saying, "He would like to see you tonight after your class."

'Oh, what have I done?' I pondered.

I had seen Wilf Finch in different meetings. It could be a union meeting, departmental meeting or any other meeting, whatever it was somehow Wilf always appeared to be the most prominent figure in the audience. He always asked viable questions, making effective comments and statements.

Wilf was the senior lecturer in pre-services courses, and the team leader of the GCSE tutors in college. Before joining Accrington & Rossendale College he had served in the British Army. With having an army background he was a rather strict disciplinarian.

After finishing my class that evening I went straight to see Wilf in his room. It was already quarter past nine and the premises on Blackburn Road were due to close within the next fifteen minutes.

After the usual greetings Wilf said, "Lyndsey and I were talking about you, we wondered if you would like to be one of the GCSE tutors?"

I was pleased, but a bit surprised too, so I asked, "Could I think it over and give you my answer tomorrow?"

"Yes of course, you know where my staff room is."

I was quite excited about it, and as soon as I reached home I mentioned it to Shahnaz and Suhail. Both were very supportive and gave me lots of encouragement.

The next day I went to see Wilf and he gave me details of a group of students. It was made up of a good mixture of young people, consisting of both English and Asian teenagers.

Wilf had five GCSE tutors in his tutorial team. They were Alan, Janice, Helen, Kath and me. In the tutorial group there were always some awkward students. The tutors dealt with most problems by themselves, but there were always some pupils who were a little extra difficult to deal with. Such students were usually referred to Wilf Finch.

If a tutor had a difficult student, he or she would first of all try to take an appropriate action to try to resolve the problem themselves. If this failed they would then write a brief report about the student concerned detailing any action taken. These reports would then be sent off to Wilf Finch, who would give a day, date and time to the tutor, as to when he could see the student in question.

Wilf had a unique way of dealing with awkward and unruly students. He used an army-style technique to deal with most people, particularly with these students.

If I ever had a problem with any students, I would accompany them to Wilf's office, ask them to sit outside and wait, whilst I went in to discuss the student's progress report with Wilf.

When Wilf was ready I would bring the student in to see him.

While the student was standing in front of Wilf's desk, I would take a seat next to Wilf. Without even a glance at the student, Wilf would busy himself reading my comments regarding the student. When he had finished Wilf would then look at the student.

If it was a male student who had his hands in the pockets of his trousers, Wilf would say in a commanding voice, "Take your hands out of your pockets."

This would put an unknown fear into the student, he would instantly obey Wilf. I noticed a few times that some students stood in almost an attention kind of position.

If a student made the mistake of having chewing gum in his mouth, Wilf's commanding voice would roar out, "Get rid of that gum."

If the student looked around wondering where he could dispose it, he would be told to swallow it. The poor student would just do it. As

I mentioned, most students feared Wilf so much, that if I said to any student that he or she would have to go to see Mr Finch, they would become very worried and nervous.

Their reaction was always, "Oh no Sir, I will do whatever you say, but please don't send me to Mr Finch. I will behave myself."

Wilf had such a unique way of correcting misbehaving students, that not only the tutors of **his** team, but other tutors also brought their students to see Wilf.

Wilf was always kind and helpful to me. Twice I made some silly mistakes professionally, on both occasions Wilf came to my rescue, sorting out the matters in such a way that nobody even knew about them.

Margot Clark was the Director of curriculum when I got to know her. I am sure she had a soft spot for me; I could go to see her in her office at any time. On a few occasions she invited me and my family to her house for the evening. Wilf and Margot both visited our house, we all spent many enjoyable evenings in pleasant company.

During the time of my difficulty in arranging and conducting the Urdu exams, I also got to know Ken Holmes the examination officer. Ken was a very pleasant and efficient man; I never had any problem with him. In fact he was very helpful to me in conducting the annual exams, as he said he had full faith in me.

"How can things go wrong with Mudassir; he has been trained by Mary Parsons," he used to say.

I came to know Ann Pilkington the director of student support. In order to conduct the A level speaking exams efficiently and with perfection, I needed an almost soundproof room, free from any interference. Ann Pilkington's office was the perfect choice for this.

The first time I asked to use her office by writing an official letter to her, Ann readily agreed for me to use it. On top of everything else, she also allowed me to use her own kettle, tea, coffee and milk; it felt like being at home.

Ann was always available for the students; she helped them to solve their problems. I witnessed her efforts in helping Asian students. I was often involved in meeting the parents of such students.

Almost every year 'The Council for the Development of Urdu' held its annual conference in different towns in England. That particular year the Council held its conference in London.

The language department of the college allowed me to attend. The day before the said conference I reached London and stayed at the Hilton Hotel.

The next morning I reached the conference centre. As I was a bit early, I began looking around in the centre's yard when I noticed a car entering the gate which then pulled up beside me.

The Englishman in the car wound his window down, in clear pronunciation he greeted me, "Assalam-o-Alaikum."

"Walaikum Assalm." I responded instantly.

Coming out of the car and speaking in Urdu he said, "Aap kaisay hain? (How are you?)"

Thinking that he had learnt some basic spoken Urdu, I replied, "Main Theek hoon, shukria. (I'm all right, thank you)"

But I was a bit surprised when he spoke in perfectly pronounced Urdu, "I believe this is the right hall for the conference?"

"Yes, I think so too," I answered, walking towards the hall.

By now our conversation was entirely in Urdu.

Climbing the steps of conference hall he said, "Can I ask your name? Your voice sounds very familiar."

I responded to his question saying, "I'm Mudassir Khan; I'm from Accrington & Rossendale College."

He stopped on the last step and almost screamed, "So *you* are Mudassir, I have been listening to your 'A' level speaking tests for EDEXEL."

I got a bit concerned, and in order to discover his reaction I asked nervously, "What did you think?"

"What did I think? They are wonderful," he told me.

By that time more people started arriving. I asked, "Can I have your name please?"

"I'm Martin Dodd," he told me.

I was both amazed and pleasantly surprised to finally meet Martin Dodd the chief Urdu examiner like that.

Dr Martin Dodd did his doctorate in Urdu, and spent some time in Karachi, Lahore, Delhi and Lucknow. For a few years he was the 'A' level's Chief Urdu Examiner for EDEXEL. He spoke better Urdu, than I could speak English. I had previously heard about another gentleman known as Ralph Russel, who also spoke good Urdu. I had never had a chance to speak to him, but apart from Dr Martin Dodd who impressed me very much with his spoken Urdu, there was Dr David Mathews, who I must admit spoke even better Urdu than some of our educated Asians.

****

As mentioned in the previous chapters, after two interviews I was appointed as a JP in 1993. The JPs appointed that year were to take an oath in Preston in the presence of two judges.

It was a big day for me and my family as we all travelled to the Crown Court at Preston. I was pleasantly surprised to meet Zubeda Chaudry and Michael Amery. Zubeda had worked in Blackburn's CAB with me, whilst Michael was my contact in Pleckgate School for Accrington & Rossendale College.

In front of Judge Bennett and another judge, one by one we stood with a raised hand to take our oath as JPs. After taking our oaths we had informal chats with the judges and fellow JPs. There I met a wonderful and happy-go-lucky person, Graham Forrest. He is a very ordinary and down-to-earth person. I later sat with him on the magistrates' bench many times, and we also went on the same training sessions in Garstang.

Mudassir and his colleagues after swearing their oaths as JPs in Preston.

I found Michael Emery to be ever so pleasant and helpful, not just in school, but also in Blackburn courts. I was so moved when Michael came to see me in Queens Park Hospital during my illness. I had always enjoyed going to see him in Pleckgate School.

During my illness and stay in hospital I received a lot of get well cards from my fellow JPs, visits by Vanessa Townson, Douglas Norris and others. I used to see Vanessa in Beardwood School, where we talked about young students.

Douglas Norris impressed me a lot as a bench chairman. He is a very intelligent, witty, and a straightforward gentleman. So many times I noticed, that even in the most difficult cases, he would consult his wingers first, before giving his own version and opinion of the case.

At the time I was appointed JP there were no mentors to look after, or take care of newly appointed JPs, as is the usual practice now. At that time however, Douglas Norris gave me a lot of moral support and his expert guidance. I always enjoyed sitting with him as his winger.

Other people I enjoyed sitting with on the magistrates' bench were Elaine Holden, Margaret Shuttleworth, the late Ann Marsden,

Edna Egleston, Susan Teal, Mrs Craven, Mrs Hill, Mr Rawcliffe, Mr Blackburn and Mr Geoff Hill; in fact the list is endless.

Amongst my Asian fellow JPs, Mian Chopdat and Mr Mohammed Sufi come to mind as I always enjoyed their company. Mr Sufi had been a very active member of the Blackburn and Darwen Bench arranging visits to the local mosques and madresahs for interested magistrates.

I have known Elaine Holden for a long time. Actually my wife Kath has worked for Mrs Holden for almost thirty years. Whenever I had time I used to go to pick Kath up from the Holden's residence. Mrs Holden always found time to talk to me.

Many times I sat with Mrs Holden as a winger, and I learnt a great deal, such as how to address the accused or a solicitor. I must admit that when I had completed my training to take the chairmanship on the bench, I was rather nervous. Again Mrs Holden came to my rescue, and sat with me as a winger, while I took the chair. On my first day as chair of the bench, she gave me a lot of support and encouragement.

It would be very wrong of me if I didn't mention Mr Laurence Loft, a barrister and clerk to the justices. Laurence is one of those people in Blackburn who are so intelligent, cheerful and have been blessed with a wonderful memory. There were more than a hundred justices in Blackburn, Darwen and the Ribble Valley while I was on the bench. What amazed me was that Laurence knew almost all of the magistrates by their first names. Not only that, but if introduced, he would remember the first names of the magistrate's partners too!

On my very first visit to observe the procedure of the courts I sat on the side bench of Court 2. On that particular day Mrs Christine Davies was the court clerk. There were three magistrates on the bench. I can't remember the name of the chairperson, but I noticed that it was a lady in the chair.

The court proceedings were moving along smoothly, Mrs Davies's powerful voice was echoing throughout the courtroom dealing with the cases. In the next case a young defendant was in the dock. After confirming his name, age and address, Mrs Davies read out the charges.

After listening to the prosecution and defence the magistrates retired to consult, and to reach their decision. After a while they came back. The chairperson was about to announce their verdict, when all of a sudden the young defendant jumped over the docks and made for the door trying to escape.

"Arrest that man," the chairperson ordered, in an authoritative voice.

The usher of the court grabbed the young man before he reached the door. He received an extra punishment for his actions. For a while there was a bit of confusion in the court, but within minutes the chairperson had restored order and continued to deal with two other cases.

Later on when the court business was over, Mrs Davies said to me, "I can assure you Mr Khan, incidents like that don't happen every day. It was just unfortunate that it happened on your first visit."

I was pleased to hear that!

During my twelve years with Blackburn, Darwen and the Ribble Valley courts, I sat with different court clerks. They were all intelligent and knowledgeable, and always helpful and supportive to the justices. After all they were well qualified in the law. Although they would explain the law to the justices, they would never make a decision for them, as the decision making is left entirely up to the justices.

Mrs Gillian Simpson, the office support officer at the Magistrate's Court kept all the JPs and other staff informed regarding meetings, training, and other events.

If I ever wanted information, or needed to change my 'sittings' on any particular day, Mrs Simpson would readily do it for me. She also gave me a lot of support prior to my by-pass operation.

Besides Mrs Davies I sat with Miss Janet Wright, Mrs Rosemary Jamieson, Mr Neil Lucas, Mr Jonathan Salem and Mr Tariq Ali.

During my twelve years in Blackburn as a JP, I also had the honour of taking a seat in the appeal courts with Judge Bennett and others in Burnley and Preston Crown Courts. It was part of my training.

CHAPTER THIRTY-TWO

I had heard of Imtiaz Patel, first as a friend and associate of Shakeel Salam in the Asian news agency, and I had briefly met him once. It was one afternoon while I was coming out of the central library that I first met Imtiaz at the main door. He is well-known for his wonderful manners and the respect he shows to his elders. Imtiaz told me that he was working for Blackburn Council as the development officer of Asian culture in Blackburn museum.

During our conversation he said, "I'm compiling the experiences of Asians in Blackburn. I'm told that you have been in Blackburn for a long time. Would you take part in recording your early experiences in Blackburn?"

I agreed to Imtiaz's request and a few days later he, along with Christine Healey, came to our house in Leamington Road with a tape recorder. Imtiaz used this recording in the Asian Art Gallery. I was told later that my early findings and feelings about being in Blackburn were listened to with interest by schoolchildren and the general public visiting the museum. This resulted in a few young students from different schools wishing to meet me.

Imtiaz collected a lot of interesting items representing Asian culture from India and Pakistan. Later on he became a councillor in Blackburn, and involved himself in national politics joining the Lib Dem Party.

One morning I received a letter from Imtiaz Patel inviting me to a meeting, which was arranged in one of the rooms in the town hall building. At that meeting I met some very familiar faces. Some I knew very well, but over the years had lost touch with them; others I knew by face but hadn't as yet been introduced to.

One of them was Mr Abdul Hamid Piracha, a very well-known figure in Blackburn. I remembered him from the time when he was in the final year of his textile course in Blackburn College, and at that time I had just arrived from Pakistan to join the textiles course myself.

In the 1950's the overseas students, particularly those from the Indian sub-continent, were keen to become even more English than the English people themselves. The senior students tended to speak more English than their own language even to their fellow countrymen. Newly-arrived students like myself, were very hesitant to speak in English because of our lack of confidence and fluency.

I followed the advice of senior students in Blackburn as I had with the senior passport officer in Karachi. Some advice was suitable and useful, such as buying a raincoat, an overcoat, a scarf and a pair of gloves, but I couldn't bring myself to buy a trilby or a flat cap. I tried on these head coverings in a few shops, but when I looked at myself in the mirror I thought I looked a proper 'Charlie'. Eventually I gave up on the idea of buying either a trilby or a flat cap.

The one single image that always reminded me of my first ever meeting with Mr Piracha so many years ago, was that I always used to see him with his trilby, always trying to blend into the background in the town centre. Unfortunately it wasn't very easy for him to blend in as not many Asians wore this headwear.

By the time I got to know the Asian students in Blackburn in 1956 and '57, the senior students had left college; however images of their faces stayed with me for a long time.

CHAPTER THIRTY-THREE

It was the middle or late 1960's, when I was working in Wm. Birtwistle's Waterfall Mill. I used to catch the Greenbank or Moor Nook bus from the railway station. A few times I had noticed an intelligent looking Asian man sitting in the bus. He would always be busy reading a book called *Friends, not Masters*. It was the autobiography of the President of Pakistan, Field Marshal Ayub Khan.

The young man reading the book never noticed that I was watching him. He used to get off the bus in Havelock Street. I later found out that he was Mr Piracha and worked at Silk Velvet.

Though he had met me during college time, he didn't recognise me on the bus, and as I'm basically a very shy person, I didn't feel like imposing myself on him. In 1982 I met Mr Piracha again when I was going to Hyderabad Sind with my family.

Mr Piracha's son Shahid had started a travel agency in Victoria Street. Mr Piracha used to help Shahid out by taking phone calls and booking seats for their customers.

I had bought our British Airways tickets to Karachi through Shahid's agency, in fact Mr Piracha himself had personally handed over the four tickets to me, but unfortunately he *still* didn't recognise me. However I got to know Mr Piracha better when I met him in a meeting at Mr Rehman Qureshi's residence.

As a graduate from the famous Muslim University Aligarh (India), and a college diploma holder in textile technology from Blackburn College, Mr Piracha's career took him to Eastern and Middle Eastern Countries such as Pakistan, Iraq, and other places. In the end he settled down in Blackburn with his family, taking an active part in local politics, but only once was he elected councillor in Blackburn Borough Council.

For his political activities and good work for the community at large, he has been recognised and awarded a few times by local and national dignitaries and authorities. In 2005 he was presented to the British Prime Minister Tony Blair and Jack Straw the MP for Blackburn in recognition of his work for the community. He is a member of several local organisations. In fact Ashiana, a housing organisation, is Mr Piracha's brainchild. He developed this organisation from scratch.

At the same meeting I met Abdul Rehman Qureshi. I had seen him at different Asian community meetings in Blackburn, but was never previously introduced. He turned out to be quite a literary man. Like me, he always enjoyed attending Mushairas (poetry reciting meetings). Mr Rehman Qureshi has a unique and likeable Urdu accent, and I have always enjoyed his company.

Amongst the others present in that meeting was Mr Afzal H. Quraishi. The very first time I noticed him was in the early 90's when he was with his family in the same Urdu drama in Blackburn College, where I met Dr Nasir-ud-Din Ahmed.

Prior to my introduction to Afzal Quraishi I had met his wife Mrs Aquila Quraishi. She worked in the town hall for Blackburn Borough Council in their housing department.

Mrs Quraishi invited us to her residence to meet her daughter Fariha. At that time Salim Sameja and I were following a story for the *Blackburn Independent.* Mrs Quraishi gave us some details regarding that story, and at the same time she told us about her daughter Fariha Quraishi, who was very interested in writing for the newspapers.

We went to Mrs Quraishi's residence where we met Mr Afzal Quraishi and Fariha. The very sociable and fearless Fariha was a Liverpool University student. Although she is outspoken, Fariha is always cultured, civil and well mannered. She joined the Independent team, and took charge of editing the women's section. Fariha became a very important member of the team, and contributed to the initial success of the *Lancashire Independent.*

In the summer of 2000 or 2001 Mr Piracha called a meeting of selected people to Mr A. R. Qureshi's residence to form a 'Friends of Pakistan Forum'. Eight or nine people attended that meeting. I was familiar with most of them, but there were one or two faces that I wasn't sure of. One face struck me as being very familiar.

Unfortunately I couldn't at that moment place as to where I had seen him before.

One by one we introduced ourselves to the meeting, one man said, "My name is Mian Mazhar Hussain, and I come from Haslingden."

I instantly recognised that it was the same person I was thinking of. In fact Mazhar Hussain had travelled with me from Karachi to Liverpool on *RMS Circacia,* and from Lime Street Railway Station Liverpool to Blackburn all those years ago. Mazhar had to change trains to go to Burnley.

At the end of the meeting, where Mr Rehman Qureshi had provided a wonderful and tasty buffet I, with my plate filled with food, went over to Mian Mazhar and asked him, "Didn't you come to England in 1956?"

"Yes," he replied.

He gave me a surprised look and to add to his surprise I said, "Did you come by Anchor Line's ship called the *Circasia?"*

Now it wasn't just Mazhar who was attentive to me, but other people in the room were also interested in our conversation.

I continued speaking to him, "You came to Burnley College for further studies."

"Yes, yes, but how do you *know* all this?" Mian Mazhar asked curiously.

He couldn't believe it when I told him, "I too was a passenger on *Circacia*. I used to be with the other students, Malik from Lahore, Rizvi from Karachi, the two brothers Ghaffar and Sattar from Karachi, Ghosh from Calcutta, Bhatti from Llyalpur and others. The two brothers Ghaffar and Sattar had already completed the first year of their diploma course in textiles at Blackburn College. Their father owned textile mills in Karachi."

Then I reminded Mazhar about himself. "You were on leave without pay from TDA textile mill. After completing your apprenticeship you worked as a supervisor in the mill. In order to improve your chances of promotion in this field you decided to go abroad for higher qualifications."

Mazhar and the other people there were listening to me in amazement. Then I reminded him about his TDA blazer. I saw him wearing it quite often on the ship and whenever I met him in Blackburn or Burnley. After completing our studies in Blackburn and Burnley colleges we somehow lost touch with each other.

I would never have thought that I would meet somebody again after forty-five years. I found out that after completing his course, Mazhar had temporarily worked for different firms in Burnley. Then he went to Pakistan with the intention of settling down there, but because of unfavourable circumstances he returned to England.

Some time later Mr Piracha and his group arranged an Eid-Party, to which my wife and I were invited. Upon reaching the venue, I was pleased to see one of my colleagues and an ex-student of mine at Accrington College, Samina Riffat. I found out that she was Mazhar's wife.

'Isn't it a small world?' I thought.

After returning from Pakistan, besides his full-time job, Mian Mazhar had decided to work for the Asian community, as well as the host community. He had set up Asian organisations and headed the CRC in Burnley and Haslingden. He devoted himself to helping Asians who settled in these towns, and worked hard to improve Race Relations.

Mian Mazhar Hussain's wife Samina Riffat had been as active as her husband. Besides her full-time job as a lecturer at Accrington College, she also organised several social activities.

At that meeting at Rehman Qureshi's house I met Mr Nisar Sayyed who had come to Blackburn as a student. I first saw Mr Sayyed at the door of a lodging house in London Road in 1956. I had gone there to see a friend, but he was not in, and Mr Sayyed informed me in English that my friend was out.

The second time I had a chance to see Mr Sayyed was in 1957. Pakistani students in Blackburn held an event at Queens Hall in Darwen Street. The main item in the programme was a snake charmer's dance, which was performed by none other than Mr Nisar Sayyed himself.

At that same meeting at Mr Rehman Qureshi's house, Mr Piracha put forward a proposal to form an organisation with the name of 'Friends of Pakistan Forum'. Mr Afzal Quraishi was elected as the general secretary of the forum, while Mr Piracha and Rehman

Qureshi were elected chairman and treasurer respectively. The rest of the people in the meeting joined the forum as members.

Afzal Quraishi, a retired successful physiotherapist, devoted himself to working for the forum as its general secretary. Mr Quraishi is a quiet sort of person, but he is filled with knowledge and enthusiasm. Like other members of the Friends Forum, Afzal Qureshi is very much interested in Urdu poetry. He is an active person, who likes things moving and constructive work being done on time.

The forum organised several Urdu Mushairas (Urdu poetry reciting meetings), Pakistan Independence Days and other important events. At one of the events organised by the Forum we had managed to gather a good crowd from both the Asian and host communities. Amongst the crowd were also some so-called Asian community leaders. They were very politely asked if they would like to join the forum. They took the membership forms with them, promising that they would join the Forum straightaway.

Within a week, the *same* so-called leaders who had promised to support us formed their own group more or less on the same basis. This action was just to sabotage the chances of success for the 'Friends of Pakistan Forum'.

I had already warned the Forum's officials about the mentality of these types of people. I have had both good and bitter experiences dealing with them since 1958, but sometimes I was terribly disappointed.

In 2003 the Friends of the Pakistan Forum organised an event to celebrate Pakistan Day. Formal invitations were sent to local host and Asian community leaders and dignitaries. The response was very encouraging, as most of the dignitaries accepted these invitations. As the date of the event approached, the forum started receiving apologies from the same leaders, particularly the Asians, who had readily accepted an invitation earlier. Actually it was an act of sabotage from other organisations and their leaders.

As I had suspected, the Asian leaders turned the forum's invitation down, because the forum's organisers did not come from the area of Pakistan that the majority of Blackburn Pakistanis come from.

In Blackburn there are two major ethnic communities, Punjabis and Gujratis. Mainly the Punjabis come from Pakistan and the Gujratis from India. If one didn't speak Punjabi, one wouldn't be accepted as a Pakistani, likewise if one didn't speak Gujrati one would not be taken as an Indian.

It was unfortunate that some of the forum's officials and members were Urdu speakers. They were taken as **neither** Indian nor Pakistani. Many times I have experienced this feeling myself as I only speak Urdu and English.

****

In previous pages I have briefly mentioned Salim Sameja as to how we met and got involved in *The Lancashire Independent.* Salim is a multi-talented man, as whatever task or situation he comes across he handles it well and comes out successfully.

While editing and running the paper Salim was offered a job in 1991 researching and producing the Asian programme in English and Urdu on BBC Radio Lancashire and BBC GMR. He accepted this position and introduced several news, current affairs and educational programmes for Asians and a wider audience.

In 1996 he applied for, and was successful in getting, the post of a recruitment officer at Staffordshire Police. He worked diligently and within two years he was transferred to Greater Manchester Police in June 1998 to take up the post of the Community Development Officer for North Manchester.

Within a year Salim had established himself as a very successful CDO. His suggestions to promote harmony and better understanding between the increasing Asian population in Manchester and the Police, were widely recognised and given full approval. He arranged meetings, seminars and conferences relating to community relations and racial awareness. At the same time he involved young people into helping him to eradicate racism.

Besides organising seminars and conferences, Salim highlighted the importance of stamping out the cultural and language barriers between the diverse Asian community and the Police. Again his bosses agreed to support his initiative to introduce tailored Asian Cultural Awareness sessions, and Basic Communication Urdu course classes over a period of twelve weeks.

One day I was approached by Salim Sameja who asked me if I would be interested in taking up a position teaching spoken Urdu to the police to help them with their communication? He told me that he had put my name forward upon hearing what the police officers needed.

I was rather interested to hear more about this kind of work, so Salim directed me as to whom I should see to get full details of the work involved.

I was informed that they needed a person to teach basic spoken Urdu to the officers, so they would be able to communicate with the growing number of Asians in their areas.

After meetings and discussions with former Superintendent Harry Campbell and former Chief Inspector Margaret Parker, I was pleased to start the lectures and Urdu classes in September 1998.

****

On my first Asian Cultural Awareness lecture, as I entered the room all the officers were sitting with their arms folded across their chests looking very disinterested.

I decided on a different approach. I introduced myself to them and started talking rather generally about my family. Then I mentioned my elder brother Muzammil who had just retired from the Karachi police.

As soon as I told them about my observations of police behaviour in the Indian sub-continent, and of the officers like my brother, they all relaxed. At the same time I asked them if they had watched *Karachi Kops* on television; they all joined me in a very lively discussion. This was a good ice-breaker.

It took about ten minutes for them to unwind, but it was well worth it, because when I started the Cultural Awareness lecture they were all attentive. As I reached the topic of 'arranged marriages' I involved the officers in acting in order to explain it properly. I chose two officers to act as the parents of the boy, and two others to pretend to be the girl's parents. Then I acted the part of being the middleman. During my explanations they were howling with laughter. I was kept very busy answering their questions during the discussion on such subjects as food and fashion.

Then we had more laughs as I explained the topic of four wives allowed for Muslims and the divorce system.

At the end of class they all applauded. I never expected any applause at all, but this was wonderful and so spontaneous.

I am proud to mention here that the officers in my class enjoyed and liked my style of delivering lectures. On completion of that twelve week session I was presented with a GMP plaque, a tie and tie-pin, as well as a set of GMP cuff-links.

To this day I still proudly wear these occasionally. Once or twice when I have attended weddings, both English and Asian, I wore the GMP tie, tie-pin and the cuff links. Quite a few people took an interest in these as they were curious about the origin of the gifts. I am always pleased to reminisce with pride, concerning my association with the police.

I must also mention that all the officers in all of my classes were courteous, very interested and keen to learn. Whenever I think back, some faces and names still come in mind, I pleasantly remember that period as being a wonderful time for me, and hopefully for the officers too.

I was reminded of an incident when one of my student officers, in full police uniform, went into an Asian shop to make some purchases. This officer greeted the shopkeeper in Urdu; then she continued to ask for some items, also in Urdu.

For about thirty seconds the shopkeeper just stared at her open-mouthed. He said, "I'll answer your question later; but please tell me where you learnt such a wonderful Urdu accent?"

The officer told him about the recent lessons, and also mentioned the Urdu lecturer from Accrington College. That was a wonderful endorsement and a credit to the officer.

There was another officer who previously had only attended seven or eight of my Urdu classes, when he was involved in interviewing a suspected illegal immigrant. This suspect didn't have an adequate knowledge of English, so the officer then used his newly acquired skill and spoke to him in Urdu! Within a short period, perhaps to the disappointment of the suspect, the officer managed to get the information he required.

Unfortunately it is not easy to remember every student, but I am able to at least acknowledge some of the many who gave me so much pleasure with their cheerfulness during the lectures.

These officers were, Simon B, Mark K, John E, Judith G, Brian D, Guy T, Colin O, Andy M, Judith S, Andy P, Gary G, Lisa M, Anna G, Lois B, Julie T, Ross H, Ron F, and last but not least, Simon G. I am terribly sorry but some names have escaped my memory, and for this I do sincerely apologise.

Finally none of this would have been possible without the support of senior officers like, Mr Campbell and Mrs Parker, Mr Cantrell and Mr Simon G. No matter which police station I used to attend in North Manchester, the welcome was always warm and friendly.

I must also add that none of this would have been possible without the foresight of Salim, who initiated the full programme to support the officers. I hold such a high regard for Salim for his professionalism, and I am sure it was fully appreciated by his colleagues.

Mastering the basics of spoken Urdu, took about ten weeks on average, which fit nicely into the twelve weeks that were allocated for each group. I was able to teach many police officers, as one batch finished their course, a new batch began theirs.

Certificate presentation to Greater Manchester police officers for successfully completing their Urdu course.

Prior to my heart attack in January 2001 Salim had arranged a twelve week Basics Communication Course for the Oldham Police in the same way as had been used for the Greater Manchester Police.

Amongst the other police officers enrolled in my class was the former Chief Superintendent Eric Hewitt. He too was very keen to learn Urdu.

Unfortunately I was taken ill after just two sessions. I received many ‘get well soon’ cards, not just from other officers, but Mr Hewitt also sent me a personal letter. I was terribly sorry that I couldn’t carry on teaching the Oldham Police.

The police officers thoroughly enjoyed the course and learnt to speak basic Urdu. They told me that they found their newly acquired language skills very helpful to them in their work, as they were now able to speak to the Asian people in their areas.

I was so delighted to have helped to bridge the gap between the two communities in my small way, in order to allow them both to converse, which naturally made things a little more harmonious on both sides, as now they could at least understand one another a little better. Furthermore with me discussing our Asian culture and our way of life, the police officers had gained a much better insight into the Asian way of life.

Mudassir being presented a gift by (North Manchester Division) Police Officers in appreciation of him teaching them Urdu.

CHAPTER THIRTY-FOUR

At the turn of the Millennium I was excited because I was going to retire in June 2000. I should have retired in 1998, as my real year of birth is 1933, and not 1935 as is stated on my documents.

At the time of my admission into primary school, with all good intentions, my father made a deliberate mistake to put my year of birth as 1935 instead of 1933. This meant that I had to work an extra two years before I could qualify for my state pension and other benefits, hence my retirement in June 2000. It would be appropriate to mention here as to why my father made this 'deliberate mistake'.

At the time of my birth the whole of India was under the British Raj. With India being a huge country, and heavily populated, certain agencies such as births, deaths, and marriage registrations were confined to the big cities. In small places or remote villages, people didn't bother going to big cities to register these events.

I was born when my father was an assistant station master. On a station of that size nobody bothered to register births, deaths or marriages. Still somebody noted down my *real* date of birth as 16th June 1933 in an old family poetry book.

Once my father explained to me why he had made this deliberate error. Apparently during the British Raj in India it was one of the Government rules that to join the Government services one had to be under a certain age. If one was well qualified for the post, but over that age limit, he or she could not apply for the job.

So my father thought that if I failed one or two of my high school, college or university exams, I would still be eligible to apply for a Government job.

****

Besides myself, Diane Waterhouse was also taking her retirement in June 2000, and Mel Chadwick, Janet Royston and Munawwar Jan Leyland were all leaving at the same time. The leaving parties started in May 2000.

In my 'Goodbye Mudassir party' the whole humanities team, headed by Mel Chadwick came to have lunch with me, and to wish me luck. It was a wonderful afternoon spent with all my colleagues. I was both surprised and delighted to receive a letter from Mr Austin inviting me to have lunch with the senior management team on the 4th July 2000. It was great to see Mr M. Austin, as well as the vice principals Mr T. Atkinson and Mrs Angela Smith, head of the personnel department and others in the Globe House Restaurant, Accrington.

During conversation over lunch I must have mentioned my early days in Blackburn as a student, and the incident in Clitheroe with a young boy who wanted to bring his young friends and show them what coloured people looked like, which had caused my friend and I to almost run from there.

It was customary in Accrington & Rossendale College that the Principal addressed the college staff twice a year. Once in the first week of July before the summer holidays, and also in December just before Christmas.

In his address Mr Austin would go through the past six months stating progresses, activities, as well as details of staff leaving and joining the college.

On the last day of the first week of July 2000 at about 11:00am, the main hall of college was filled with lecturers, staff from maintenance, catering, administration, security as well as staff from other sites of college. As it was my last day in the college Kath came along with me. She was going to sit in my staff room during the Principal's speech, but Margo Clark spotted her there and dragged her out into the hall.

Mr Austin came to the rostrum to deliver his speech. Everybody was quiet and attentive to him as usual.

Mr Austin started his speech by saying, "I would like you to imagine 1956 when Elvis Presley was just coming up and it was the Teddy Boys era, when a young man and his friend were passing through an area in Clitheroe…"

****

At that moment I knew what he was going to say, so I put my head down. Mr Austin went through the whole incident in such a way that the whole hall was filled with loud laughter. Then he said some wonderful words about me, my services to the college, and my GCSE and 'A' level results with 100% passes in grades A-C every year. It was a wonderful day for me and my wife. We spent the whole afternoon in student services.

****

Some of my close Asian friends accuse me of having too much admiration and praise for the British people, British Government and British departments for their sense of priorities, responsibilities and honesty.

I would like to mention here the unexpected pleasant surprise I got in May 2000. On the 9th or 10th May 2000 I received a letter from Blackburn Benefits Agency, stating that a firm called Lambert Fenchurch had been trying to locate me for a while in connection with a pension. The Benefits Agency wanted me to get in touch with Lambert Fenchurch at Preston as soon as possible. On hearing this I promptly contacted them.

Upon meeting a young lady in Lambert Fenchurch, she told me about an insurance policy that had been taken out on my behalf by Blackburn Cord Company in 1975. Then she showed me the amount I was going to receive. Looking at the amount I was going to get, I almost dropped, for it had accumulated into a rather large sum.

I had forgotten about Blackburn Cord and its insurance. They could have easily claimed that they had tried to locate Mudassir Khan but couldn't find him. But this insurance company had kept on trying, so in the end through the Benefits Agency they were able to trace me. They not only presented me with the cheque, but they also offered me their expert investment advice.

This is just one of so many reasons why I have placed my trust in the integrity of the majority of the British people, hopefully this helps to explain why I hold such a high regard for them.

****

Although I had taken my retirement in June 2000, I had some students in their second year of 'A' level Urdu. I didn't want to disappoint anyone by leaving them halfway through, so I accepted that I would teach that class only, to allow them the opportunity of getting good grades in their final exams.

CHAPTER THIRTY-FIVE

I have always enjoyed taking part in 'live' phone-in programmes of different local and national radio stations. Through the regional radio I came into contact with, and got to know some wonderful and interesting people. Like many other listeners I enjoy taking part in political and social programmes, as well as participating in debates, discussions and reading selected poetry of Indo-Pakistan's famous poets. Many times I would enjoy taking the 'other view', sometimes with tongue in cheek, just to stimulate different views.

Over the past twelve years or so since I developed my interest in local and regional media, some of the listeners who have become familiar with my voice 'on air' have wanted to meet me personally, but nearly always I kept evading them. One of these listeners was Suraiya Bahen. I had heard she was so keen to meet me, that she had instructed her grown-up children to keep a look out for a Mudassir Bhai. She told them that I could be in the town centre, library or in a car park. The amazing thing was that neither she nor her family had any idea who I was, let alone what I looked like.

All that changed when she eventually spotted me with my wife Kathleen, when we both appeared in the audience of a BBC Television programme, *'Kilroy'*. It was after appearing on this programme that she finally managed to persuade me to make contact with her. When we eventually met, we soon became good family friends and have remained on good family terms ever since.

The other young person who impressed me a lot is Faiqa. Although she was new to being on the air, her style of reading poetry and taking part in live radio discussions was different and unique. Being young, modern and enthusiastic, she formed a group of listeners and callers for the radio station. The group holds light-hearted events twice a year where Faiqa puts in a great deal of work. She is a multi-talented girl, and is always busy creating something new for her family and friends.

Hafeez Bottar and I have a high regard and respect for each other. Although he is a highly educated person he never brags about it. He has full command over all three languages, English, Urdu and Punjabi. In fact he holds a Master's degree in the Punjabi language.

Many people like to listen to his Punjabi poetry on the radio. As I have always been very fond of this language myself, but didn't have a chance to learn this sweet language in a proper manner, I asked Hafeez to teach it to me with a proper accent. I am proud to say that now I can communicate in Punjabi, and sometimes I have even recited Punjabi poetry on the air.

****

Since my retirement in 2000 I have had three heart attacks. The first one in November 2000 was a mild one, which was taken as a warning to me to slow down. It kept me in Queens Park Hospital for a week. I suffered the second one in January 2001, which this time was a severe one.

It was about 3:30 in the afternoon of 22nd January 2001; I was listening to Tahir Khan's phone-in programme on Asian Sound Radio. Tahir Khan used to give very interesting topics to discuss on the air. On that particular day he had given a very touchy and controversial topic to talk about on the air.

I wished to take part in the programme so I phoned Asian Sound Radio; I was placed on hold waiting to come on the air. I waited for quite a long time. Tahir Khan kept talking to other callers, who in my opinion were talking rubbish.

At this point I was getting worked up; I could feel the tightness in my chest. I kept grumbling to my wife who was in the same room watching television. I was listening to the programme on a walkman radio wearing earplugs.

I was listening, but all of a sudden I lost interest in the programme and started to feel breathless. At the same time I felt I needed to go to the bathroom, but as I rushed I became even more breathless.

I shouted to Kath from the landing, "Will you bring some pillows for me?"

Kath brought the pillows for me, as I thought I wanted to lie down. I don't remember everything properly, but I do have a vague idea. I lay down on the landing with the pillows under my head, but I just couldn't stay there as I was feeling very restless, and whilst lying down I could feel I was becoming more breathless.

At this point I realised there was something very wrong with me. I asked Kath to ring for an ambulance. Within seven minutes the ambulance arrived. There were two paramedics, one a middle-aged man, and the other a girl in her twenties.

They were both very cheerful and put me at ease straightaway. The girl prepared a soluble aspirin in a tumbler, while the man got an injection ready. Unfortunately the man was having difficulty in locating any veins on my wrist for this injection.

They talked to each other then decided to wheel me to the ambulance. For twenty odd minutes we were in the ambulance, during which time the paramedics were constantly in touch with the hospital. In the end the male paramedic managed to find my vein and injected something into me.

Kath opted to follow the ambulance in our car, so that without troubling anybody at the hospital, she could get home.

Our son Suhail reached home at about 6:15pm but couldn't understand why the furniture in the room was not in its proper place, or why the doors of the living room and hallway were left wide open. Unfortunately in the midst of the upset, Kath had forgotten to leave a note for him.

As soon as we reached Blackburn Royal Infirmary's heart-care ward, two nurses immediately attended to me, giving me some more injections in order to stabilise me.

It would be a lie if I stated here that I wasn't scared; in fact I was terribly frightened, as I was constantly getting short of breath and the pain in my chest was increasing, but after the last injection I felt a lot better. As I was in good hands and needed to rest, Kath left at about 8:00pm.

It was about 11:00pm when I had another attack of pain in my chest. I managed to tell the nurse and she gave me a tablet to put under my tongue which helped to reduce the pain in my chest. However within a few minutes I was running short of breath again and feeling restless.

As the nurses were monitoring my condition closely, one of them noticed a change in my condition, and placed an oxygen mask on my face covering my nose and mouth. I was quite aware of what was going on, but I remained breathless.

At that moment I did think, ‘Am I dying?’

Having that thought in my mind I recited the ‘Kalima’ and threw my head back onto the pillow. I vaguely remember there were at least three doctors and three or four nurses round my bed. I’m sure they must have also thought that I was taking my last breath.

The last voice I heard was a female saying, “Give him 95%.” After that I didn’t remember anything.

It was just a coincidence that the patient on the next bed to me was having a second heart attack. A team of doctors and nurses were working hard to stabilise him. They told me the next day that he had recovered within an hour.

It was about five o’clock in the morning when I woke up and saw two nurses sitting one on either side of my bed. As soon as they saw me awake, one of them leaned over me saying, “You had a rough night, didn’t you? How do you feel now?”

“I’m all right, thank you. Have you been at my bedside all night?” I enquired.

At their affirmative answer, I was filled up emotionally.

I thought to myself, ‘I’m not even known to them, I have never met them, I’m not related to them in any way, so how come these young nurses would spend the whole night sitting beside me? I will never forget their kindness and continuous reassurance that I’d be all right and recover to the full.’

One nurse brought a bowl and a jug of warm water for me to have a shave and wash; then later on a much welcomed cup of tea. I must mention here how dedicated and caring these nurses and doctors are to their profession. They deal with all their patients with a smile; they don’t lose their cool even with awkward patients.

One of the nurses got in touch with Victoria Hospital in Blackpool, so that I could be sent there for an Angiogram. It is another story how the heart specialist at Blackburn Infirmary overruled her decision.

I was kept in the Coronary Care Ward in Blackburn Infirmary for two days, before being moved to Queens Park Hospital on 24th January 2001. They kept me there for sixteen days. During my stay quite a few doctors and heart specialists came to examine me. The heart specialist informed me that my most recent heart attack was probably caused by a clot in the left ventricle of my heart. He assured me that it could be dissolved with medication. At the same time Dr Chatterji a heart consultant, also informed me that the muscles of my heart were very weak, but with some gentle exercises the weakness could be overcome.

During my sixteen day stay at Queens Park Hospital I got to know most of the nurses, auxiliaries and other staff. On Ward 3 the patients were mostly elderly. As most of the time I felt fine, I thought I would use my time to talk to these patients. Because I had lived in Blackburn, Bolton and Preston since 1956, I could speak to them about the late 50's era easily, and get them thinking and talking about the times when they themselves were young.

One morning a nurse came to me and said, "Do you know any lady in the next female bay?"

"No not really," I answered.

With a big smile the nurse said, "A woman in the next bay has asked me to ask 'that nice Indian gentleman' to come and talk to her."

I went over to the bay to see her. She was feeling a bit depressed, but when I started talking to her about her childhood and the times when she was of a younger age, she soon came round. She started talking about the time when she was a teenager; in those days she used to go to King George's Hall, Tony's Ballroom or the cinemas. I started naming the cinema halls in Blackburn. Within minutes she became very cheerful and started laughing with me.

The same nurse came over to us with a big smile. "Do you feel all right now?" she asked the lady.

"Oh yes I feel really good. Didn't I tell you he is a grand chap," she said.

I talked to her for about three quarters of an hour; in the end she was really cheerful and talkative. Word must have gone round to others about me, for during my stay in Ward 3 I started getting 'requests' to visit fellow patients in other bays.

Whilst I was in the hospital, word must have got around outside that I was unwell and had been admitted into the Infirmary, as soon a few of my students came to visit me. Amongst them were Mahmoor, Alvina, Eileen, Nagina, Naseem, Kauser, Najma, Nazreen, Waheed, Majid, Wasim and others. I apologise to the students whose names I haven't included, it is not intentional, it is due to my poor memory.

Since I joined Accrington & Rossendale College in 1992 as an Urdu lecturer, whilst I came to know some college lecturers, I also got to know a great many Asian and English students over the years. Although it is a long time since I retired from college quite a few of my old students still ring me. Instead of calling me Sir, they address me as Uncle.

Amongst the young people who regularly call me is Kauser. It is a long time since she was my student, but it is wonderful to hear her speaking fluent Urdu on the phone with me. Whenever she rings me we always talk for a long time. Some students ring me for advice, others just want to chat. Amongst the young people who were at one time my students and still ring me are Nagina and Nasim. They tell me all about the lives they are leading now. Amongst the boys I am delighted to say that Shamim, Wasim and Mahruf still keep in touch with me.

****

Kath devotedly visited me every day from 2:00pm to 8:00pm. On the third day Shahnaz came from Kemberley; she stayed for a week, but had to go back because of work.

On 9th February 2001 I was going to be discharged from hospital, when a wonderful chatty and beautiful nurse named Sylvia came in with a bag full of medicines. I was fully dressed ready to go home and sitting on my bed.

Sylvia in her usual cheerful and chatty way started to explain the medications to me.

Kath had also arrived to take me home that evening, and was sitting in the bedside chair. As usual I was in a good mood.

To humour Sylvia I said, "Me no understand English, tell this lady."

Sylvia looked at me with a big grin and surprise on her face. She retorted, "Hey, don't you come with that caper to me. I know you better than that. Don't forget I have dealt with you for ten days."

I had to give in, and the three of us had a good laugh about my pretence at not understanding the English language.

During my stay in Ward 3, Sylvia and I used to talk a lot on different subjects. She was already full of knowledge, but she particularly liked to discuss Asian religions, culture and values. I used to explain to her that Islam is a religion that could be practised in any part of the world; we also had regular discussions about other faiths.

Following my discharge from hospital, cardiac nurses Judith and Sylvia visited me a few times at my home. I also made regular visits to the blood clinic for a month or so, until I was discharged from there when my blood was stabilised.

Once after giving blood in BRI, I was with Kath in the waiting area ready to see the doctor, when I saw a nurse passing through the gangway. I recognised her as she worked in the Coronary Care Unit.

Thankfully the nurse also recognised me, and came over to us. "Hello, how are you?"

"I'm fine, thank you," I replied standing up.

I introduced the nurse to Kath asking, "Have you met my wife?"

Then I introduced Kath to her, "This is the nurse I was telling you about. She and another nurse sat at my bedside all through the night."

Then I turned to the nurse and asked her, "Tell me the truth nurse, what really happened to me?"

"Actually you died that night for ten minutes or so," she told us. "In fact we thought we had lost you; there were no signs of a pulse, you stopped breathing, your lips turned blue and your colour changed altogether. But we don't give up easily, so we managed to revive you."

I had always wondered what colour a dead body changes to; I couldn't resist this opportunity and said, "What colour did I turn to?"

"Well, usually English bodies change to a light grey, you changed to dark grey," she replied

All three of us laughed about it, and I thanked her once again for looking after me.

After those heart attacks I couldn't carry on teaching. But after recovering from this illness I kept to my commitments as a JP and attended the Magistrates' Courts at least once a week.

CHAPTER THIRTY-SIX

On January 3rd 2002 I travelled to my home town of Hyderabad for eight weeks to visit my brothers, sisters and other relatives. My doctors were kind enough to give me enough medication to last my planned stay of about eight weeks. I was too nervous to go to Hyderabad without a supply of my much needed drugs from my GP in England.

It is very difficult to get genuine medicines in these parts of the world. Luckily I was all right throughout my stay except for minor coughing, or a temperature once or twice.

Fortunately, there is British trained Dr Haroon in Hyderabad. My family have known him for years. Looking at my minor ailments, he just blamed the polluted air in Hyderabad for my troubles.

The main cause of pollution in Hyderabad and the other cities of Pakistan are rickshaws and cars with no exhausts. Rickshaws are the cheapest and fastest means of transport in Pakistan, and throughout India and Bangladesh. Basically a rickshaw is a motorbike, but it is modified in such a way that instead of its back wheel there is a little carriage. This carriage is designed to carry two passengers, whilst the driver sits in front.

****

In Hyderabad wherever I went I was always accompanied by my grown-up nephews. Even if I wanted to, I never got a chance to be on my own. This was mainly as a mark of respect to ensure that all my needs were met, but partly also because they were aware of my recent heart attacks, which meant they wanted to ensure I was never at risk of being alone. Perhaps rather cheekily one day I did manage to dodge my nephews and walked on my own to my old high school in New Fort, which was situated at the end of the famous shopping centre Shahi Bazaar.

Walking down Shahi Bazaar towards my old school I imagined my old school friends walking beside me in the days when we used to go to school without a single care in the world. We were the cheeky bunch with presence of minds.

I was completely lost in my thoughts, when all of a sudden I found myself in front of my old G.H. High School. The students were on holiday on account of Eid-ul-Adha and Christmas winter holidays. The head teacher, with only an administrative and skeleton teaching staff was in the school.

The main gates looked the same, the building was still there, and appeared to be in a very decent condition, even the sun falling on the walls looked more or less the same. I stood in front of the gates for a few minutes. For a little while I got lost again in my past. I could clearly hear the noise of children entering the gates. I was thoroughly absorbed in the past, but all of a sudden I was startled and brought back to reality by the loud noise of a passing rickshaw.

I composed myself and felt ready to enter the gates, but I could feel my heartbeat racing with some exciting and mixed feelings. Crossing the gates I reached the forecourt where we used to have our morning assembly before going to classes.

The forecourt was still the same, although it must surely have been repaired a few times in the last forty-eight years. It was still surrounded by buildings on three sides. As I turned to my left in the forecourt I could see our Matric classroom behind the familiar verandah. At the other end of the verandah the steps leading up to the first floor were still there. At that moment I was filled up emotionally. With a heavy head, mind and feet, I started walking to my old classroom.

As I stood at the door I could clearly imagine our maths teacher Mr Rashid and my classmates Baqui, Sabir, Abdul Haque, Saeed, Mannan and others, as time seemed to have somehow travelled back almost fifty years.

Leaning over the railings of the verandah, I could see our old headmaster Mr Abdul Mabood with some books, looking down and walking to his office. Then I could see our other teachers Mr Mohammed Ayub, Mr Misbah, Mr Younus, and Mr Yasin.

Just as I was wandering in my little innocent world, I heard a polite voice, "Excuse me Sir, but are you looking for something?"

"Yes, I'm looking for my childhood. I left it here some years ago," I replied without thinking clearly.

The man was an orderly to the head-teacher of the school. At first he couldn't understand what I meant. He had a blank expression on his face.

I explained, "Nearly fifty years ago I was a student here. I did my Matriculation from this school. This was our classroom and I used to sit near that window."

I was getting emotional, a few tears were beginning to brim up in my eyes; my voice became quite hoarse.

To bring me out of this state the man said, "Would you like to meet our headmaster Sir?"

"Yes, of course. I would like that very much." I replied giving him my visiting card.

I followed him to the headmaster's office. I waited outside while the man went in. Within a minute the headmaster appeared at the door.

"Ass-Salam-o-Alakum. Welcome, welcome. Please come in," he invited.

"Walaikum-Ass-Salam. Thank you very much." I replied, walking with him to his office after our greetings.

I told the headmaster about myself, saying that I was in G. H. High School from 1948 to 1950. He was very interested in my stay in England. Amongst other things, we talked extensively about the educational systems in Pakistan and in England. He was shocked to learn how the teachers were disrespected and undervalued in the UK by a small percentage of their pupils. Frankly he could not understand how a society that provides the opportunity of free education for every child up to sixteen years of age, could possibly allow this to develop into an opportunity for a generation of disrespectful adults. The headmaster was not aware that in these changing times corporal punishment had become illegal, so lessons are often interrupted by the unruly minority, and to a certain degree the teachers' hands are tied. Children who do not wish to be educated are often dismissed from their school and are sent to special ones where they are encouraged to work harder to improve themselves, thus allowing the majority of children to do well in their studies.

He then showed me around all the classrooms, pointing out to me the developments that had taken place since I had left that school.

Before leaving I thanked him for the guided tour of my old school. I talked about some of the cheeky things we used to do in and out of the classroom. Sometimes we were caught, but mostly we used to get away without any punishment; but more importantly, it was indeed a wonderful moment for me to reminisce about my childhood and appreciate the educational opportunities that were to provide me with a firm foundation for life in a foreign country.

I left the headmaster, and as I walked along the same street as I had almost fifty years ago, I remembered the time when I had my first smoke. It happened when I was with five or six friends and we had visited our school in August 1950 to collect our official results to get admission into Government College, Hyderabad.

During that particular week each of us had received extra pocket money from our parents. Intoxicated with the success in our Matric exams and the idea of going to college, these factors had combined to make us feel, and perhaps act like grown-ups.

We decided to go to a café, after sitting down we ordered cold drinks for us; at the same time we ordered the waiter to bring us some Capstan cigarettes and a light, after all, this was going to be our very first experience, so none of us had a match or a lighter.

We were non-smokers, so we smoked without inhaling, and just blew the smoke into the air. This made us feel like we were *real* adults. I stood at the spot where that café used to be; this had now been turned into a small shop for rickshaw's spare parts.

****

After a week or so, I dodged my nephews again and headed for my good old Government College on the banks of the famous Phuleli Canal.

The rickshaw driver taking me from Tilak Incline to College was quite talkative; he guessed that I had left Hyderabad a long time ago. At the end of the journey I wanted to give him a tip of ten rupees, which sounds very little, but was a reasonable tip over there.

Very politely he kept saying, "No Sir, you are our guest. I can't accept more than we agreed on."

I was quite moved by his honesty and said, "All right, but please buy something for your children from me."

He agreed to do that, and dropped me off at the huge main iron gates of Government College. The posts on both sides of the gate looked so familiar to me. Standing there for few moments my thoughts took me back almost fifty years when in September 1950 I had stood on the very same spot with my friends. We had gone to enrol ourselves into first year Science classes. I was with Baqui, Raees, Sabir, Abdul Haque, and Umar.

With my heart pounding I passed the gates and approached our old Physics Lecture Hall. I could clearly hear Professor Ayer explaining the Micro Metre Gauge. I looked into the hall; nothing seemed to have changed in there, even the entrance doors for students and lecturers were still in the same places.

I moved forward; I was in front of our huge library. I couldn't resist, so I stood on the steps where I used to sit with some friends and watch the female students passing by.

In my vision I could see Amina, Noor Jahan, Razia, Fehmida, Feeroza, Azim-un-Nisa, Khurshid and others. None of the boys would dare speak to these girls.

There were a few reasons for boys not to talk to these girls. Firstly it was because these girls came from the upper class rich families; secondly the boys lacked the much needed confidence to talk to the girls, and lastly the cultural barrier still existed. Most of these girls were my class fellows in our last years of B.Sc.

Going across from our Chemistry Labs to the new Zoology Lab buildings, I could hear Naseer, Baqui, Inayat, Hadi, Abdullah, Khair Mohammed, Zari, Usman and others. They all sounded to be laughing and joking as if they didn't have one care or worry in the whole wide world.

Passing these buildings I could now see an image of Dr Duarte and his English wife coming out of their bungalow. Eventually I reached our football and cricket grounds. There I could see Prof. Nasir Raza, Prof. Ayer, and a ground full of enthusiastic spectators, all cheering and supporting their teams.

The same old pond was still there where some mischievous student had drowned a professor's cycle, and there was a big inquiry. However no one was ever found guilty of this act.

Returning back to reality I was filled up emotionally and had damp eyes, 'What happened to those good old days? Oh God, will they never return?'

Once again I found myself on the main road outside the college boundaries. On the banks of the Phuleli Canal, I was near the same old tree where in summer I had sat thousands of times under its cool shadow. I moved forward to the trunk of that tree. To my amazement, my name engraved nearly fifty years earlier as a boy, was still clearly visible there. I put my right hand palm on it, and caressed it lovingly for a few minutes. At the same time I looked across the Phuleli Canal. A few young carefree children were running on the other bank of the canal; I was soon lost in my thoughts again.

All of a sudden I was jolted into the present by a voice, "Would you be going to town, Sir?" A rickshaw driver was asking me.

"Oh yes, of course," I replied, wiping my wet eyes.

I climbed into his rickshaw. Once again I glanced at the 'good old college' and the rickshaw set off.

While remembering Dr and Mrs Duarte, all of a sudden my mind went back to the time when I, with my two friends Inayat and Qureshi used to go to Prem Park in Hyderabad. We would stay there in the park for about an hour then we would go for a walk on the Civil Lines area. Civil Lines in Hyderabad was, and still is, an exclusively residential area for the gentry of the town. There we would see an elderly couple coming out of their bungalow and going for a walk.

There is nothing unusual in that one would have thought. What was unusual? It was just that the couple were Allama Dr I. I. Quazi and his European wife.

Allama I. I. Quazi was our Sind University's Vice-Chancellor. Allama Quazi and his wife would emerge from their bungalow and walk down the road very gracefully.

At that time I wondered as to what it would be like to have a European wife? In my wildest dreams I would have never thought I would come to England, let alone get married to an English girl from Lancashire. The rest, as they say, is history!

****

During my stay in Hyderabad, I did feel unwell a couple of times, but generally I got over these little setbacks without making any fuss. But once in Hyderabad I woke up as usual in the morning, as far as I can recall, I was going to the bathroom when I fainted at the door.

Every day I would attend to my toiletries in the bathroom, get changed and go downstairs where Shahida (my youngest sister-in-law) would have prepared my breakfast for me.

On this particular morning Shahida was waiting downstairs for me as usual. After waiting a little while she became worried and wondered why I was so late, and came upstairs to check up on me.

As soon as she saw me lying at the door, she shouted for Aapi, who was still asleep in her room. Hurriedly Aapi came from her bedroom, when she saw me on the floor she was very shocked.

Eventually I came round, finding myself on the floor with my head in Aapi's lap. She was wiping the perspiration off my forehead with her dupatta (headscarf). I was looking round for my mother and was wondering where she was; every time I was ill at home, Mother was always the one to comfort me, so where was she?

My mind moved on and I don't remember anything except Aapi asking me what I was doing there. My reply was that I was in my own house; obviously I wasn't quite myself.

I recovered fully within minutes. During that time my nephews Zahid, Majid and Sajid came upstairs. They wanted to send for Dr Haroon, but I told them that I was feeling all right, so there was nothing for them to worry about.

The second time I felt ill there was when we went to visit our parents' graves in Hyderabad Cemetery. Mubashir and Hafiz Soomro were with me. Although it was early March, it was pretty hot that afternoon. The two gentlemen were quite used to the heat, but it was really unbearable for me.

I missed my parents very much, but I knew that they would be upset to see me like this, but I felt that they were both very close to me at that moment in time.

We hurried home, and as soon as we arrived there I was sick. Once more everyone was very worried about me, but after a little rest and a cold drink I felt much better, but it was arranged that I would go to see Dr Haroon. He told us that there was nothing to worry about and gave me some medicine.

The day following my arrival in Blackburn I went to see one of our GPs. After a thorough checkup, the doctor informed me that all was well.

****

After spending eight weeks in Karachi and Hyderabad I returned to Blackburn on 6th March 2002. The journey from Karachi to Manchester was as comfortable and enjoyable as it had been going to Karachi. This was the first time I had travelled to and from Pakistan by Pakistan International Airlines.

It is sometimes alleged amongst the Pakistani community in Britain that the aircrew of PIA does not treat its Pakistani passengers in a proper and polite manner. I was told they are rude to their passengers. I was therefore very reluctant and hesitant to travel by PIA, but at that time a seat was only available on that airline. Considering my heart condition and problems, we had decided to book a seat in Club Class.

On the outward journey from Manchester, as soon as I entered the departure lounge I was directed to the area for First Class and Club Class passengers. It was a sort of self-service cafeteria where one could get free snacks and soft drinks. After having a cup of tea there, I wanted to have a look round.

I came out again in the departure lounge and noticed a huge jumbo aircraft standing at Gate 10. To my shock and surprise it was the PIA aircraft destined for Karachi. After a while the passengers started to board the aeroplane. As I entered the aircraft a Pakistani air hostess with a beautiful smile, welcomed and directed me to my allocated seat. Far above and beyond my belief, my journey from Manchester to Karachi was pleasant, enjoyable and faultless.

I was curious about that unpleasant relationship between the aircrew and passengers of PIA, so I asked a regular traveller of that airline about this. What I was told horrified me, but it made sense.

He told me, "On PIA, the aircrew are generally from Pakistani middle classes. The air hostesses are usually from the upper middle classes. Now the majority of passengers mainly come from the villages of Pakistan. These people left their villages for America or England to better their own and the rest of their family's lives."He added, "They worked hard, and most of them became successful in their businesses or chosen professions. Through their successes they consider themselves to be amongst the Pakistani middle classes. Unfortunately the aircrew still think of themselves as better than the passengers in the Asian class system. But the passengers regard themselves as British Citizens and better off financially than the crew."

I was told that they don't ask the air hostess for items; instead they actually *order* them to bring items to them. That's how the rift starts. It's ignorance on *both* sides. Contrary to experiences by some travellers, my own experience of travelling with PIA turned out to be a very pleasant one. Some people might just say that this was because I travelled in Club Class, but I am of the opinion that the cause of any alleged behaviour by some staff, could be completely understandable and justified, simply because of the poor and nasty attitude of a small minority of travelling passengers. Quite simply, we should all treat others as we ourselves would wish to be treated. My personal experience with the PIA staff and Pakistani passengers during my journey was wonderful.

****

Although I had enjoyed the 'cruise of my life' during my maiden journey to England in 1956, Kath had never had a chance to experience a cruise holiday.

It was the end of March 2002 when Kath and I spotted an offer in a travel agents window in Preston advertising a 'bargain offer' for a Carribean Cruise. I decided to book it there and then.

We flew from Manchester to Montigue Bay and boarded the ship called *Sun Dream*. We visited different islands namely Montiguebay, St. Martin, St. Lucia, St. Catalina and others. Although once or twice I felt unwell during the cruise, I didn't let it spoil our enjoyment at all. It was a wonderful cruise, which we both thoroughly enjoyed for the whole week.

Although I was visiting my GPs regularly, I also suspected that I was going downhill rather fast. During one visit to my GP, I enquired if he could refer me to a heart specialist as a private patient. He named one or two specialists in Blackburn, Manchester and Blackpool.

Afzal Quraishi, one of my trusted friends had also recommended a heart specialist in Blackpool Victoria Hospital to me. I therefore asked my GP if he could write to that specialist on my behalf at his earliest convenience. Within two weeks I went to see this specialist in his private surgery.

He gave me a thorough examination before explaining to me, "The grafting done by the surgeon in 1987 is not working properly and I suspect that there are some more blockages. I'll have to arrange an Angiography for you for further investigation."

In October 2002 he arranged an Angiography for me as a private patient in Blackpool Victoria Hospital. The specialist himself performed the Angiography and I recovered in the Lancashire Suite ward.

Later he came to speak to me. "I'm sorry Mr Khan," he told me, "you have three blockages, and they are the real reasons why you are having heart and breathing problems."

He then said, "One blockage could be cleared by Angioplasty, but for the other two blockages you will need to undergo a by-pass operation."

Without any hesitation I agreed with him.

He told me, "That's fine I'll refer you to one of the surgeons in Blackpool."

It was only a few weeks later when I received an appointment to go to see the surgeon. My family and I were willing to have the operation privately and pay for it ourselves, but the surgeon himself told me that he had just a little backlog of operations, but as soon as he had cleared these, he would send for me for my operation.

He then said, "However, should you have any problems in the meanwhile which require you to go to hospital, then you should let the hospital staff know which surgeon's patient you really are."

Although I never felt right, I tried to put on a brave face for everybody. As usual Shahnaz came home during the Christmas holidays. On Christmas Eve Shahnaz noticed that I didn't look so good, and asked me how I was feeling.

I told her that I didn't feel so good.

She insisted that I went to see my doctor. So Shahnaz, Kath and I went to the surgery and I saw the doctor. After examining me, the doctor assured me that the only thing that I had was anxiety, otherwise there was nothing to worry about.

It was Christmas Day, December 25th 2002; I woke up at about 5.45am with a terrible chest pain. I knew it was either a heart attack or a warning of one. I woke Kath up; she promptly took me downstairs.

After putting an oxygen mask on me, she rang for an ambulance; it reached our door within seven minutes. Once again there was a male and a female paramedic. The lady took our oxygen mask off my mouth, replacing it with one of theirs before attaching me to their oxygen cylinder. While she was doing this the man prepared a medicine for me to drink. The lady paramedic kept talking to me all the time, assuring me that everything would be all right.

By this time Shahnaz had also got up. Kath came with me in the ambulance while Shahnaz followed us in her car.

There wasn't a soul around the hospital at that time. While they wheeled me through the corridors I noticed only one person passing and wishing us a 'Happy Christmas'.

As soon as we reached the cardiac care ward Shahnaz told the staff that I was under the Blackpool surgeon.The nurses in that ward are so wonderful and caring. Within minutes they gave me the necessary injections and medicines, and I was soon resting in bed peacefully.

While the world and hospital patients were busily celebrating Christmas, and were having or getting ready for their Christmas dinner, I sat in my bed looking at two cheese sandwiches, but nobody could do anything for me because the meals are ordered on the previous day. But in the evening, due to the kindness of an on duty nurse, I got a hot meal, and joined in the Christmas's celebrations with the ward nurses.

After two days I was transferred to Queens Park Hospital, where I joined in wishing a Happy New Year to the patients and nurses to welcome in the New Year of 2003. I spent three weeks in the ward where I was well looked after by those caring nurses.

Every evening after visiting time, the patients used to have good discussions on various subjects. During those three weeks in Queens Park Hospital sometimes I felt ill, but with the care and assurances of doctors and nurses I got plenty of encouragement which helped me to carry on.

This time too I enjoyed both English and Asian meals. After an English breakfast I would have English meals at lunch time and Asian meals at teatime.

I was supposed to be transferred to Blackpool Hospital straightaway, but because of some bug on the cardiac wards in Blackpool, the ward had to be isolated, which meant I had to wait an extra three weeks. Eventually I was taken to Blackpool Victoria and given a bed on Ward 11. When I reached there I found that I was one of only two patients in the whole ward. After Kath, Shahnaz and Suhail left I felt really lonely, but it did not take me long to make friends with the other patient and the nurses.

After a day or two, more patients started coming on the ward. I met some wonderful people in that ward. Most patients were over fifty-years old. Mr Isherwood from Lytham St. Annes was in his eighties and was ever so cheerful. Mr Isherwood had spent a few years in India in his earlier life, which meant that he and I had a lot in common and plenty to talk about. He would tell me and the other patients about his experiences in India.

Then there was a patient from Burnley, who was a loyal supporter of Burnley football team. He had a few posters and badges put on the wall near his bed.

Although I was satisfied with the Asian food in the hospital, I still felt there was something missing. One lunch time somebody came from the hospital restaurant and got talking to me. During our conversation I must have mentioned my concern about the Asian food in the hospital.

Later that afternoon the chef of the restaurant came to me and asked me a few questions about Asian food. I told him whatever I knew without thinking of it as important.

Later on the nurse who came every day with the usual slip for next day's meal orders said, "Oh, you are going to have a treat tomorrow. The chef is preparing a special meal for you."

The next day at teatime when the food arrived, mine was not on the usual trolley. My family were there too, they noticed that all the other patients had been served. Kath became rather concerned, she was just about to get up to speak to one of the canteen staff, when a man from the restaurant came towards my bed holding out a huge tray which he then placed onto my side table.

I was very surprised to see the items on that tray. There were two types of curry, Biryani, Pilao rice, Naans, three Samosas, mango chutney, Yogurt Raita and other Asian delicacies.

When my son and wife saw the tray and its contents, they commented that it was no wonder I liked staying in hospital. One of the patients in that ward made some funny remarks that are not really worth mentioning, except to say that later on the chef himself put him right.

I was told that my operation was going to be on 29th January 2003, and would be performed by surgeon Mr Sogliani. Three or four days before my operation Mr Sogliani's anaesthetist and Mr Sogliani himself came to see me. They each explained what was going to happen.

Although I was frightened, I somehow managed to keep up a very brave face, as I had already gone through the same operation almost sixteen years earlier.

On 29th January 2003 my operation was successful, but they kept me in ICU for two or three days which was unusual. They told me later on that it was due to my blood pressure and temperature, as both kept going up and down. As soon as these were stable I was transferred to the high dependency cardiac care ward where I recovered very quickly. During my stay on that ward, it wasn't just the nurses on duty who cared for me, the surgeon and the heart specialist also visited me regularly.

During my stay in both Blackburn and Blackpool hospitals my family and friends regularly visited me. These visits helped me immensely in keeping up my spirits. However there were patients there who got depressed all the time. On 4th February 2003 I was discharged from Blackpool Hospital.

It took me almost three months to recover before I could once more resume my duties as a JP in the Blackburn Courts. Following the advice of the surgeon, heart specialist and my GPs, I started taking it easy, and only doing things that I enjoyed most, such as meeting friends whose company I thoroughly enjoy, and going to the town library or for a walk with my wife. I now try to steer away from debates and arguments.

****

However in 2004 I once again started having some problems, such as shortness of breath, and having difficulty in climbing stairs. Luckily the specialist saw me straightaway and he prescribed some wonderful medication which worked wonders for me.

I was due to retire from the Blackburn courts on 15th June 2005, but due to my poor health I could no longer carry out my duties as a JP. Therefore with deep regret I had to resign. In recognition of my services, on the 17th May 2005 I was presented with a decanter and a reference, whilst Kath was presented with a beautiful bouquet.

After a further change of medication by the specialists in Blackpool in 2005 my health began to improve a lot. I felt better than I had done for some time.

Now I do what I **want** to do, and not what I **have** to do, which is really wonderful.

Final update

Time has now moved on to 2008, so it is now over fifty years since I first arrived in Blackburn, England from Pakistan. This means I have now experienced fifty plus wonderful years of meeting many wonderful people of all different nationalities, customs, cultures and faiths.

During this wonderful journey, I met and married my beautiful wife Kath, and together we have been blessed with such a lovely family

****

Not forgetting my origins, and together with Kath and our children, we have managed to visit Pakistan, thoroughly enjoying the times we spent there with our relatives.

I have worked with, and for many different people, gained so much knowledge through College Education and hands-on experiences, enjoying several careers.

I now like both English and Asian food, and I have almost, but never quite learned to tolerate the English weather that very nearly forced me to turn back and return to Pakistan after my first day in Lancashire. Thankfully I soon learned and experienced a different side to England, that it is indeed a green and pleasant land.

Whilst India was indeed the Country of my birth, and where I was brought up until I was fourteen-years old; and Pakistan is the country where my family still dwell; England has become my adopted home for the past half a century. Way back in 1956 when I first arrived at Blackburn Railway Station and caught that bus to Alexandra Road to stay with my first landlady, life has indeed turned full circle, for my family and I now have our own house on Alexandra Road. It is not as large as the one I first stayed in as a lodger, but to me and my family it is truly important, as it is indeed the place we have chosen to call our home, and as such it is very dear to us all.

Throughout all of this and more, even after over fifty years, and such changeable weather, plus and all the general ups and downs of life, I can truly and proudly say that I am STILL HERE.

****

Kath (Fernaz) and Mudassir Khan
Still here after 46 years